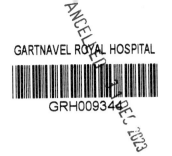
CBT for Schizophrenia

LIBRARY

Learning
Resource Centre

CBT for Schizophrenia

Evidence-Based Interventions and Future Directions

Edited by

Craig Steel

*Charlie Waller Institute for Evidence-Based
Psychological Treatment, University of Reading*

WILEY-BLACKWELL

A John Wiley & Sons, Ltd., Publication

Wiley-Blackwell is an imprint of John Wiley & Sons, formed by the merger of Wiley's global
Scientific, Technical and Medical business with Blackwell Publishing.

Registered Office
John Wiley & Sons, Ltd, The Atrium, Southern Gate, Chichester, West Sussex, PO19 8SQ, UK

Editorial Offices
350 Main Street, Malden, MA 02148-5020, USA
9600 Garsington Road, Oxford, OX4 2DQ, UK
The Atrium, Southern Gate, Chichester, West Sussex, PO19 8SQ, UK

For details of our global editorial offices, for customer services, and for information about how
to apply for permission to reuse the copyright material in this book please see our website at
www.wiley.com/wiley-blackwell.

The right of Craig Steel to be identified as the author of the editorial material in this work has been
asserted in accordance with the UK Copyright, Designs and Patents Act 1988.

Library of Congress Cataloging-in-Publication Data

CBT for schizophrenia : evidence-based interventions and future
directions / edited by Craig Steel.
     pages   cm
  Includes bibliographical references and index.
  ISBN 978-0-470-71206-1 (cloth) – ISBN 978-0-470-71205-4 (pbk.)
1. Schizophrenia–Treatment.   2. Cognitive therapy.   I. Steel, Craig, editor of compilation.
  RC514.C5782 2013
  616.898–dc23
                                                    2012032289

A catalogue record for this book is available from the British Library.

Cover image: Close-up of Meadow Goatsbeard seed head © Radius Images/Corbis.
Cover design by Simon Levy Associates.

Set in 11/13pt Minion by SPi Publisher Services, Pondicherry, India

Printed in Singapore by Ho Printing Singapore Pte Ltd

1   2013

Contents

Contents

About the Editor

Craig Steel is a Senior Lecturer based at the Charlie Waller Institute of Evidence-Based Psychological Treatments, School of Psychology and Clinical Language Sciences, University of Reading, UK. Since he gained his PhD from the Institute of Psychiatry, London in 1998 he has been an active clinician and researcher within the area of cognitive behavioral interventions for schizophrenia. He has extensive experience within clinical trials including as a trial therapist, clinical supervisor, and as principal investigator. He has published numerous experimental and clinical research articles.

List of Contributors

Max Birchwood,
School of Psychology,
University of Birmingham, UK.

Christine Braehler,
Institute of Health and Wellbeing,
University of Glasgow, UK.

Simon Burton,
Norfolk and Waveney Mental
Health Foundation Trust, UK.

David Fowler,
Norwich Medical School,
University of East Anglia, UK.

Daniel Freeman,
Department of Psychiatry,
University of Oxford, UK.

Paul French,
Greater Manchester
West Mental
Health Foundation Trust, UK.

Brandon Gaudiano,
Alpert Medical School,
Brown University, USA.

Paul Gilbert,
Mental Health Research Unit,
University of Derby, UK.

Jennifer Gottlieb,
Department of Occupational
Therapy,
University of Boston, USA.

Eric Granholm,
VA San Diego Healthcare System &
Department of Psychiatry,
University of California,
San Diego, USA.

Andrew Gumley,
Institute of Health and Wellbeing,
University of Glasgow, UK.

Amy Hardy,
Department of Psychology,
Institute of Psychiatry,
King's College London, UK

Janice Harper,
NHS Greater Glasgow & Clyde,
UK.

Gillian Haddock,
School of Psychological Sciences,
University of Manchester, UK.

Jason Holden,
Department of Psychiatry,
University of California, San Diego,
USA.

Jo Hodgekins,
Norwich Medical School,
University of East Anglia, UK.

Rebecca Lower,
Norfolk and Waveney Mental
Health Foundation Trust, UK.

Alan Meaden,
Birmingham and Solihull Mental
Health Trust, UK.

Anthony Morrison,
School of Psychological Sciences,
University of Manchester, UK.

Kim Mueser,
Department of Occupational
Therapy,
University of Boston, USA.

Elissa Myers,
Department of Psychiatry,
University of Oxford, UK.

Neil Rector,
Department of Psychiatry,
University of Toronto, Canada.

Nicola Smethurst,
Greater Manchester West Mental
Health Foundation Trust, UK.

Ben Smith,
North East London NHS
Foundation Trust, UK.

Helen Startup,
South London and Maudsley NHS
Trust, UK; Department of
Psychiatry,
University of Oxford, UK.

Craig Steel,
School of Psychology and Clinical
Language Sciences,
University of Reading, UK.

Ruth Turner,
Norfolk and Waveney Mental
Health Foundation Trust, UK.

Jon Wilson,
Norfolk and Waveney Mental
Health Foundation Trust, UK.

Preface

The development of evidence-based psychological interventions for schizophrenia has been rapid. The first clinical trials were taking place in the United Kingdom in the early 1990s, and within 10 years the evidence base had grown to the point that CBT for psychosis was becoming a routine part of mental health services.

During the past 10 years clinical researchers have moved on from the core application of CBT for the positive symptoms of psychosis. A growing number of research groups have developed protocols aimed at specific phases, symptoms or co-morbidities within this group. The momentum within these developments has reached the point where there is sufficient material to form the basis of the current book. Each chapter highlights an intervention that is embedded within the context of the relevant evidence base. The aim is to enhance access to the protocols used within research trials, and therefore to optimize clinical outcome.

Craig Steel, June 2012

Acknowledgements

This book is the dissemination of a large number of clinical trials, which will have included hundreds of people diagnosed with a psychotic disorder. Each person will have signed up to be part of a research project and to undertake detailed assessments without any guarantee of immediate therapy. It is hoped that this book will help to increase other peoples' access to the products of those trials.

Needless to say this book is a combined effort from a wide range of contributors. Each one is highly valued and I am indebted to them for their hard work and patience. There are also a number of people I have worked with who have not contributed directly, but have provided inspiration to me, and the field as a whole. These include Christine Barrowclough, Paul Bebbington, Philippa Garety, David Hemsley, Elizabeth Kuipers, Emmanuelle Peters, Nick Tarrier and Til Wykes.

There are also those at home who have provided their own special kind of encouragement and support, Kerry, Frankie and Joss.

1

CBT for Psychosis: An Introduction

Craig Steel and Ben Smith

Introduction

Many readers of this book will recall a time when the predominant view within psychiatry was that talking therapies were not recommended for people diagnosed with schizophrenia. The past 10 years have seen a rapid expansion of an evidence base that has overturned this traditional view. Cognitive behavioural therapy (CBT) for schizophrenia is now recommended as part of routine clinical practice within a number of countries, including the United Kingdom and the United States. One consequence of this rapid rate of change is the need for widespread dissemination of this psychological intervention. Attempts have been made to meet this need through the publication of a number of treatment manuals, as well as an increase in the availability of training events.

The evidence base of CBT for schizophrenia was first developed through a generic intervention aimed at the relatively stable 'medication-resistant' group. However, as those readers who are trained clinicians will be aware, a diagnosis of schizophrenia is associated with a wide range of presentations. Consequently there have been recent developments within distinct protocols aimed at specific presentations and phases of the disorder. The aim of this book is to bring together these recently developed evidence-based protocols.

CBT for Schizophrenia: Evidence-Based Interventions and Future Directions,
First Edition. Edited by Craig Steel.
© 2013 John Wiley & Sons, Ltd. Published 2013 by John Wiley & Sons, Ltd.

Although the interventions described within this book have key differences, which have been developed for specific target groups, they all rely on the basic engagement skills that are required when working with individuals diagnosed with a psychotic disorder. This chapter therefore aims to cover generic information, which will form the background to all following chapters. The chapter will cover four main areas: (i) a brief introduction to the symptoms associated with schizophrenia, (ii) the generic cognitive model of schizophrenia, (iii) generic clinical skills required when adopting CBT for schizophrenia, and (iv) a brief review of the evidence base of CBT for schizophrenia.

Schizophrenia

Schizophrenia is the most commonly diagnosed form of psychotic disorder. The most common symptoms are hallucinatory experiences and delusional beliefs. These are often referred to as the 'positive' symptoms of schizophrenia. The vast majority of CBT protocols for psychosis are aimed at these positive symptoms.

Hallucinations

Hallucinations are frequently considered to be sensory perceptions of stimuli that are not really there. While auditory hallucinations are the most common form, and have received the most attention from clinical researchers, they may occur within any sensory modality. Although the perceived auditory stimuli may be of general noises or music, they are most often in the form of a voice, or voices. They may be judged to originate from either inside the head or outside the head, may be experienced as male, female or alien voices, and there may be either single or multiple voices. The type of communication originating from the voice may come in many forms including 'voices commenting' in which the perceived voice makes frequent comments on the actions and thoughts of the voice hearer and 'command hallucinations' in which the voice-hearer is given direct instruction on how to act (see Chapter 2).

The work of Marius Romme and Sandra Escher in the late 1980s helped to highlight the relatively prevalent occurrence of voice hearing and to challenge the traditional psychiatric view, in which voices are the symptom of an illness. Their seminal work started with Romme, a social psychiatrist, and one of his voice-hearing patients appearing on a Dutch television programme and inviting viewers to contact them if they had heard voices. Hundreds of viewers responded with the majority having never received psychiatric attention. This event led to a research programme focussing on how individuals, who had heard voices, but remained outside the psychiatric system differed to those who had received a diagnosis (Romme and Escher, 1989).

Since then, several studies have suggested that around 3 percent of the population will experience hearing a voice at some point during their lives (Johns *et al.*, 2004). These experiences will vary enormously within a number of different dimensions, and require careful assessment. One aspect of the voice-hearing experience which has received attention is that voice-hearers develop relationships with their voices, and that these relationships need to be considered during therapy. This perspective makes sense when one considers that an individual may have heard the same voice, which they attribute to a single person, every day for many years.

Perhaps the main impact of the work of Romme and Escher was to introduce the concept of 'normalization' into therapy. That is, to discuss with voice hearing clients the fact that there are many other voice-hearers, many of whom cope with or even enjoy their voice hearing experiences. This can often liberate a client from feeling trapped and alone with their experience. An introduction to voice-hearing groups can further facilitate this process.

The main issue for all therapists to consider would seem to be whether an individual's voice hearing experience is causing them distress. Traditional psychiatry would have viewed all voice hearing experiences as a symptom of illness, which required treatment. However, recent work suggests than we cannot assume a voice-hearing experience is distressing. Given that therapy is aimed at the reduction of distress, it would seem than non-distressing voices should not be a target for therapy. However, it should be remembered that voice-hearing experiences can fluctuate rapidly and that careful assessment is required.

Delusions

Delusions are the most common symptom associated with a diagnosis of schizophrenia, being present in around 75 percent of those receiving hospital care (Maher, 2001). A common definition of a delusion is that of a fixed false belief that is held in the face of evidence to the contrary. Delusional beliefs often need to be understood within the context of hallucinatory experiences. For example, a belief that someone is themselves the son of God may be fuelled by the experience of hearing a voice that tells them so. The most common of these beliefs are *Delusions of Persecution*, which tend to be associated with a paranoid presentation. Such delusions typically involve the belief that one is being spied on and/or is under threat due to some kind of organized conspiracy. The sufferer may feel threatened by government agencies, God or the Devil, their neighbours or by family members. Fenigstein (1996) described paranoia as a disordered mode of thought dominated by an intense, irrational, but persistent mistrust or suspicion of people and a corresponding tendency to interpret the actions of others as deliberately threatening or demeaning. *Delusions of Grandeur* are associated with a belief that one is a powerful and/or famous figure (e.g. Jesus). It is quite common for such individuals to also believe that they are being persecuted, and that the persecution is a result of their famous identity. Another form of this symptom is *Delusions of Control*, in which an individual believes their thoughts and actions are being controlled by an outside agent. A commonly reported experience within schizophrenia is that certain external events are perceived to contain special messages, for example within a news broadcast or within the lyrics of a song on the radio, and these are termed *Delusions of Reference*.

As with auditory hallucinations it is important to consider whether the symptoms associated with a diagnosis of schizophrenia are found within a non-clinical population, and if so what this means regarding clinical interventions. Several surveys have highlighted the prevalence of beliefs in the paranormal and other unusual beliefs within the non-clinical population. One important study highlighted how the beliefs of a psychiatric population could not be distinguished from those of new religious movements on the basis of content alone, but only by consideration of the dimensions of controllability and distress (Peters *et al.*, 1999). There are also reports of a range of paranoid beliefs occurring throughout the non-clinical population (Freeman *et al.*, 2005).

As with hallucinations, the therapist needs to consider whether the experiences an individual is reporting is distressing or not, and therefore whether they should be a target of therapy. While an individual may be expressing highly unusual beliefs, for example, relating to alien abduction, this may not be a cause of concern to them. Again, careful assessment is required.

Cognitive Behavioural Models of Psychosis

The early application of psychological models to schizophrenia was predominantly a simplistic application of learning theory, which gave rise to basic interventions. However, the development of cognitive behavioural models for affective disorders had a significant impact on psychosis research within the late 1990s. This work highlighted the extent to which the development and maintenance of a psychotic presentation could be understood with reference to psychological processes already associated with anxiety and depression. The traditional psychiatric view of schizophrenia was challenged in that therapists were encouraged to engage directly with the content of psychotic symptoms.

Early work was based on the view that the basic cognitive model could be applied to the symptoms of psychosis. Perhaps the primary rule within the cognitive approach is that it is not experiences which distress you, but the way you make sense of them. Thus, someone ignoring you is only upsetting if you believe that they saw you and that they ignored you on purpose. The same principle was applied to voice hearing experiences by Paul Chadwick and Max Birchwood (1994, 1995). They showed that the distressing affect and behaviour arising from hallucinations were not simply the result of the content of the voices, but reflected the voice hearers' appraisal of the voices. They suggested that the hallucination is, therefore, seen as an activating event (A), which is then appraised by the individual in the context of their belief system (B), and which consequently leads to emotions and safety behaviours (C). The authors argue that this forms a cognitive-emotional-behavioural mechanism that maintains the belief in the power and dominance of the voice.

Two influential cognitive models of the positive symptoms of psychosis have since been proposed by Philippa Garety and colleagues (2001) and Tony Morrison (2001). Both of these models incorporate the role of negative core beliefs, hypervigilance for threat, scanning for confirmatory evidence and safety behaviours. In essence they concur that a psychotic presentation may evolve out of the presence of unusual experiences, with a critical factor being how these experiences are interpreted. Such experiences may include hearing voices, strong déjà vu, dissociative experiences such as derealization and intrusive thoughts or images. Psychosis is associated with such experiences being interpreted as negative, threatening and external and leading to hypervigilance and safety behaviours. For example, an individual who 'hears a voice', and decides that this perceptual experience is due to a lack of sleep is likely to have a different outcome to an individual who decides that the Devil is speaking to them with bad intent.

While many of the treatment implications of these two models overlap, one of the key theoretical distinctions is the extent to which the core unusual experiences are 'normal' or are anomalous biologically based phenomena. Garety *et al.* (2001) refer to the potential role of a genetic vulnerability for the propensity to some of these experiences, whereas Morrison focuses on the extent to which these phenomena are normal and that it is the interpretation of these experiences that is critical. In particular, Morrison focuses on the role of common 'intrusive experiences' such as intrusive thoughts and images that may form the basis of an unusual experience for some individuals. However, both models highlight the critical role of the appraisal of the unusual experience in determining whether an individual arrives at a 'psychotic' explanation. Therefore, while incorporating the generic cognitive model of anxiety and depression, these models also enable the formulation of the development of psychotic symptoms. A major strength of these models is that they incorporate a wide range of psychological processes that have been associated with psychosis, and have the potential to be flexible enough to enable the formulation of the heterogeneous range of psychotic presentations.

Cognitive behavioural models of psychosis (e.g. Birchwood, 2003; Garety *et al.*, 2001; Morrison, 2001) all emphasize the central role of emotional dysfunction as a precursor, and consequence of, the symptoms of psychosis. These influential models also suggest that cognitive appraisals and perceptions concerning the nature of psychotic symptoms (including hallucinations) will influence the maintenance or recurrence of symptoms through coping responses, emotional dysfunction and cognitive processes such as reasoning biases.

CBT for Psychosis

In recent years a number of predominantly UK based clinical researchers have publicized the potential for an individualized formulation based cognitive behavioural approach to schizophrenia (e.g. Morrison, 2002; Kingdon and Turkington, 2005). Such an approach, as for other disorders, is based on the integration of developmental experiences and current beliefs and behaviours. The aim is to develop a personal account of the development and maintenance of currently distressing experiences that is less threatening than the beliefs that are currently held. This aim is particularly relevant for people diagnosed with schizophrenia, as their current explanations are usually limited to, for example, in persecutory delusions, either (a) 'It is all true, people are out to get me' or (b) 'I am insane, I cannot trust my thoughts, I must take medication for ever'.

It is important to note that cognitive behavioural therapies for psychosis have developed in line with theoretical developments in our understanding of psychotic phenomena. CBT for psychosis aims to help an individual make sense of psychotic experiences by making links between emotional states, thoughts and earlier life events. Assisting people to make sense of psychotic and emotional experience by discussing psychological formulations can help them make connections between seemingly unconnected events or beliefs and disabling, distressing psychotic symptoms. The individualized, emotion-focussed nature of CBT for psychosis facilitates the engagement process. However, there are a number of generic issues that therapists need to be aware of when working with individuals diagnosed with a psychotic disorder.

Engagement within CBT

Fowler *et al.* (1995) suggest that CBT starts with a comprehensive engagement and assessment phase. This establishes a working collaborative therapeutic relationship, and allows for the collection of information that will inform cognitive-behavioural formulation. Specifically, therapists must be sensitive to issues of mental state, active hallucinations and specific delusional beliefs when engaging, assessing, sharing formulations and conducting interventions.

The clinician should be mindful that a voice hearer, for instance, may initially not wish to discuss their experiences and that a level of trust may first need to be gained. Problems for engagement may include the voice hearer being concerned that they may be sectioned or have their medication increased if they discuss their voices. This issue can be addressed overtly with the clinician stating whether or not these assumptions are correct. It may also be the case that the voice is telling the voice hearer not to discuss anything with the clinician, and may even make threats of violence or death. The clinician will not be in a position to know this information until trust is gained, and they should therefore be mindful of this possibility and observe any discomfort or anxiety when they enquire as to voice content.

The clinician will need to establish a level of trust before the client will disclose their specific and sometimes delusional beliefs. As well as being fearful of how the clinician may respond, it may be that the client has incorporated the clinician and the psychiatric system into a paranoid belief. As with hallucinations, the clinician should not be too distracted by the level of conviction a patient exhibits for a belief that has been diagnosed as delusional. A wider assessment should be conducted in order to clarify the clinical problems of most significance.

When individuals have experienced traumatic events it is especially important to allocate time early-on in CBT for the opportunity to discuss this. Therapists should be mindful of sensitively assessing trauma-related intrusions (e.g. intrusive memories, dreams), arousal (e.g. heightened startle response, hypervigilance) and avoidance symptoms (e.g. specific behavioural avoidance of reminders, thought and memory suppression). Also, therapists should assess the meaning of any trauma to an individual and any trauma related secondary appraisals (e.g. 'I will never get over this' or 'I just can't trust myself anymore').

Sometimes individuals will understandably and deliberately avoid discussion of their traumas or indeed their symptoms more generally. Trauma memories (which might relate to previous experiences in the psychiatric system such as being sectioned) can be accompanied by extreme emotional responses. A gentle approach in the assessment stage, assisting and facilitating feelings of safety when disclosing information about traumatic experiences, can become a systematic strategy to help to overcome avoidance and manage the processing of strong emotion and extreme negative thinking that can accompany disclosure. Sometimes it may be appropriate for the therapist to directly address the client's negative thinking about what the therapist may think of the client after the disclosure. Often trauma or symptom disclosure can be accompanied by thoughts that the therapist will regard the person negatively. Reality testing of such views within sessions using careful and systematic cognitive therapy approaches (where the therapist's opinions can be regarded as a test) can be useful in starting work on addressing extreme negative views of self (e.g. I am bad, dirty, unclean, disgusting) and others (e.g. others will view me as bad and dirty and reject me).

Individuals who have been abused are likely to find it particularly difficult to establish trust within a therapeutic relationship, and this should be acknowledged. There is also the possibility that the client may have previously disclosed their trauma history, but not been believed, which will further complicate the development of trust. More specifically, the clinician should be mindful of the setting of their clinical sessions. If this is within a psychiatric institution, the client may have experienced some traumatic events within such an institution that may contribute to heightened vigilance, the triggering of stressful memories and avoidance. This should be dealt with as early as possible by openly discussing whether this issue is relevant to the particular client, and how it can best be dealt with.

The initial aim for the clinician will be to establish engagement but also simultaneously educate the patient into the broad framework of the cognitive behavioural approach. That is, collaborative, goal focussed and time-limited. Given that CBT usually involves a certain amount of homework, and the need to build on the contents of previous sessions, care should be taken to ascertain whether any cognitive functioning deficits interfere with this process. Should this be the case then, wherever possible, adaptations should be made. This is likely to include repetition of the contents of a session, and making sessions shorter. As CBT interventions are short-tem it is useful to include other professionals involved in the long-term care of the patient in the process, especially towards the end of the intervention. This will be essential if the sessions have focussed on some form of relapse prevention plan or crises plan to be implemented, if required, in the future.

Any therapeutic intervention should begin with a collaborative development of treatment goals, so as the patient feels some ownership of the process. This process will be of particular importance for those who have experienced many years of coercion within the psychiatric system, including involuntary sections and forced medication. These individuals are likely to be suspicious of any offer of help from a professional they consider to belong to that system, and extra effort must be made to create a collaborative therapeutic relationship.

The clinician should be alert to the possibility of the patient trying to get them to offer help that they cannot provide. For example, this may include wanting the therapist to help them get the police to arrest their neighbours who are believed to be persecuting them. The clinician should adopt an empathic position, but are unable to act until having heard more about the problems. Inexperienced therapists may fear saying anything that may seem to collude with the contents of the patients symptoms, out of fear of reinforcing their 'madness'. However, if the therapist states that they (currently) simply do not know enough about the situation to be able to be sure what is going on, then they are likely to maintain the therapeutic relationship without committing themselves to any specific belief.

Assessment within CBT

There are a range of issues to consider when conducting a full assessment. It is likely that an individual diagnosed with schizophrenia will suffer with emotional and functional problems, and the clinician should be cautious not to assume which of these are the most significant. Although the content of this chapter focuses on positive symptoms, any initial assessment should also cover physical health, social and occupational functioning and suicidal ideation.

Although an individual is diagnosed with schizophrenia and for instance, experiences auditory hallucinations, the clinician should not assume that the hallucinations are a source of significant distress. A careful assessment is needed in order to assess what the most significant problems are, and whether hallucinations and delusions are involved. In the example of voice hearing, the patient may experience a number of different voices that are attributed to different individuals. Some of these voices may be friendly and helpful, while others are more threatening and cause distress. In this scenario, if the clinician appears to assume that the patient would be better off not hearing any voices at all then this may distance them from the goals of the patient.

The initial assessment should be conducted with flexibility and in an environment where the patient feels most comfortable. This may mean going for a walk while the patient has a cigarette, or meeting in their own home. There will be many areas to cover in an assessment, and it may help to let the patient start with whichever area they feel is most important. This may be current symptoms, current social problems or earlier life events.

The clinician can guide the conversation towards those issues that have been missed in later sessions. During the early sessions the therapist should be building a model of how the patient constructs their position. There are many possible models the patient may hold. These include believing they have a genetic vulnerability to their current mental health problem, that medication does help, that stress can exacerbate symptoms, and that they do not believe their delusional beliefs when well. Whereas another individual may believe their condition is purely stress related and not biologically based, and that medication is useless. Other people may believe that there is nothing wrong with them, but that they do hear voices which *sometimes* trouble them, and would like some coping strategies for this. It is important to consider what the clinician and patient need or need not agree on, in order to help the patient achieve their goals. The patient does not need to believe they are suffering from a biologically based illness called schizophrenia in order to benefit from a therapeutic intervention. Attempting to induce such 'insight' is likely to cause many to drop out of the process. Therefore, the clinician can be flexible as to what model of mental illness they collaboratively share with the patient, in order to help them achieve their goals. During the course of therapy, new information and reconsideration of old information may cause this model to evolve.

The Evidence Base for CBT for Psychosis

Although single case reports of psychological interventions for psychosis date back more than 50 years (e.g. Beck, 1952), significant developments in this area did not occur until the 1980s. Early behavioural interventions were aimed at symptom management and were predominantly embedded within the traditional psychiatric view of schizophrenia. During the mid 1990s a small number of mainly UK based researchers conducted the first trials in cognitive behavioural therapy for psychosis (CBTp). The encouraging results led to clinical trials being conducted within other countries, and to large scale randomized controlled trials being funded within the UK. The rapid growth in the number of clinical trials aimed at evaluating CBTp has led to an increasing number of meta-analyses. The most recent and comprehensive review has been able to incorporate a large enough number of clinical trials in order to investigate the role of a number of variables that may be associated with outcome (Wykes *et al.*, 2008). Of the trials 34 met inclusion criteria, with 22 of these being individual CBTp (i.e. one to one therapy) aimed at the positive symptoms of psychosis. The overall effect size for CBTp was moderate, and was broadly similar (around 0.4) whether the analysis was based on outcome in relation to positive symptoms, negative symptoms, mood or social functioning.

The evidence to date predominantly provides support for CBTp as an intervention for individuals suffering from 'treatment-resistant' psychosis in a chronic, but stable phase. However, most trials have adopted a generic approach to CBTp and despite being aimed at the positive symptoms of psychosis, there has been little differential impact between psychotic and non-psychotic symptoms. Consequently, relatively little is known about the effectiveness of CBTp for other phases of the disorder. Also, little is known as to which elements of CBTp are the most important in producing change, and there are few markers as to who would benefit most from this intervention.

The modest overall outcomes of most CBTp trials may be, in part, a product of the choice of measure used for the assessment of outcome. The most widely used assessment tool has been the Positive and Negative Syndrome Scale (PANSS, Kay *et al.*, 1987) for schizophrenia, which is predominantly a symptom-based measure developed for use in drug trials. It has been shown to be a poor measure of the psychological distress associated with psychotic symptoms (Steel *et al.*, 2007). The use of the PANSS is in contrast to the view that CBTp should not be considered a quasi-neuroleptic (i.e. targeting symptoms) but seen as an intervention aimed at reducing emotional distress (Birchwood and Trower, 2006). Also, the use of a generic form of CBTp aimed at a heterogeneous population may contribute to limited effect sizes. This limitation would seem all the more significant given that a large number of clinical researchers question the scientific validity of the diagnosis of schizophrenia (Bentall, 2007) upon which most trials are based. Of interest, the study which exhibited the largest effect size within the Wykes *et al.* (2008) review, adopted a specific protocol for a specific from of psychotic presentation (command hallucinations) and used an appropriate outcome measure (Trower *et al.*, 2004).

References

Beck, A.T. (1952) Successful outpatient psychotherapy of a chronic schizophrenic with a delusion based on borrowed guilt. *Journal for the Study of Interpersonal Processes, 15,* 305–312.

Bentall, R.P. (2007) *Madness Explained. Psychosis and Human Nature.* Penguin, London.

Birchwood, M. (2003) Pathways to emotional dysfunction in first-episode psychosis. *British Journal of Psychiatry, 182,* 373–375.

Birchwood, M. and Trower, P. (2006) The future of cognitive behavioural therapy for psychosis: not a quasi-neuroleptic. *British Journal of Psychiatry, 188,* 107–108.

Chadwick, P. and Birchwood, M.J. (1994) The omnipotence of voices: A cognitive approach to auditory hallucinations. *British Journal of Psychiatry, 164,* 190–201.

Chadwick, P. and Birchwood, M. (1995) The omnipotence of voices II: The beliefs about voices questionnaire. *British Journal of Psychiatry, 166,* 773–776.

Fenigstein, A. (1996) The paranoid personality. In C.G. Costello (ed.), *Personality Characteristics of the Personality Disordered* (pp. 242–275). New York: Wiley.

Fowler, D. Garety, P. and Kuipers, E. (1995) *Cognitive Behaviour Therapy for Psychosis: Theory and Practice.* Chichester: Wiley.

Freeman, D., Garety, P.A., Bebbington, P.E. *et al.* (2005) Psychological investigation of the structure of paranoia in a non-clinical population. *British Journal of Psychiatry, 186,* 427–435.

Garety, P.A., Kuipers, E., Fowler, D. *et al.* (2001) A cognitive model of the positive symptoms of psychosis. *Psychological Medicine, 31,* 189–195.

Johns, L., Cannon, M., Singleton, N. *et al.* (2004) Prevalence and correlates of self-reported psychotic symptoms in the British population. *British Journal of Psychiatry, 185,* 298–305.

Kay, S.R., Fiszbein, A. and Opler, L.A. (1987) The positive and negative syndrome scale (PANSS) for schizophrenia. *Schizophrenia Bulletin, 13,* 261–269.

Kingdon, D. and Turkington, D. (2005) *Cognitive Therapy for Schizophrenia.* New York: Guildford.

Maher, B. (2001) Delusions. In P.B. Sutker and H.E. Adams (eds), *Comprehensive Handbook of Psychopathology,* 3rd edn. New York: Kluwer Academic/Plenum.

Morrison, A.P. (2001) The interpretation of intrusions in psychosis: an integrative cognitive approach to psychotic symptoms. *Behavioural and Cognitive Psychotherapy, 29,* 257–276.

Morrison, A.P. (ed.) (2002) *A Casebook of Cognitive Therapy for Psychosis.* Hove: Routledge.

Peters, E., Day, S., McKenna, J. *et al.* (1999) Delusional ideation in religious and psychotic populations. *British Journal of Clinical Psychology, 38,* 83–96.

Romme, M. and Escher, S. (1989) Hearing Voices. *Schizophrenia Bulletin, 15,* 209–216.

Steel, C., Garety, P., Freeman, D. *et al.* (2007) The multi-dimensional measurement of the positive symptoms of psychosis. *International Journal of Methods in Psychiatric Research, 16,* 88–96.

Trower, P., Birchwood, M., Meaden, A. *et al.* (2004) Cognitive therapy for command hallucinations: randomised controlled trial. *British Journal of Psychiatry, 184,* 312–320.

Wykes, T., Steel, C., Everitt, B. *et al.* (2008) Cognitive Behaviour Therapy for schizophrenia: Effect sizes, clinical models, and methodological rigor. *Schizophrenia Bulletin, 10,* 1–15.

2

Cognitive Therapy for Reducing Distress and Harmful Compliance with Command Hallucinations

Max Birchwood and Alan Meaden

Introduction

The most distressing, high-risk and treatment resistant of all symptoms of schizophrenia are command hallucinations (Nayani and David, 1996). They occur frequently, with over 30 percent complying directly with their commands. A further 30 percent will attempt to resist (Shawyer *et al.*, 2003), but will 'appease' often by complying with less serious commands (Beck-Sander *et al.*, 1997); but nonetheless placing themselves at risk of later compliance (Shawyer *et al.*, 2003). While findings from the MacArthur Risk study funded by the MacArthur Foundation and reported by John Monahan and colleagues (2001) found no link between the presence of command hallucinations and violence, a recent secondary analysis by Rogers (2004, 2005) found that the perceived need to 'obey' hallucinations was significantly associated with increased risk of violence. In our own research we have shown that cognitive mediation (the process whereby cognitions or beliefs generate distress and subsequent behavioural responses) is one of the key processes in understanding and managing risk in clients with command hallucinations and not experiencing commands per se (Trower *et al.*, 2004). Consequently they are an important target for treatment.

In this chapter we provide a brief overview of our research which shows how distress and harmful behaviours such as violence to others, self-harm

CBT for Schizophrenia: Evidence-Based Interventions and Future Directions,
First Edition. Edited by Craig Steel.

and suicide can be successfully reduced through our form of cognitive therapy. We go on to highlight the key features of our approach which we have termed Cognitive Therapy for Command Hallucinations (CTCH) and describe how this has developed into a trial treatment protocol. The protocol is subsequently illustrated in more detail through a case study drawn from our routine work.

Clinical Trial Evidence

In our first, and the only published, study explicitly targeting command hallucinations (Trower *et al.*, 2004) we focused on measuring compliance behaviour and distress in addition to standardized symptom measures; compared to treatment as usual (TAU). We set out to establish whether targeting power beliefs could reduce harmful compliance or safety behaviour use and distress, and increase resistance to voice commands. Thirty eight participants all reported at least two voices they experienced as commands from their 'dominant' voice, at least one of which was categorized as a 'severe' command. Participants were considered at high risk of compliance on the basis of their risk histories, use of the Mental Health Act (1983) and the need for detention. Five participants in the sample had been prosecuted or cautioned for behaviour linked to voice commands. Behaviours included causing actual and grievous bodily harm, theft and common assault. Three participants had been hospitalized for attempting to kill someone in response to voices within the past 3 years. Those included in the trial were further characterized by the heavy and prolonged consumption of TAU, both during the trial and as sampled 1 year prior to the trial.

The group receiving CTCH completed a median of 16 sessions and dropped from 100 percent compliance (the selection criterion) over 12 months to only 14 percent compared to 53 percent for the TAU group. Voice related distress was also significantly impacted upon by CTCH in the treatment group at 6 months. By 12 months, depression had risen significantly in the TAU group but not in the CTCH group.

The CTCH group reported a large and significant reduction in their power beliefs (as described below), compared to the TAU group who showed no change. This effect was maintained at the 12-month follow-up. When the effect of the power beliefs was statistically removed the treatment effect disappeared, providing clear evidence that it was a reduction in conviction in participant's beliefs about their voices that was responsible for the reduction in compliance. Conviction in omniscience beliefs (that the voice is all seeing and all knowing) fell significantly only in the treatment group. This benefit was also maintained at 12 months. Those receiving CTCH also showed significant improvement in perceived control over their voices, compared to the TAU group who again showed no change. This too was a benefit sustained at the 12-month follow-up.

Our first trial produced an effect size of major clinical significance (see Wykes *et al.*, 2007) in the context of good quality and high-level TAU services. CTCH exerts a major influence on the risk of compliance, reduces distress and prevents the escalation of depression, compared to TAU alone. From our previous research (Birchwood *et al.*, 2000) depression is known to be high in this group, and was evident in the participants within this study. Depression alone (e.g. in the absence of command hallucinations) may lead to further risk behaviour; especially suicide.

The CTCH Model

Building on early work that showed how cognitive approaches could be successfully applied to psychosis (Chadwick and Lowe, 1990; Chadwick and Birchwood, 1994) we employ a now widely accepted ABC model. Here 'A' represents the activating event, 'B' the beliefs about the 'A' and 'C' the emotional (Ce) and the behavioural consequences (Cb) of these beliefs. This core model owes much to Rational Emotive Behaviour Therapy (REBT) pioneered by the late Albert Ellis (2004) and we have incorporated further elements of REBT into our approach as illustrated in our case study. The ABC model is deceptively simple. It enables us to remain clear about the targets of our therapeutic efforts. Problems are located firmly at C, in CTCH terms these constitute voice-related distress and compliance or safety behaviours that pose a risk to self or others. These are the target for therapy and not the broader symptoms of psychosis.

Case example: Lilly

Lilly hears the voice of a powerful demon (B: the power and identity beliefs) saying 'Kill your partner' (the A);

She believes that she should act but not fully comply (B: the compliance belief) since she 'must do what my voice says otherwise it will harm me' and 'hitting my partner will keep the demon quiet;'

Lilly was distressed (the Ce), as she felt afraid;

Lilly assaulted her partner (the Cb), she slapped him round the face.

Delusional symptoms in CTCH are inferences since they constitute 'if . . . then' propositions, guesses or predictions about what is or may be happening which can be true or false: either as secondary to voices (voice-related inferences or beliefs): The spirit of Princess Diana (whose voice I hear) wants to take over the world . . . she is always talking about grand plans she has. Or in their own right (delusional inferences): there is a conspiracy involving spirits to take over the world.

Positive symptoms in CTCH arise from attempts to defend against negative person evaluations (see Chadwick *et al.*, 1996 for a more detailed discussion) or underlying rules and assumptions regarding, for instance, the mistrust of others, underlying specific paranoid beliefs that others are involved in active attempts to harm them (Chadwick and Trower, 2008) rather than being purely a misinterpretation of anomalous experiences as in other models (see Chapter 1). Positive symptoms are also explained in CTCH by the incorporation of social rank theory (Gilbert, 1992; Gilbert and Allan, 1998). This proposes that evolved mental mechanisms operate as internal signals: 'attack the weaker and submit to the stronger'. These internal signals are experienced in psychosis in the form of derogatory, controlling and powerful voices requiring submissive behaviour including appeasement and compliance in order to avoid punishment (see Birchwood *et al.*, 2010, for a more detailed account). Voice-hearers subsequently develop a set of inter-related beliefs (which we have termed the power schema) about these experiences that can be understood in terms of an interpersonal relationship. This process of personification has itself been linked to an increased likelihood of harmful compliance (Junginger, 1990). The overarching theme of power runs through all therapeutic efforts and is used both implicitly and explicitly in the therapeutic relationship.

The notion of power concerns the voice's ability to harm (sometimes referred to as omnipotence). Power is also a broader concept, incorporating other voice beliefs (e.g. identity and intention to harm; sometimes expressed as malevolence) that imply power and for this reason we use have adopted the term power schema. The perceived need to obey seemingly powerful voices is crystallized in the voice power schema. The target of therapy is to deconstruct this power schema. Our model can be most readily conceptualized within our standardized formulation template as shown in Figure 2.1 for Brian. Here voice activity at A is appraised within a dominante–subordinate schema, person evaluations, dysfunctional assumptions and other interpersonal rules at B. These give rise to power beliefs, which in turn elicit emotional distress and safety behaviours; the latter maintain voice beliefs by preventing their disconfirmation. This formulation drives all treatment efforts and is a useful tool for socializing the client into the CTCH model.

Findings from our own and others research (Birchwood *et al.*, 2000; Birchwood *et al.* 2004; Mawson *et al.*, 2010), suggest that the client's own evidence for powerful voices stems from a number of sources:

- An inability to keep one's own thoughts, experiences and feelings private (thought broadcast);

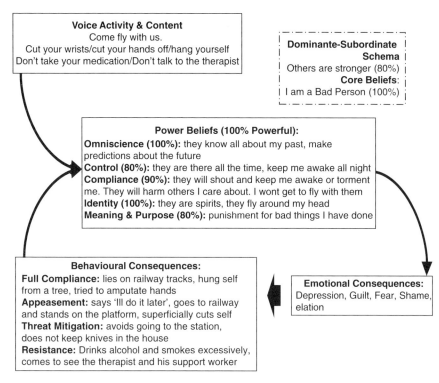

Figure 2.1   CTCH formulation template for Brian

- Voices appear to know the person's present thoughts and past history (omniscience) and may threaten to expose them (e.g. shaming them, which may constitute a psychological threat);
- Voices apparent ability to predict the future (omniscience);
- Who the voice is, in other words identity beliefs (the Devil being seen as intrinsically powerful) and related purpose beliefs (malevolence or benevolence: intention);
- The ability of the voice to cause or claim to harm others or the client or inflict psychological distress upon them (e.g. keeping the person awake all night): omnipotence;
- The perceived consequence of non-compliance (the compliance belief).

It is crucial to understand this aspect of the voice-hearers' relationship with their voice since the greater the perceived power and omnipotence of the voice, the greater the likelihood of compliance (Beck-Sander *et al.*, 1997). This relationship is in turn moderated by appraisal of the voice's intent and consequences of resisting. Those with benevolent voices virtually always comply regardless of its severity (Beck-Sander *et al.*, 1997) whereas those with malevolent voices are much more likely to resist. Resistance, however, increases if the command involves a major social transgression or self-harm (Chadwick and Birchwood, 1994).

In line with other models, during our trial and other work we have noted how behavioural Cs or consequences would not only result in various types of risk behaviour that are harmful, even potentially lethal, to the person and others, but also how they served to maintain the individual's power beliefs about their voices and therefore their symptoms (as shown in Brian's case in Figure 2.1). In this sense they served as a type of 'Safety Behaviour', which functioned to keep them safe from and reduce anticipated negative consequences from their powerful voices. At the same time however these safety behaviours also prevented disconfirmation of voice beliefs. In our work with colleagues (Hacker *et al.*, 2008) we predicted that distress and safety behaviours would follow from beliefs about power. In a cross-sectional study of 30 individuals with hallucinations, three sources of threat were identified: fear of physical harm, shame, and loss of control. Of these individuals 26 reported use of safety behaviours in the last month. The degree of use of such safety behaviours (and voice-related distress) was associated with beliefs in voice omnipotence; mood and voice characteristics did not account for this relationship. Crucially we found that the association between safety behaviour use and increased distress was mediated by beliefs about voice omnipotence: power.

This body of research and trial work carried out over a decade or more has informed our ongoing research efforts and our intervention protocol described below.

The Trial Protocol

We currently conceptualize CTCH in terms of eight levels of intervention (see Table 2.1). Ideally the client and the therapist collaboratively work through these 8 levels in order, building engagement and shifting the power balance away from the voice and towards the voice hearer themselves. However, we have taken a pragmatic approach in our trial work accepting that some individuals will wish to work more quickly on advanced levels (7 and 8) while for others progress may be limited to levels 1 to 5. Similarly more attention may need to be paid to some levels such as promoting control and building engagement while for others change may be best facilitated by focusing on broader interpersonal power issues at level 6. Ideally clients will progress to levels 7 and 8 since, according to REBT practice and theory (Walen *et al.*, 1992), such work is vital to consolidate lasting change. Core belief work in CTCH terms focuses on dominate–subordinate schemas (I am weak, others are stronger; in line with social rank theory); negative self- or person-evaluations (I am Bad, others are

Table 2.1 Summary of the 8 levels of CTCH and the main strategies

CTCH Level	Key Tasks
1. Assessment and engagement	1. Sensitively and non-judgementally elicit a detailed account of psychotic experiences and development of beliefs about voices 2. Anticipate and address engagement problems and beliefs – keep the focus on the C 3. Provide a 'panic button' allowing stopping of the session/change of topic (to model control early on and promote engagement) 4. Offer normalizing analogies: nosey neighbours, school bullies
2. Promoting control	1. Reframe current strategies employed by the client as evidence for control 2. Identify what increases and decreases voice activity and content 3. Introduce/teach new coping strategies – including establishing initial boundaries (e.g. regarding compliance, availability) 4. Reframe new coping strategies as evidence of control and evidence of power shift
2. Socializing into the ABC/ CTCH model	1. Explore the advantages and disadvantages of voice beliefs being true and false 2. Elicit/offer lower conviction beliefs/ones that have changed in their level of conviction: Father Christmas, favourite band 3. Normalize the role of beliefs in everyday life: cat in the night versus a burglar and link to different likely affective and behavioural responses 4. Reframe difficulties in 'ABC' terms
3. Developing and sharing the formulation	1. Develop power schema, compliance behaviours and distress elements of the formulation (including evidence for each), 2. Hold back on sharing subordination schemas and core belief for later reformulation and advanced CTCH work
3. Setting goals for therapy	1. Agree goals focused on reducing distress and the use of safety/compliance behaviours
4. Reframing and disputing power beliefs	1. Exploit the client's own doubts that their beliefs may be wrong 2. Discredit the truth of what the voice says by pointing out their mistakes and their ability to make predictions (challenging their omniscience) 3. Question the voices capacity to carry out their threats (challenging their omnipotence) and therefore the need to comply

(Continued)

Table 2.1 (*cont'd*)

CTCH Level	Key Tasks
5. Reducing the use of safety behaviours	1. Address discomfort intolerance beliefs – using coping strategies and cognitive disputation to build tolerance of discomfort (when the voices do carry out their threats) 2. Use metaphors (e.g. Garlic and Vampires – the spinning tribe) 3. Emphasize the benefits of resistance → Use a graded approach to reduce safety behaviours → Reality test belief via behavioural experiments
6. Raising the power of the individual	1. Making the client aware (through Socratic questioning) of the increasing power shift 2. Identifying the clients own mastery and control 3. Helping the client to question the voice's commands and threats directly 4. Developing alternative powerful self beliefs 5. Extending strategies other power (dominate–subordinate) relationships.
7. Addressing Identity, purpose and personal meaning	1. Agree goals focused on addressing Identity, Meaning/Purpose beliefs 2. Use Socratic questioning to reframe beliefs about Identity, Meaning and Purpose 3. Highlight logical inconsistencies in the belief system (e.g. is this consistent with what God would do; would the school bully have aged?) 4. Draw upon the client's own doubts (e.g. has the voice ever said that this is its purpose?) 5. Encourage consideration of alternative explanations 6. Devise true tests
8. Reframing and disputing core beliefs	1. Revisit/clarify/elicit developmental history 2. Highlight potential key experiences, stressors or traumatic experiences that may have led to the development of psychotic experiences and beliefs 3. Clarify and agree that these were key emotional and developmental experiences 4. Share the reformulation as a personal model of psychotic experiences 5. Explore and identify core beliefs through thought or inference chaining for psychotic beliefs. Clarify core beliefs and the evidence used to support them 6. Use Socratic questioning, highlight logical inconsistencies and draw upon the client's own doubts about core beliefs 7. Use specific philosophical disputation techniques: Big I little I; evaluating behaviour Vs whole person evaluations; changing nature of self? 8. Help the client to develop emotional insight by acting in accordance with emerging new core beliefs

worthless); interpersonal rules and dysfunctional assumptions (in order to be worthwhile I must always do things perfectly/be liked by others, others are not to be trusted), which can give rise to and serve to reinforce negative person evaluations (drawing on the earlier work of Chadwick *et al.*, 1996) or may be implicated in their own right in delusional thinking (e.g. Chadwick and Trower, 2008). How a person responds emotionally and indeed behaviourally reflects interplay between person evaluations and inferences (the beliefs about voices and what is or what may be happening).

In order to assess suitability for CTCH we routinely use a comprehensive set of measures to elicit the defining features of the client's belief system about their voices, their degree of resistance and engagement with their voices along with their distress and compliance behaviours. The measures we use are:

1   General psychosis measures
    a   Positive and Negative Syndrome Scale (PANSS; Kay *et al.*, 1987). This is a widely used, well-established and comprehensive symptom rating scale measuring mental state.
    b   Psychotic Symptom Rating Scales (PSYRATS; Haddock *et al.*, 1999) measure the severity of and distress associated with a number of dimensions of auditory hallucinations and delusions.
    c   Calgary Depression Scale for Schizophrenia (CDSS; Addington *et al.*, 1993) is specifically designed for assessment of the level of depression in people with a diagnosis of schizophrenia.
    d   Evaluative Beliefs Scale (EBS; Chadwick *et al.*, 1999). This scale measures global and stable negative person evaluations.
2   General voice measures
    a   The Beliefs about Voices Questionnaire-Revised (BAVQ-R, Chadwick *et al.*, 2000) was developed initially as a cognitive assessment of voices to examine the mediating role of voice beliefs in distress and behaviour. The revised questionnaire now includes ratings of Disagree, Unsure, Slightly Agree and Strongly Agree to rate key beliefs about auditory hallucinations, including benevolence, malevolence and two dimensions of relationship with the voice: 'engagement' and 'resistance.' Like its companion assessment The Cognitive Assessment Schedule, it is usually completed for the most dominant and distressing voice.
    b   The Cognitive Assessment Schedule (CAS; Chadwick and Birchwood, 1995) is used in conjunction with the BAVQ-R to further assess the individual's feelings and behaviour in relation to the voice, and his/her beliefs about the voice's identity, power, purpose or meaning and in the case of command hallucinations, the most likely consequences of obedience or resistance.

3   CTCH specific measures
  a   Voice Compliance Scale (VCS; Beck-Sander *et al.*, 1997). This is an observer rated scale to specifically measure the frequency of command hallucinations and level of compliance/resistance with each identified command within the previous eight weeks.
  b   Voice Power Differential Scale (VPD; Birchwood *et al.*, 2000). This measures the perceived relative power differential between the voice (usually the most dominant voice) and the voice hearer, with regard to the components of power including strength, confidence, respect, ability to inflict harm, superiority and knowledge. Each is rated on a five-point scale and yields a total power score.
  c   Omniscience Scale (OS; Birchwood *et al.*, 2000). This scale measures the voice-hearer's beliefs about their voices' knowledge with regard to personal information.
  d   Risk of Acting on Commands Scale (RACS; Byrne, Birchwood, Trower and Meaden, 2006). This rating scale was specifically designed to identify the level of risk of acting on commands and the amount of distress associated with them.

Those suitable for CTCH should have all of the following:

1   An ICD-10 diagnosis of schizophrenia, schizoaffective or delusional disorder under the care of the clinical team (F20, 22, 23, 25, 28, 29);
2   Command hallucinations (PANSS P3 hallucinations score $\geq$ 3) with a history of command hallucinations lasting at least 6 months with harmful compliance (voice compliance scale score $\geq$ 3) including: appeasement, harm to self; others; or major social transgressions;
3   Collateral evidence of 'harmful' compliance behaviour liked to command hallucinations (e.g. reported by other professionals or evident from case notes);
4   Distress associated with compliance or resistance;
5   Be 'treatment resistant' (prescribed at least two neuroleptics without response but on a stable dose of medication for a period of 3 months) or 'treatment reluctant' (refusal to accept optimal medication (e.g. Clozapine);
6   *Not have* organic impairment or addictive disorder considered to be the primary diagnosis.

Case Example: Marcus

Marcus is in his late thirties with a history of psychosis starting in his early teenage years. He reported experiencing a very unhappy childhood

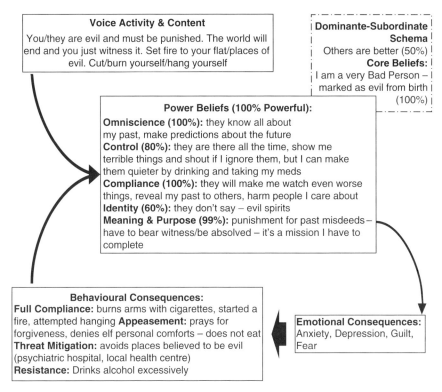

Figure 2.2 CTCH formulation template for Marcus

characterized by emotional neglect and extreme physical abuse including involvement in occult rituals by his stepfather. He often failed to attend school and related poorly to his peers. Marcus was an isolated child and describes having imaginary friends who were a great comfort to him. His younger sister was taken into care and also has mental health problems. His stepfather died some years ago and Marcus spent much of his time with an aunt who was supportive and kind to him. She died when Marcus was in his late teens and it was around this time that he began experimenting with alcohol and cannabis. Sometime later Marcus recalled that he began experiencing malevolent voices and intrusive visual images (of people dying and being tortured, their bodies rotting and being eaten by insects) that he attributed to the voices. He was subsequently found attempting to hang himself from a tree in the local park and was taken to his local psychiatric unit. This was the first of several admissions, some precipitated by further suicide attempts or episodes of self-harm and some due to worsening of his mental state. Marcus is currently compliant with his medication but continues to experience significant symptoms and distress with frequent examples of compliance (see Figure 2.2). He lives alone in the community and is unemployed.

Assessment

During the initial assessment phase (employing the trial protocol assessments listed above) Marcus described hearing many voices, both male and female, mostly of a malevolent nature. He said that the voices occurred almost continuously and were extremely loud and that they often resorted to shouting at him if he ignored them. His prolonged heavy substance use (predominantly alcohol) and medication were reported as helping to make them quieter and less distressing; producing a 'numbing effect'. He reported that the voices frequently commanded him to harm himself: 'Cut /burn yourself/hang yourself' and telling him to 'Set fire to your flat/places of evil'. Unsurprisingly, he found the voices extremely distressing. These voices were interpreted by him as being very powerful and would punish him for non-compliance by keeping him awake and showing him 'terrible' scenes of death 'like on a movie screen' of bodies rotting and being consumed by insects. Marcus also believed that it was his duty to watch these and comply since he was 'a very bad person' and 'marked as evil from birth' and would be rewarded by them by being 'forgiven'.

The findings from this assessment process were developed into our standardized CTCH formulation template first shown in Figure 2.1 and completed for Marcus in Figure 2.1.

Engagement

Engagement is the key to successful CTCH. In Marcus's case trust was gradually established through empathic listening and addressing his engagement beliefs that he would be taken back into hospital which he saw as a 'place of evil'. It was carefully explained that if the therapist believed that he was at risk of serious harm to himself or others this would need to be communicated to his team, but that it would not be necessary to report in detail Marcus's experiences, beliefs and personal history or minor incidents of compliance.

Marcus reported early on that the voices were very angry at him for talking so much about them to his therapist. A further important engagement strategy therefore was to pass a message to the voice that the aim of meeting was to enable Marcus to cope better and lessen his distress and NOT to get rid of the voices. Marcus was also concerned, following the angry reaction of his voices, that therapy would make things worse and increase his voices and distress. The notion of a symbolic panic button was introduced. This aims to give the client control over the process of therapy, (promoting the notion of taking control in other relationships) with the option to disengage at any point and ensuring that Marcus felt free to disagree, remain silent or withdraw.

Time (over 6 sessions) was devoted to eliciting his theories about the voices and his belief system about the world as an evil place watched over by spirits, along with his place within it. This was explored sensitively and carefully, valuing Marcus's struggle and attempts to cope thus far. In addition, the session arrangements were kept flexible, with the option to meet in non-NHS premises and for shorter or longer sessions.

Finally attempts were made to normalize his experiences drawing upon analogies such as nosey neighbours; which Marcus identified as having.

Promoting control

Promoting control is an important practical and conceptual step in CTCH, serving to consolidate the initial engagement phase and build optimism for change. Crucially it begins the process of undermining the perceived power of the voice, building evidence against it and the individual's own powerlessness. This process begins by reviewing and enhancing any existing coping strategies which for Marcus was very limited and chiefly involved consuming large amounts' of alcohol (as much as one 70cl bottle of vodka every 1–2 days) and avoiding particular places which he believed to be evil (a threat mitigation safety behaviour). Mostly however he engaged with his voices and listened (in accordance with his compliance beliefs) to what they said and watched what they showed him on 'the movie screen'.

Supported by the therapist Marcus developed three initial coping strategies enabling him to gain some sense of control over and relief from the voices and reducing his conviction in lack of control to 70 percent. Marcus learned that he was sometimes able to ignore what the voices were saying by focusing his attention away from them and concentrating on something else: the beauty of a tree or a flower (also challenging his belief that the world was totally evil). He was very interested in a variety of different music styles, and found that listening to music on an iPod was a useful distraction technique. For Marcus media reports of bad things happening triggered the voices and he was therefore encouraged to take some time off from his mission (to bear witness) and 'clock off' each day at 5 p.m. (modelling an end to his day of working on the mission).

A further function of developing effective coping strategies is to build discomfort tolerance. This can then be employed in subsequent CTCH work. This was especially important here since for Marcus the voices often did carry out their threats for non-compliance: keeping him awake all night and showing him terrible images.

This evidence of increased control was then reframed as evidence that the voices were not quite as powerful as he previously thought they were (reducing conviction by 10 percent). Having developed some control

Marcus was encouraged to begin to set boundaries with his voices by telling them 'That's enough today'.

Two subsequent further coping strategies were then introduced. First, he was supported to go for long walks (helping to counter his belief that others were watching him and knowing he was evil and in league with the spirits and so would harm him). The second involved reading recipe books building on his previous interest in cooking. This served as preparation for targeting appeasement behaviours as described in later stages.

Socializing into the ABC/CTCH model

Relocating the problem at B is a key stage, which if not accomplished makes progress in disputing power beliefs and reducing the use of safety behaviours less effective since the client will not be working to the same agenda. Marcus was encouraged to distinguish between facts and beliefs and to see how viewing them in this way meant that they could be changed (addressing his sense of hopelessness, helplessness and depression). He was however not particularly persuaded by this and so another approach was taken. A belief (elicited when the panic button was used and the focus of the session was on non-voice talk) that he had now changed was reviewed: that the band Led Zeppelin were the best band in the world which he no longer thought was true now believing that there were many great bands. The disadvantages of his beliefs about his voices being true or false were then considered. There were some benefits to both but overall Marcus conceded that he would be better off if they were false.

Developing and sharing the formulation

The ABC formulation is a powerful tool capable of expressing and distilling most aspects of client's psychotic concerns and distress and is embedded within our CTCH formulation template first shown in Figure 2.1. The process of formulation may involve separating out the various As, Bs and Cs; mindful of the fact that there may be several As (e.g. derogatory comments, commands to harm self, commands to harm others), which may all lead to different or the same Bs. For Marcus being told that he was evil and that he must be punished reinforced both his core beliefs and compliance beliefs (resulting in depression and guilt). Statements such as 'The world will end' and 'You just witness it' caused anxiety and revealed their purpose, while 'Set fire to your flat/places of evil, cut /burn yourself/ hang yourself', constituted direct and unambiguous commands and caused much anxiety and fear. Each of these ABC formulations was shared with

Marcus before sharing the final completed template with him. This helped to not overwhelm him, keep him engaged and allowed feedback and any modifications to be made.

Agreeing and Setting Therapy Goals in CTCH

The goals in CTCH are always to reduce distress and safety behaviour use. The process of sharing the formulation with Marcus described above made it easy to agree the goals of his therapy:

1   Reducing anxiety and fear (the initial targets);
2   Reducing depression and guilt (the latter an advanced therapy target, levels 7 and 8);
3   Reducing the use of his safety behaviour:
    a   Beginning with threat mitigation that was already linked to a coping strategy intervention;
    b   Appeasement: cooking nice meals (again linked to a coping strategy intervention);
    c   If a and b were successfully attained subsequent safety behaviour goals could then be focused upon reducing more harmful forms of compliance beginning with self-harm.

Reframing and disputing power beliefs

The overall aim of this phase of CTCH is to address the perceived power imbalance which underpins compliance and distress. A number of key conceptual stages are adopted. These aim to:

- Reduce the perceived power of the voice and increase the perceived power of the voice hearer;
- Reduce compliance, appeasement and other safety behaviours and increase resistance;
- Weaken the conviction that the client is being and will be punished or harmed;
- Weaken the conviction about the identity of the voice (level 7).

The key conceptual stages may vary in individual cases but typically involve:

- Exploring the origin or source of the belief, tentatively and sensitively seeking clarification;

- Listing and critically examining support, reasons and evidence for the belief;
- Seeking and fairly examining conflicting views (alternative points of view).

Throughout this process the therapist draws upon the client's own doubt, past or present, and any of the client's own contradictory evidence and behaviour. 'Evidence' is questioned starting with the least convincing piece of evidence first; a disputation hierarchy.

Marcus, though often reluctant to go into detail, described a long history of abusive experiences that the voices seemed to know all about. He also cited numerous incidences of supporting evidence for his beliefs frequently bringing newspaper clippings to sessions and on one occasion his own social security number, which had three consecutive sixes in it providing (in his eyes) final proof of his badness. Rather than attempting to address each piece of evidence in Marcus's case (since the 'evidence' was numerous and likely to be replaced by new examples or inferences) it was decided to tackle his power beliefs using two key disputes. The first of these involved discrediting the omniscience of the voices and revealing that they are fallible and make mistakes (just like everyone else). This is an important CTCH strategy in down-ranking the voices and loosening their hold over the individual. It was noted how his voices were not correct in their prediction of the end of world in 2000. It was proposed that they were therefore fallible. This created doubt in Marcus's mind and he was then able to note other instances. It was suggested subsequently that the voices make lots of claims but cannot back them up and that if they were wrong about this and other predictions what else could they be wrong about?

The second important test was to build discomfort tolerance. More usually we would engineer a situation whereby the voice hearer would withhold a safety behaviour and when no harm occurred use this as a dispute to suggest that the voices cannot carry out their threats and so are less powerful than previously thought. Past examples where the individual has already done this can be elicited as further evidence. In Marcus's case however the voices generally did carry out their threats: keeping him awake all night, abusing him and subjecting him to terrible images. Asking Marcus to act against his voices' commands or challenging their claims could therefore result in his belief being reinforced when the voices did in fact punish him by keeping him awake or tormenting him. For Marcus the key cognitive manoeuvre focused on helping to identify how he would tend to tell himself that he could not *stand it* thereby increasing his distress. It was then suggested that more accurately he could say to himself 'I can stand it and have done so before. I can now use my coping strategies rather than drink'. The images he saw were in fact flashbacks and reflected an involuntary activation of his traumatic memories (Waters *et al.*, 2006) of his aunt's death and finding her decomposing body. It emerged that although he routinely submitted to this experience he was actually subtly avoiding reprocessing and exposing himself to the traumatic images and would use praying as a distraction technique. In line with Nelson (2005) it was suggested at a later stage of therapy (see below) that the brain sometimes makes mistakes and can replay such events, which can be then become distorted. In general, we have found introducing the concept of the brain 'making mistakes' as a very helpful way of building evidence to support the alternative explanation: that the voices might reflect memories of past events. In Marcus's case it was suggested that the voices had exploited this event and fed off his guilt about not having been there for his aunt. The event had been so disturbing that understandably he had tried not to think about it. Accepting this explanation made it possible to go on to explore his guilt and reappraise and reprocess this traumatic experience.

Safety behaviours are adopted by the individual to reduce perceived threat and provide short-term relief. In this they are effective and their value should be explicitly recognized. However for Marcus it was noted that they also served to prevent him from learning the extent of the voices true power. In order to build further motivation for change Marcus was asked to consider how not eating helped him to comply with the voices' demands and through Socratic questioning building the insight that 'it will leave me weak and unable to bear witness'. This command from the voices was therefore exposed as logically inconsistent with their plans for him and therefore further proof of their fallibility.

Reducing the use of safety behaviours

The reduction of two safety behaviours were prioritized for Marcus, these were chosen and agreed from a hierarchy of most to least distressing/difficult to withhold. These built upon on the disputes and coping strategies of previous phases. The first involved extending his walks (building on this now established coping strategy) past places that Marcus considered to be evil (at first using his iPod as an additional coping strategy) in order to reduce this threat mitigation safety behaviour. During the walk Marcus was also encouraged to note something of beauty (e.g. a tree in autumn) and how this was further evidence against the world being a totally evil and bad place.

The second safety behaviour targeted was that of eating. Again drawing on Marcus's previous interest in cooking it was agreed that he had to cook a nice meal for himself (building on his coping strategy of reading cookery books) initially once a week; in order to reduce his appeasement behaviour of not eating and not preparing nice food.

For each safety behaviour experiment Marcus was asked to note afterwards how he had felt and importantly what the reactions of the voices had been and how he had coped with these. Marcus reported that although the voices had at times been difficult he had coped with them and that actually when out walking they had soon stopped commenting on places as being evil. They had been quite nasty when Marcus had cooked a nice meal for himself but after repeatedly cooking meals had been less intrusive and distressing, especially when Marcus had pointed out the flaw in their argument and that he needed to keep well.

Raising the power of the individual

Most of the preceding interventions are not only aimed at challenging beliefs about the power of the voice but also establishing that the client has mastery and control, not the voice. The previous experiments served to reinforce Marcus's beliefs that he now had more control over his voices, that they were fallible and that he could choose not to follow everything they said or commanded and, crucially, that he could tolerate the consequences. This was reframed as evidence of a changing power shift. It was also noted that Marcus's beliefs about other people when out on his walks had not been borne out and that they were also like him, no better and no worse, but rather going about their own daily business.

Subsequently Marcus was encouraged to question more harmful commands directly and thereby act against his remaining dysfunctional power beliefs and in line with the new functional beliefs. Marcus found this extremely difficult since he believed that he was deserving of punishment. The rationale for further advanced work at levels 7 and 8 was quickly established and agreed.

Addressing identity, purpose and personal meaning beliefs

It was evident, even from the initial stages of therapy and the shared formulation that his voices fed off guilt for not having saved his aunt and finding her dead in a state of decomposition. It was suggested that this experience would be very distressing for anyone but in his case had turned his voices into malevolent ones (from benign childhood friends) as a result of his guilt at not being there for her and that the images they showed him reflected this theme. It was proposed that Marcus had been punished enough. A trauma explanation was explored (as described above) and accordingly beliefs in identity (which were the least convincingly held power beliefs) dropped to 20 percent; Marcus continued to hold beliefs about the spirit world in general however.

Reframing and disputing core beliefs

REBT theory posits that work at the core belief level is needed in order to effect longer term changes. Clients may also not respond fully to interventions targeted just at power beliefs that are inferential beliefs and this is evident in Marcus's case. Time was spent exploring Marcus's belief that 'I am a very bad person' and that he was 'Marked as evil from birth'. It was formulated that work at this level was key to further reducing compliance and deconstructing the power relationship with his voices.

Past deeds: involvement in occult rituals and starting a fire (following commands to do so from his voices) were all cited as proof of badness. As a first step Marcus was encouraged to consider how it followed that others treating him badly made him bad. It was suggested that maybe they were simply wrong to do this; especially since he was only a child. It was also highlighted how while he had committed an act of arson this was driven by voices and that he had few other ways of coping or refusing their demands at that time. Making whole self judgements and rating one's whole self on the basis of past behaviours (even 'bad' ones) was explored as a logical error and Marcus was encouraged to see 'the self' as an evolving process and helped to recognize that people can change and are not 'forever bad or evil'. Subsequent reduced conviction in this core belief (to 40 percent) enabled final reduction in compliance behaviour with no further incidents reported post therapy and at 6 months.

Outcome

Marcus still used alcohol but less heavily, with, by the end of therapy, a bottle of Vodka lasting for up to a week. He also stopped smoking cannabis and was referred at the end of therapy for ongoing support with substance use. Marcus continued to hear voices but found them much less distressing since he now saw that he had more control over them (80 percent) than they did over him (20 percent), he now also saw his voices as fallible and only 20 percent omniscient. Furthermore Marcus now believed that he did not have to comply with their commands but that they may still be spirits (20 percent) trying, wrongly, to punish him.

Limitations and Future Directions in CTCH

The sample size of our first study, a single blind intention to treat proof of theory trial, was small and conducted only in one (though ethnically and economically diverse) part of the United Kingdom (the West Midlands). We are currently completing a 3-year multicentre trial to address this issue. We hope this will replicate the findings from our first study using different loci and different therapists. In our current trial the average number of sessions required to produce such outcomes as that seen in Marcus has extended to 24 sessions.

Finally, it should be evident by now that we do not make any claims regarding any reduction of symptoms for CTCH. These often persist as shown in other trials; though they may be reduced or even disappear in some individual cases.

References

Addington, D., Addington, J. and Maticka-Tyndale, E. (1993) Assessing depression in schizophrenia: the Calgary Depression Scale. *British Journal of Psychiatry, 163 (suppl. 22)*, 39–44.

Beck-Sander, A., Birchwood, M. and Chadwick, P. (1997) Acting on command hallucinations: A cognitive approach. *British Journal of Clinical Psychology, 36*, 139–148.

Birchwood, M. Gilbert, P., Gilbert, J. *et al.* (2004) Interpersonal and role-related schema influence the relationship with the dominant 'voice' in schizophrenia: a comparison of three models. *Psychological Medicine, 34*, 1–10.

Birchwood, M., Meaden, A., Trower, P. *et al.* (2000) The power and omnipotence of voices: subordination and entrapment by voices and significant others. *Psychological Medicine, 30*, 337–344.

Birchwood, M., Tower, P. and Meaden, A. (2010) Appraisals. In Larøi, R., and Aleman, A. (eds) *Hallucinations: A Practical Guide to Treatment.* Oxford: Oxford University Press.

Byrne, S., Birchwood, M., Trower, P. *et al.* (2006) *Cognitive Therapy for Command Hallucinations: A Social Rank Theory Approach.* New York: Brunner-Routledge.

Chadwick, P. and Birchwood, M.J. (1994) The omnipotence of voices: A cognitive approach to auditory hallucinations. *British Journal of Psychiatry, 164*, 190–201.

Chadwick, P. and Birchwood, M. (1995) The omnipotence of voices II: The beliefs about voices questionnaire. *British Journal of Psychiatry, 166*, 773–776.

Chadwick, P., Birchwood, M. and Trower, P. (1996) *Cognitive Therapy for Delusions, Voices and Paranoia.* Chichester: Wiley.

Chadwick, P., Lees, S. and Birchwood, M. (2000) The revised beliefs about voices questionnaire (BAVQ-R) *British Journal of Psychiatry, 177*, 229–232.

Chadwick, P.D. and Lowe, C.F. (1990) Measurement and modification of delusional beliefs. *Journal of Consulting and Clinical Psychology, 58*, 225–232.

Chadwick, P. and Trower, P. (2008) Person-based cognitive therapy for paranoia: The challenges of 'poor me.' In D. Freeman, R. Bentall, and P. Garety (eds) *Persecutory Delusions: Assessment, Theory and Treatment*, (pp. 411–425). Oxford: Oxford University Press.

Chadwick, P., Trower, P. and Dagnan, D. (1999) Measuring negative person evaluations: The evaluative beliefs scale. *Cognitive Therapy and Research, 23*, 549–559.

Ellis, A. (2004) Why rational emotive behaviour therapy is the most comprehensive and effective form of behaviour therapy. *Journal of Rational Emotive and Cognitive-Behavior Therapy, 22*, 20–38.

Gilbert, P. (1992) *Depression: The Evolution of Powerlessness.* Hove: Lawrence Erlbaum.

Gilbert, P. and Allan, S. (1998) The role of defeat and entrapment (arrested flight) in depression: An exploration of an evolutionary view. *Psychological Medicine, 28*, 584–597.

Hacker, D., Birchwood, M., Tudway, J. *et al.* (2008) Acting on voices: Omnipotence, sources of threat and safety-seeking behaviours. *British Journal of Clinical Psychology, 47*, 201–213.

Haddock, G., McCarron, J., Tarrier, N. *et al.* (1999) Scales to measure dimensions of hallucinations and delusions: The psychotic symptom rating scales (PSYRATS) *Psychological Medicine, 29*, 879–889.

Junginger, J. (1990) Predicting compliance with command hallucinations. *American Journal of Psychiatry, 147*, 245–247.

Kay, S.R., Fiszbein, A. and Opler, L.A. (1987) The positive and negative syndrome scale (PANSS) for schizophrenia. *Schizophrenia Bulletin, 13*, 261–269.

Mawson, A., Cohen, K. and Berry, K. (2010) Reviewing evidence for the cognitive model of auditory hallucinations: The relationship between cognitive voice appraisals and distress during psychosis. *Clinical Psychology Review, 30*, 248–258.

Monahan, J., Steadman, H.J., Silver, E. *et al.* (2001) *Rethinking Risk Assessment: The MacArthur Study of Mental Disorder and Violence.* New York: Oxford University Press.

Nayani, T.H. and David, A. (1996) The auditory hallucination: A phenomenological survey. *Psychological Medicine, 26*, 177–189.

Nelson, H.E. (2005) *Cognitive-Behavioural Therapy with Delusions and Hallucinations. A Practice Manual,* 2nd edn. Cheltenham: Nelson Thornes Ltd.

Rogers, P. (2004) Command hallucinations and violence: Secondary analysis of the MacArthur Violence Risk Assessment Data. PhD diss. Institute of Psychiatry, Kings College, London.

Rogers, P. (2005) The association between command hallucinations and prospective violence: Secondary analysis of the MacArthur Violence Risk Assessment Study. *Presentation at the Institute of Psychiatry Medium Secure Unit Conference.* January 2005.

Shawyer, F., MacKinnon, A., Farhall, J. *et al.* (2003) Command hallucinations and violence: Implications for detention and treatment. *Psychology, Psychiatry and the Law, 10*, 97–107.

Trower, P., Birchwood, M., Meaden, A. *et al.* (2004) Cognitive therapy for command hallucinations: Randomised controlled trial. *British Journal of Psychiatry, 184*, 312–320.

Walen, S.R., DiGiuseppe, R. and Dryden, W. (1992) *A Practitioner's Guide to Rational-Emotive Therapy*. New York: Oxford University Press.

Waters, F.A.V., Badcock, J.C., Michie, P.T. *et al.* (2006) Auditory hallucinations in Schizophrenia. *Cognitive Neuropsychiatry, 11*, 65–83.

Wykes, T., Steel, C., Everitt, B. *et al.* (2007) Cognitive Behaviour Therapy for schizophrenia: Effect sizes, clinical models, and methodological rigor. *Schizophrenia Bulletin, 10*, 1–15.

3

CBT for Post-Traumatic Stress Disorder and Psychosis

Amy Hardy, Ben Smith, Jennifer Gottlieb,
Kim Mueser and Craig Steel

Introduction and Current Evidence-Base

The potential role of trauma in the development and maintenance of psychosis has been increasingly recognized in recent years, with studies indicating higher rates of trauma exposure and Post-Traumatic Stress Disorder (PTSD) in people with psychosis compared to the general population (see Grubaugh *et al.*, 2011 for a review). Further, evidence suggests that PTSD is associated with more severe symptoms, worse functioning and increased use of services in people affected by psychosis (Resnick *et al.* 2003; Mueser, Salyers *et al.*, 2004; Lysaker and LaRocco, 2008). Mueser and colleagues (2002) propose an interactive model to account for the detrimental impact of trauma on psychosis, where the direct effects of PTSD (e.g. re-experiencing, hyperarousal and avoidance symptoms) and the indirect effects (e.g. relationship difficulties, substance use and re-traumatization) are hypothesized to exacerbate symptoms, functional problems and service engagement difficulties. Given the marked negative impact of trauma on people with psychosis, developing effective interventions for PTSD in this client group is a treatment priority.

Cognitive-behavioural approaches provide the basis for the recommended psychological interventions for PTSD (Foa *et al.*, 2000a, 2000b; NICE, 2005). The evidence-based treatments for PTSD can be divided into two

CBT for Schizophrenia: Evidence-Based Interventions and Future Directions,
First Edition. Edited by Craig Steel.
© 2013 John Wiley & Sons, Ltd. Published 2013 by John Wiley & Sons, Ltd.

categories, exposure therapy, involving imagined or actual exposure to trauma-related stimuli, and cognitive restructuring, consisting of evaluation of trauma-related cognitions and beliefs. There is an ongoing debate over the relative effectiveness of these therapies, with the available evidence suggesting that both approaches are equally effective (Marks *et al.*, 1998; Tarrier *et al.*, 1999; Resnick *et al.*, 2002). Few studies have examined the use of these therapies in treating PTSD in people affected by psychosis, and no studies have directly compared exposure and cognitive restructuring approaches in this population. Frueh *et al.* (2009) delivered an exposure-based CBT package (also consisting of group sessions for psychoeducation, anxiety management and social skills training) using an open trial design to a sample of 20 people with co-morbid PTSD and schizophrenia or schizoaffective disorder, and found it significantly reduced PTSD diagnostic status and symptoms at 3-month follow-up, although no differences were found for general anxiety, depression and physical health. In another open trial design, Van den Berg and Van der Gaag (2012) found that a brief EMDR intervention was effective in reducing symptoms of PTSD, psychosis, low self-esteem, anxiety and depression in 27 people with co-morbid schizophrenia and PTSD. While these exploratory studies suggest that exposure approaches may be effective for people with PTSD and psychosis, more systematic research is needed before any firm conclusions can be drawn.

Further, concerns have been raised about the suitability of exposure-based approaches for individuals with complex needs, who may already be experiencing heightened levels of anxiety and sensitivity to stress. Mueser and colleagues (Mueser, Rosenberg, Jankowski, Hamblen & Descamps, 2004; Mueser, Rosenberg and Rosenberg, 2009) developed a Cognitive Restructuring (CR) treatment programme as a potentially more tolerable approach for people with severe mental health problems. The programme also targets common treatment obstacles that occur when working with psychosis, such as cognitive difficulties and social care needs. The focus on CR is based on findings suggesting that the technique can be an effective means of reducing distress in a range of difficulties including psychosis. CR may be a necessary component of addressing complex trauma-related emotions such as guilt and shame, as exposure therapy is less effective for treatment of PTSD when the dominant emotion is not anxiety (Pitman *et al.*, 1991; Smucker *et al.*, 2003). In support of the use of CR in treating PTSD in psychosis, changes in trauma-related cognitions have been shown to mediate changes in PTSD symptoms in people with schizophrenia-spectrum diagnoses (Mueser, Rosenberg, Xie, Jankowski, Bolton, Lu, *et al.*, 2008).

The CR programme has been evaluated in a randomized controlled trial in the US of 108 people with severe mental health problems, and was shown to be helpful in reducing symptoms of PTSD, depression and anxiety, and improving engagement (Mueser *et al.*, 2008). While only 15.7 percent of the sample had schizophrenia-spectrum diagnoses, two pilot studies of the programme had a higher proportion of these clients and also showed high feasibility and reductions in PTSD symptoms at follow-up. To further explore if these findings can be generalized to the psychosis population as a whole, the treatment programme is currently being evaluated by the authors in a randomized controlled trial with a UK sample of people affected by psychosis. This chapter describes a treatment case from the trial in which a client, Helen, worked together with the first author (AH) to manage the impact of her experience of physical, sexual and emotional abuse on her life. The treatment protocol is first described, together with an overview of Helen's presentation and background history. A module by module narrative of the therapy is given, highlighting the progress of key tasks, process issues and impasses during sessions. The chapter concludes with a critical reflection on the use of the protocol to treat Helen's trauma-related problems in the context of her complex mental health needs.

The Protocol

Drawing on cognitive-behavioural models of psychosis and PTSD (Ehlers and Clark, 2000; Garety *et al.* 2001; Morrison, 2001) that highlight a central and key role for *interpretations* of experiences in determining how people *feel*, the main focus in the treatment programme is on cognitive restructuring (CR) – a skill that clients can use to manage distressing feelings, including those arising from trauma-related thoughts and beliefs. The emphasis in the programme is on teaching clients how to use CR independently as a self-management skill, as opposed to the therapist taking responsibility for CR through Socratic questioning. While the teaching of CR is structured, there is a focus on flexibly adapting the approach to suit the specific needs of the individual client and their range of problems (e.g. simplifying for clients with cognitive difficulties, addressing housing or financial problems, and developing ways of coping with symptoms of psychosis). The programme was designed for use with clients who have a primary diagnosis of severe mental health problems (i.e. psychotic, mood and personality disorders) and meet diagnostic criteria for PTSD, although it has also been used in a variety of other vulnerable populations, such as people with PTSD in substance use treatment (McGovern *et al.*, 2011). It is used as an adjunct to the care the individual is already receiving, usually from multidisciplinary secondary mental health services. There is an emphasis on working collaboratively with the client's care team, or others in their social network, during treatment so as to support progress, promote safety and ensure generalization of skills to outside of therapy sessions.

Session Structure

The programme consists of 12 to 16 sessions of individual CBT, starting with weekly meetings and tapering off to biweekly as the work progresses. Individual session structure follows a standard CBT format. Sessions start by collaboratively setting an agenda, reviewing the previous session and the homework task, covering session content, setting and planning a between session task, then reflecting on the session including what has been learnt and addressing any questions. The relationship between out of session skills practice and outcome is highlighted throughout the work, with the therapist using modelling, rehearsal, problem solving, graded scheduling, reinforcement and the client's social support network to promote homework adherence. Worksheets and handouts are also used to support clients' learning in and outside sessions.

Monitoring

To assess the client's presentation and progress during the work it is recommended that symptoms are monitored at regular intervals (i.e. at sessions 1, 4, 7, 10, 13 and 16). The Clinician Administered PTSD Scale (CAPS, Blake *et al.*, 1995) is widely accepted to be the "gold standard" method of assessment of PTSD, and has been shown to be reliable and valid in people with complex mental health needs (Gearon *et al.*, 2004). However, this measure is lengthy and a self-report measure of PTSD can suffice to assess progress, particularly during treatment, such as the PTSD Checklist (PCL, Weathers *et al.*, 1999). Given the high co-morbidity of PTSD and depression, depressive symptoms are assessed using the Beck Depression Inventory (BDI-II, Beck *et al.*, 1996). We have also found it helpful to use the Post-Traumatic Cognitions Inventory (PTCI, Foa *et al.*, 1999), a measure of dysfunctional appraisals about the self, world and others following trauma. The PTCI provides a means of identifying and monitoring key post-traumatic cognitions that can be a focus for CR, and which are likely to be contributing to the client's distress and symptomatology. Sessions incorporate feedback and discussion of the findings of the monitoring, to highlight areas of progress and targets for further work.

Protocol Content

The therapy protocol consists of 8 modules drawing on core cognitive-behavioural ideas and skills, adapted to target the trauma-related difficulties of people with complex needs:

1 *Overview of treatment programme (Session 1)* The main skills learnt during the treatment programme (breathing retraining, psychoeducation and CR) are discussed, including how people with similar difficulties have found these techniques helpful. The importance of homework is highlighted, together with an exploration of the client's attitude to between session practice.

2 *Crisis plan (Session 1)* This involves establishing safety through collaboratively developing a crisis plan with the client to support them in managing any difficulties that may arise and have a negative impact on their ability to complete the treatment programme (including signs, triggers, management strategies and social support).

3 *Breathing retraining (Session 1)* A relaxation technique is taught early in the treatment programme to help the client immediately start to manage their anxiety and instill hope that the therapy will support them in coping with their problems.

4 *Psychoeducation 1 (Session 2)* Information about the symptoms of PTSD is discussed, with a focus on eliciting the client's experience of these symptoms, to highlight their reactions are common, understandable and therefore amendable to change. The psychoeducation module also allows for collaborative agreement of the key trauma-related symptoms to target during treatment.

5 *Psychoeducation 2 (Session 3)* The second module of psychoeducation involves talking through the client's experience of problems associated with PTSD (i.e. distressing feelings such as anxiety, sadness, guilt/shame and anger, relationship problems and substance use), focusing again on empathising with the client's experience and collaboratively identifying treatment goals. The module concludes with a discussion of the client's hopes for therapy, including the identification of functional changes they would like to happen in their life as a result of participating in the programme.

6 *Cognitive restructuring 1 (Session 4 to 6)* The client is introduced to the cognitive-behavioural model through discussion of the impact of subjective interpretations of events on feelings and behaviour, and the influence of traumatic experiences on our thoughts and beliefs. The client learns about and is encouraged to reflect on their own experience of "common styles of thinking", or cognitive biases, that may understandably, yet unhelpfully, be reflected in thoughts, particularly in people with trauma-related problems.

7 *Cognitive restructuring 2 (Session 5 to 14)* The '5 steps' technique is introduced as the framework to help manage thoughts that are associated with distressing feelings. The 5 steps are summarized briefly as:
   1 *Identify situation*: what happened that made me feel upset?
   2 *Identify feeling*: what is the strongest feeling associated with the situation?

3 *Identify thought*: what am I thinking that is leading me to feel this way?

4 *Evaluate evidence*: what is the evidence for and against the thought?

5 *Take action*: does the evidence support my thought or not? If no, what is an alternative thought? And if yes, what can I do to cope with or manage the thought/situation? Develop an action (i.e. problem solving) plan.

The technique is taught to the client in a graded way, with the therapist shaping the client to become increasingly more independent in using the skill, using a Socratic and collaborative engagement style. Clients are encouraged to notice, in and outside sessions, situations in which they feel upset and use the 5 steps technique to address that situation. Initially the therapist focuses on everyday examples of upsetting thoughts to support the client in becoming familiar with the process of being more aware of their thoughts, identifying cognitive biases and evaluating related evidence. The therapist looks out for, and reinforces, any change in distress resulting from the 5 steps technique. As the work progresses, the 5 steps skill is applied to trauma-related thoughts and beliefs to more directly target symptoms of PTSD (e.g. thoughts of self-blame, mistrust and worthlessness, sleep problems, re-experiencing symptoms, avoidance, anger, relationship difficulties and substance use). Sessions are used to apply the 5 steps to ongoing distress and symptoms, problem solve any difficulties the client has experienced using the 5 steps outside sessions and target cognitions identified during monitoring.

8 *Generalization and termination (Sessions 12 to 16)* The final module involves supporting the client to plan how to continue using the skills they have learnt after the sessions have finished. This includes, if possible, the client rehearsing and then teaching the CR skills to their care co-ordinator (or others that provide support to the client) in the penultimate session. The client is encouraged to review the progress they have made, identify helpful strategies, highlight targets for further work towards personal goals, and problem solve and agree plans for addressing any anticipated problems.

Presentation

Helen was a 54-year-old woman with an extensive history of abuse, who identified her most distressing traumatic experience as a sexual assault by her grandfather when she was 10 years old. This incident happened in the context of persistent physical and emotional abuse and neglect from her mother and siblings during Helen's childhood. She ran away from home two times during childhood to escape the abuse and spent time in care where she was also mistreated. Helen was raped by an acquaintance of her sister's when she was 18 years old, and had experienced further incidents of emotional, sexual and physical abuse in adulthood, particularly with her partners.

In relation to the index sexual assault, Helen met diagnostic criteria for PTSD on the Clinician Administered PTSD Scale (CAPS, Blake *et al.*, 1995), endorsing 4 out of 5 re-experiencing symptoms, 5 out of 7 emotional numbing/avoidance symptoms and 4 out of 5 hyperarousal symptoms, giving a total symptom score of 74, reflecting severe PTSD (Weathers *et al.*, 1999). She strongly agreed with a number of distressing cognitions about herself, the world and self-blame on the PTCI, obtaining a score of 176 out of 231.

Helen's re-experiencing symptoms consisted of memories, dreams, flashbacks, thoughts, feelings, smells and sensations related to previous abuse, such as having dreams where she felt that she was back in the care home or experiencing sensations and smells associated with abuse. Related to this, Helen had high levels of tension, hyperarousal and irritability, such that she often felt on guard and unable to relax. Helen understandably avoided people and places that reminded her of the traumatic experiences, such as her family or her local town centre, and felt emotionally numb, finding it harder to get pleasure from and be interested in things.

Helen also had a diagnosis of schizoaffective disorder. She described experiencing ideas of reference and persecutory beliefs in that she often perceived other people to be bullying and intimidating her (e.g. saying the word 'paedophile' when she walked past them, breaking into her house and moving items around) and thought other people, including her neighbours and possibly the authorities, were deliberately conspiring against her. These symptoms impacted on Helen's functioning and strengthened her low mood, such that she obtained a score of 32 on the Beck Depression Inventory (BDI-II), indicating a severe level of depression.

Background

Helen was born and grew up in England with her mother, who was from Nigeria, and her 3 younger sisters. Helen's mother's relationship with her White British father ended before she was born and Helen did not have any contact with him. Helen described her childhood as abusive and neglectful. She was not in contact with her mother or her sisters, who she said would not communicate with her unless she was willing to deny their abusive upbringing. She said she had tried hard to overcome the impact of her childhood on her life, working in catering while bringing up her two children. She reported that her relationship with her first husband, the father of her children, ended when he had an affair. Her relationship with her second husband was abusive and they had separated 15 years ago, although they maintained occasional contact. Helen described struggling throughout her life to cope with trauma-related difficulties, regularly having periods of marked depression and anxiety. She said she started feeling increasingly anxious and unsafe 10 years ago, when she became increasingly isolated after losing her job, her youngest child left home and she was involved in a dispute with her neighbours. Helen was then referred to secondary mental health services following a crisis in which she took an overdose of antidepressant medication. Her medication at the start of treatment was Quetiapine, 400mgs o.d, and Propanol, 5mgs PRN.

Treatment programme

Module 1 – Overview (session 1)
Helen and I began by discussing an overview of the treatment programme, highlighting the key skills that she would be supported to learn during therapy (breathing retraining, psychoeducation and cognitive restructuring) and emphasizing the importance of practicing between sessions. As part of the overview, we reflected on Helen's attitude towards the treatment and motivation. On the one hand she was positive and motivated to do the work, saying 'I do not want others' mistreatment to pull me down; I have worked hard before to get over difficult times, bringing up my children and working . . . I want help to get my life back to the way things used to be'. She had previous experience of a brief CBT group for managing emotions, which she had found helpful but difficult to continue using in her daily life, and said she was keen to build on these skills. On the other hand, Helen described often being overwhelmed by feelings of anger, sadness, shame and fear, which left her doubting whether change was possible. She told me how the abuse she experienced made her think that 'others will always mistreat and force their negativity onto me'. To reinforce this point, Helen spoke about the problems she experienced with people on her estate, becoming more agitated and upset as she did, describing how they were always gossiping about her behind her back and trying to ruin her life. She was caught between feeling angry that they were bullying her and sometimes tried to fight back, while at the same time felt trapped and fearful of facing them or making any other changes in her life. Helen also said she blamed herself for her situation, commenting 'it's my fault my life is so worthless', adding to her sense of hopelessness about change.

Module 2 – Crisis plan (session 1)
When completing the crisis plan, Helen was able to readily identify signs (i.e. increased anxiety/panic and sadness, being more on the lookout for danger, intrusive memories of abuse, nightmares, suicidal ideation and withdrawal), triggers (i.e. being exposed to reminders of the abuse, relationship problems and social stressors, such as housing, finance and employment difficulties) and coping strategies (e.g. contact family, listen to the radio, consider going to see GP) to manage difficult periods. Helen was keen to make it clear that she did not trust statutory services ever since an incident when her children were taken into care during a period of family conflict. This meant she did not think services could be helpful in supporting her during a crisis, although agreed it might be helpful to record key contact numbers (care co-ordinator and crisis team) as well those of her family.

Module 3 – Breathing retraining (session 1)
We introduced the final part of the first session by discussing Helen's current experience of anxiety (she was particularly distressed by chest pain and tension) and how this impacted on her life (avoiding going outside her immediate local area, which limited her opportunities for socializing and employment). She reported having found relaxation exercises using an audio recording helpful in the past, although said this was less useful when she was actually experiencing panic in her daily life. The breathing retraining was introduced as a straightforward technique that, once practiced, could be used to regulate breathing as a way of reducing arousal in any situation. Helen noticed that when fearful she breathed more quickly, and we discussed how this increases oxygen intake and intensifies anxiety. I modelled and then we practiced breathing more slowly as a means of helping our bodies to relax, with a short breath in through the nose, exhaling slowly through the mouth while saying a relaxing word in our minds, then pausing before repeating. Helen reported feeling self-conscious and found it difficult to relax in front of another person, although thought it could be relaxing and collaboratively agreed to practice daily before bed, using the handout as a reminder and a prompt. I highlighted that we would review Helen's experience of the practice next week, and work together to address any difficulties that arose.

Helen ended the session by noting that while she had reservations about whether the work would be helpful she was willing to 'give the programme a go', and had some confidence that she would be able to learn the skills and try them out in her life. As Helen had raised lack of support from others and mistrust of health and social services as an obstacle to engagement, we agreed it would be helpful to liaise with her care co-ordinator, particularly to get a clearer picture of the circumstances surrounding her social stressors and consider how the treatment programme may support her care plan.

Module 4 – Psychoeducation 1 (session 2)

At the start of session 2, Helen reported that she had found the breathing retraining helpful, with it being easier to get to sleep and to calm herself down when she woke from nightmares about the abuse. She reiterated that she did not think that the skills would be helpful in managing all of her problems, but said she was would continue practising it and start applying it to anxiety that she experienced during the day. We agreed to spend the session focusing on learning about Helen's experience of post-traumatic stress symptoms, so that we could better understand her difficulties and identify goals and obstacles to focus on during the programme. Using a hand-out describing the main symptoms of PTSD, we explored and documented Helen's post-traumatic difficulties on worksheets, with her highlighting nightmares about the abuse ('a mixture of too many thoughts, pictures, and feelings which continue when I wake up, so the panic builds'), breathlessness and social isolation as her most frequent and distressing problems. Helen understandably became distressed when discussing her experiences, shifting between feelings of shame, sadness and fear, blaming herself for what happened and perceiving herself as vulnerable to harm – to then feeling angry, becoming more mistrustful and rejecting of others. She was prompted to briefly initiate the breathing retraining skill to help her manage feelings of anxiety as she became distressed. At the end of the session, Helen said it had been difficult to discuss her experiences, although found it reassuring to know that her problems made sense and that she could learn to manage them. We agreed it had been helpful to identify her most upsetting PTSD symptoms so we could focus on addressing them in the remainder of the work.

Module 5 – Psychoeducation 2 (session 3)

Reviewing the homework task, Helen reported that she had been using the breathing retraining more regularly and was finding that instead of being overwhelmed by distressing emotions she would 'stop and breathe'. She said this reduction in her arousal allowed her to think 'more clearly' about what to do to cope with difficult situations and agreed to continue using the technique. We then moved onto the second psychoeducation module, considering Helen's experience of distressing emotions and relationship problems (she did not report any substance use so we omitted this aspect of the protocol). Helen strongly agreed that she was affected by fearful, angry, shaming and sad thoughts and feelings, for example, reporting 'others are going to hurt me', 'people take advantage of me', 'I am a failure' and 'everything is hopeless so long as I have to deal with the neighbours'. She spoke at length about the impact of her problems on her relationships, how she could not trust others and was always let down, becoming increasingly angry and preoccupied by past events. We concluded the module by exploring Helen's hopes and goals for the treatment programme. She was readily able to identify a number of goals across a range of areas (e.g. getting back into education or work, going to the gym, taking more care in her appearance, spending time outside her local area and decorating her home). At the end of the session, Helen agreed to review the work we had done so far on being aware of and making sense of her trauma-related difficulties, to prepare for the next session in which we would start learning a technique to help her cope with distressing feelings.

Module 6 – Cognitive restructuring 1 (sessions 4, 5 and 6)
Helen and I initially made good progress in the first cognitive restructuring module. While she spent much of the first session feeling upset and angry about the events of the previous week (disagreements with friends and harassment by her neighbours), she reported the breathing retraining was still helpful and had started trying to make some plans for the future (e.g. sorting finances to buy paint and finding out about a local employment service). When introducing Helen to the cognitive-behavioural approach, she was able understand the relationship between past experiences, thoughts and feelings, and somewhat able to consider how her trauma history affected her thoughts, although she found it difficult to focus on a specific thought instead tending to report a whole stream of rumination. Nonetheless, she connected to the idea of 'Common Thinking Styles', particularly recognizing that she was vulnerable to 'catastrophizing . . . thinking the worst' when having panic attacks about leaving her home. Helen spontaneously suggested the between session task to build on her learning from the session, to start monitoring her distressing thoughts and any related common thinking styles. We went through a worksheet to support her in doing this and planned when she would do the task.

Helen then missed several sessions and when we met for session 5 she appeared more depressed and angry. She reported that she was finding the breathing retraining 'helpful . . . but it's only ever going to help up to a point'. Helen said she had not done the between session task of monitoring her distressing thoughts and common thinking styles, as she had recently spent the weekend with her family and then felt isolated when this was over. She explained the incident had made her realize that the treatment programme 'was not going to help with my reality, it's not just about my thoughts, I'm lonely and no one's helping me'. I introduced the idea that the main skill we were building towards learning allowed us to deal with social problems (through the use of action plans) that were contributing to upsetting feelings as well as working through less helpful, distressing thoughts. We reviewed the material we had covered during the past session, and Helen showed she had retained an understanding of the cognitive-behavioural approach. However, when encouraged to identify any common thinking styles connected to any of her recent upsetting thoughts, Helen became increasingly frustrated by the approach and withdrew her consent to continue with the task. We spent the remainder of the session validating her distress and making plans to help her cope during the following week, drawing on the crisis plan and reinforcing her progress with breathing retraining.

At session 6, after liaison with the care co-ordinator to start making plans for daytime activity, Helen presented as somewhat less overwhelmed, reporting she was now using breathing retraining to more effectively manage her panic attacks and sleep. She reported finding the last session a 'helpful opportunity' to express her 'genuine' problems, and thought that the programme could be useful for managing her mental health difficulties so long as she also had assistance with her social needs. We completed the module by agreeing we had developed a shared understanding of her difficulties, acknowledging both the social and psychological consequences of her traumatic experiences. Helen reported that she was keen to start the next module and start learning the 5 steps technique for managing her upsetting feelings.

Module 7 – Cognitive restructuring 2 (sessions 7 to 12)
Teaching Helen to use the 5 steps technique involved a gradual process of modelling, rehearsing and then supporting her to independently practice the skill. As demonstrated in module 6, Helen was usually readily able to identify upsetting situations, associated feelings and the related thoughts. We worked through more straightforward examples to start ('I am going to be attacked on the way to the bus stop' and 'I am never going to be able to get to sleep') and she was able to generate alternative, less distressing thoughts using the 5 steps ('I might be feeling scared but there's no actual threat' and 'I can use the time to rest and relax, and I usually do get to sleep in the end'). However, she sometimes became overwhelmed, finding it difficult to slow down her thinking and focus on identifying the strongest feeling, most connected thought, and/or evaluating the related evidence. Helen found it difficult at first to do step 4 (evaluating evidence) at home and so struggled with homework tasks, and when we explored this she reported 'I'm too stupid . . . not logical enough to be able to think things through by myself, I need to do it with someone'. We addressed this impasse using the 5 steps (leading to the alternative thought, 'I have already found the 5 steps helpful and everyone takes time to learn to do something new') helping Helen to feel more confident about using cognitive restructuring independently and improving her homework adherence. A theme throughout sessions 8 to 12 was a persistent focus on the aspects of the 5 steps that Helen found more difficult in order to build her competence in using the technique (e.g. developing a prompt sheet to help her learn to do step 4 more independently, including questions such as, Am I overestimating the likelihood of something bad happening? Am I underestimating my

ability to cope? What would I say if one of my children was having the thought? What do I think the teacher I trusted would say about the thought? Am I considering all the factors that might be contributing to the situation?) Helen started to personalize and adapt the CR approach, such as using the statement 'stop the train rolling down the hill' to remind herself to start using the 5 steps technique, and spending more time 'dealing with and breaking down my thoughts to cope with difficult feelings' outside of sessions. She generally found that she used the technique more frequently if she did it mentally in the mornings and afternoons, and then in the evenings went through her upsetting thoughts from that day in detail and recorded the process on the 5 steps sheets, referring to the previously completed 5 step examples to remind her how to use the approach.

Helen's trauma-related thoughts and beliefs had been apparent throughout the work, particularly those about being a 'worthless, hopeless failure' and 'others taking advantage' of her. As mentioned previously, Helen could become increasingly agitated and preoccupied when discussing these thoughts, getting caught up in analyzing the potential meaning and implications of past and recent events. During these times Helen found it difficult to consider alternative perspectives. When doing the 5 steps on thoughts that reflected her trauma-related beliefs, she initially tended to decide the evidence supported her thoughts (e.g. 'my friend was trying to make me look stupid', 'they are going to watch and gossip about me' and 'nothing will ever change') and so we opted to focus on developing actions plans to help her deal with these problems (e.g. asserting herself with her friend, coping with anxiety about going outside, and planning ways of working towards her goals such as being more active during the day). We regularly reviewed her progress on these actions plans, with her reporting she was more able to deal with daily stressors (such as seeing her neighbours without getting so scared and angry) from which Helen drew two main conclusions. First, that she 'needed to collect more evidence and not jump to conclusions' about stressful daily events and also that 'being chilled out and letting things go, with myself and with others, makes life easier'.

Helen integrated these learning points into her approach to the 5 steps, and at session 10 we started to directly focus on addressing her trauma-related beliefs. At this stage in the work, Helen reported noticing common themes in the thoughts that she identified doing the 5 steps. We framed these as trauma-related beliefs (e.g. 'I have not put my past behind me', 'I should have done things differently and stopped the abuse' and 'others will treat me badly and take advantage') that were providing the 'fuel' for her upsetting thoughts. Helen was increasingly able to independently evaluate her thoughts, developing less distressing trauma-related cognitions (e.g. 'I have tried and mostly been successful in putting my past behind me', 'I did what I could to help myself, but others were not there for me and played a role in what happened to me' and 'not everyone's the same, some people have helped me and the future could be different from the past'), which she practiced using outside sessions when situations triggered her trauma-related feelings and thoughts. An example of a 5 steps worksheet completed by Helen, on the thought 'I should have done things differently and stopped the abuse', is shown in Figure 3.1.

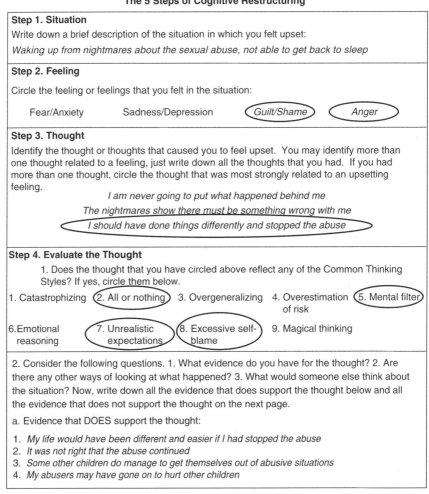

The 5 Steps of Cognitive Restructuring

Step 1. Situation

Write down a brief description of the situation in which you felt upset:

Waking up from nightmares about the sexual abuse, not able to get back to sleep

Step 2. Feeling

Circle the feeling or feelings that you felt in the situation:

Fear/Anxiety   Sadness/Depression   (Guilt/Shame)   (Anger)

Step 3. Thought

Identify the thought or thoughts that caused you to feel upset. You may identify more than one thought related to a feeling, just write down all the thoughts that you had. If you had more than one thought, circle the thought that was most strongly related to an upsetting feeling.

I am never going to put what happened behind me

The nightmares show there must be something wrong with me

I should have done things differently and stopped the abuse

Step 4. Evaluate the Thought

    1. Does the thought that you have circled above reflect any of the Common Thinking Styles? If yes, circle them below.

1. Catastrophizing   (2. All or nothing)   3. Overgeneralizing   4. Overestimation   (5. Mental filter)
                                                of risk

6. Emotional   (7. Unrealistic)   (8. Excessive self-)   9. Magical thinking
  reasoning   expectations   blame

2. Consider the following questions. 1. What evidence do you have for the thought? 2. Are there any other ways of looking at what happened? 3. What would someone else think about the situation? Now, write down all the evidence that does support the thought below and all the evidence that does not support the thought on the next page.

a. Evidence that DOES support the thought:

1. *My life would have been different and easier if I had stopped the abuse*
2. *It was not right that the abuse continued*
3. *Some other children do manage to get themselves out of abusive situations*
4. *My abusers may have gone on to hurt other children*

Figure 3.1   Example of using the 5 steps cognitive restructuring technique to address a trauma-related belief

Adapted from *Treatment of Posttraumatic Stress Disorder in Special Populations: A Cognitive Restructuring Program*, by K.T. Mueser, S.D. Rosenberg, and H.J. Rosenberg, 2009, Washington, DC: American Psychological Association. Copyright 2009 by the American Psychological Association.

Step 4. Evaluate the Thought continued.

b. Evidence that DOES NOT support the thought:

1. *I did try to tell my mum but she did not listen*
2. *I tried to talk to my teacher but it is understandable that I was too scared*
3. *Given what happened to me during my early life, it makes sense that I did not expect anyone would be able to help me*
4. *I was only a child, I would not expect another child to take responsibility for preventing abuse*
5. *The people that abused me were responsible for what they did*

Step 5. Take Action

Look at all the evidence for the thought. Do things mostly support the thought or do things mostly not support the thought?

☑ No, the evidence does not support my thought.

If the evidence does not support the thought, come up with a new, more balanced and realistic thought that is supported by the evidence.Write down the new thought below. Remember to replace the unhelpful and unbalanced thought with the new, more balanced and realistic thought if it comes to mind again in the future.

I did what I could to help myself, but others were not there for me and played a role in what happened to me

Does the new thought change how you feel? Please tick a box below.

☑ **Less** distress   ☐ **More** distress   ☐ **Same** distress

If the new thought makes you feel less distressed, remember to replace the unhelpful and unbalanced thought with the new, more balanced and realistic thought if it comes to mind again in the future.

☐ **Yes,** the evidence *does* support my thought.

If the evidence does support the thought, decide what you need to do in order to deal with the situation. Do you need to get more information about what to do? Do you need to get some help? Do you need to take steps to make sure you are safe? Write down your action plan for dealing with the upsetting situation or complete the Action Plan (Worksheet 12).

Figure 3.1   *(Continued)*

Module 8 – Generalization and termination (Session 12 to 16)

During the final module, Helen was supported to consolidate the new ideas and skills she had developed during the treatment programme. She continued to experience psychosocial stressors throughout this period, relating to conflict with her children and housing problems, struggling at times to consistently use the programme techniques and missing several sessions. We reviewed the work by summarizing the progress Helen thought she had made during the programme (e.g. managing re-experiencing and avoidance symptoms, dealing with distressing feelings particularly panic and anger, coping with relationships better and making progress towards goals in life), strategies for dealing with persistent PTSD symptoms using the 5 steps approach (e.g. graded exposure to build up vocational activity, spending time with a friend she could trust, focusing on more realistic, less distressing thoughts) and planning how she

CBT FOR PTSD SUMMARY

THE FIVE STEPS. WHEN I AM UPSET – ASK MYSELF:

1. What situation am I in?
2. How am I feeling?
3. What am I thinking? Are there any common thinking styles – is the thought real or not?
4. Does the evidence support the thought or not support the thought?
5. DEAL WITH IT. What's a more helpful, balanced thought OR what can I do to cope better?

COMMON COPING STRATEGIES

1. Learn to let it go – recognise the people and things that I cannot change – worrying does not help
2. Be as chilled out/tactful as possible
3. Get support from people/staff that I trust
4. Think about the positives
5. Don't jump to conclusions
6. Gather as much information about the situation as possible
7. Pay attention to what's actually happening not how I feel

DEALING WITH MY TRAUMA-RELATED THOUGHTS

Trauma-related thought	*Balanced, realistic thought*
I have not put my past behind me	I have done a lot to try and put my past behind me, and have mostly been successful
I should not be talking about my family and past traumatic experiences	It's my right to talk about my family, everyone does It makes sense to discuss the past if it helps keep my children safe
I should have done things differently and stopped the abuse	I could not have done things differently, others are responsible for what happened to me When I could, I tried to do things differently but others did not help me out
I'm a bad person and that's why bad things have happened to me	Bad things happen because it's part of life, they can happen to anyone I was not protected by others, I did not have the chance to learn how to cope and assert myself
I am a worthless, horrible and bad person	I am a worthwhile person and have lived a productive life
Others will treat me badly and take advantage	Not everyone is the same, I know there are people around who are more like me Just because people have treated me badly in the past does not mean that people will behave the same in the future
Things will never change and only get worse in the future	It is just a bad time, things could be worse, I've been here before, things will be ok.

Figure 3.2 Therapy blueprint developed collaboratively with Helen: CBT for PTSD summary

could be supported to continue using the techniques after the work had finished (e.g. storing electronic copies of therapy documents on her electronic medical record, using her therapy folder as a prompt and resource during difficult times, asking her care co-ordinator to assist in using skills). The therapy blueprint collaboratively developed with Helen is shown in Figure 3.2. When reflecting on the work, Helen reported that she felt more positive about the future and able to manage her problems, stating 'now I can wake up feeling rubbish and understand what's happening and deal with my thoughts, to help me get on with my life'. We planned a joint session with the care co-ordinator to handover the work done during the treatment programme, with Helen guiding them through the 5 steps approach and summarizing the work to date. Helen was keen to identify action plan points for which she needed ongoing support (e.g. housing concerns, finances, joining a gym and finishing her decorating) while also highlighting the skills she had learnt for managing her thoughts, and how the care co-ordinator could prompt her to use them. Helen and I also produced audio and written copies of the therapy summaries, which she wanted to review regularly to remind her of the work and continue applying it in her daily life.

Outcome

Helen's progress was assessed at the end of treatment and at a follow-up meeting 6 months after the end of therapy. At the end of the intervention, Helen no longer met diagnostic criteria for PTSD on the CAPS, endorsing 1 out of 5 re-experiencing symptoms, 1 out of 7 emotional numbing/avoidance symptoms and 3 out of 5 hyperarousal symptoms, with a total score of 39 reflecting mild PTSD (compared to 76 at the start of therapy, which was indicative of severe PTSD). Her depression ratings on the BDI-II had reduced from 32 to 9 at the end of the programme, reflecting a shift from a severe to mild, non-clinical level of depression. Importantly, Helen's responses on the PTCI demonstrated a more realistic and balanced thinking style, with a score of 102 out of 231, compared to 176 at the beginning of the work. The improvement in Helen's symptoms and trauma-related cognitions was more apparent at the 6-month follow-up assessment with a total score of 10 on the CAPS (endorsing no re-experiencing or numbing/avoidance symptoms, and 1 out of the 5 hyperarousal symptoms), a score of 11 on the BDI-II and an overall rating of 86 on the PTCI.

Discussion

The treatment programme provided an effective approach to support Helen in learning skills to significantly reduce her symptoms of PTSD and distress.

At the beginning of the work, there was a concern that Helen's emotions may be too overwhelming for her to be able to work on the programme tasks, and her trauma-related beliefs regarding others (e.g. 'they cannot be trusted, they will let me down') would be an obstacle to developing a secure therapeutic rapport. However, the protocol actually provided a consistent and coherent framework within which these issues could be identified and worked through while maintaining the focus on treating Helen's trauma related problems. Supervision to reflect on the balance between process (i.e. attending to Helen's affect) and content issues (i.e. working through the protocol tasks) was helpful in ensuring she felt supported during the work while also being assisted to effectively learn the treatment programme skills. The framework was sufficiently flexible to allow us to support adaptations that worked better for Helen so long as they were in the interests of reducing Helen's distress and generalizing skills learnt.

While there was no explicit focus on reliving, through the process of CR there was a sense that Helen's traumatic memories had been brought 'on-line', supporting her in being aware of and processing less helpful trauma-related appraisals. As Helen started to cognitively integrate this new information when having re-experiencing symptoms, it could be hypothesized that she was addressing her traumatic 'hotspots' as they occurred in-vivo in her daily life (see Grey *et al.*, 2002). The protocol also allowed for working with the persecutory thoughts that Helen was convinced of, by first developing actions plans to cope with anxiety-provoking situations which then indirectly provided new information to integrate into the re-evaluation of those thoughts and their underlying trauma-related beliefs. For example, Helen often reported thoughts that 'the neighbours are gossiping and spreading rumours about me' which seemed connected to her trauma-related belief that 'others cannot be trusted and will take advantage of me'. She was initially very convinced that the available evidence supported these thoughts, and so developed an action plan to help her cope with distressing situations involving the neighbours (e.g. using breathing retraining to manage symptoms of panic when seeing them, practising interpersonal effectiveness techniques, and activity scheduling to build up positive social contacts). In applying these coping strategies, Helen was able to gather more evidence relating to her distressing persecutory thoughts, leading her to alternatively conclude 'I cannot be certain the neighbours are gossiping about me and it's better to focus my time and attention on people who will treat me better'. Helen then incorporated this conclusion and the supporting evidence into the cognitive restructuring of her trauma-related belief that others would mistreat her, leading her to develop an alternative, less distressing belief that 'not everyone is the same and the future does not have to be like the past'.

The liaison with the care co-ordinator was critical to the effectiveness of treatment. It was reported that repeated attempts had previously been made to set up care plans to deal with Helen's social needs, although it had been difficult to make progress as Helen was often preoccupied and distressed by new social stressors. Understandably Helen also found it hard at times to work with the care team due to her thoughts that the future was hopeless and she could not trust others to support her. It seemed the treatment protocol had allowed a clear and focused approach to care planning. Helen's care co-ordinator reported their sessions were more productive as Helen was less affected by feelings of sadness and anger, and they were both more confident about supporting Helen's recovery.

Acknowledgements

We would like to thank Helen for her participation in the therapy and research.

References

Beck, A.T., Steer, R.A. and Brown, G.K. (1996) *Manual for the Beck Depression Inventory-II*. San Antonio, TX: Psychological Corporation.

Blake, D.D., Weathers, F.W., Nagy, L.M. *et al.* (1995) The development of a clinician-administered PTSD scale. *Journal of Traumatic Stress, 8,* 75–90.

Ehlers, A. and Clark, D.M. (2000) A cognitive model of posttraumatic stress disorder. *Behaviour Research and Therapy, 38,* 319–345.

Foa, E.B., Ehlers, A., Clark, D.M., Tolin, D.F. and Orsillo, S.M. (1999) The posttraumatic cognitions inventory (PTCI): Development and validation. *Psychological Assessment, 11,* 303–314.

Foa, E.B., Keane, T.M. and Friedman, M.J. (2000a) Guidelines for the treatment of PTSD. *Journal of Traumatic Stress, 13,* 539–555.

Foa, E.B., Keane, T.M. and Friedman, M.J. (eds) (2000b) *Effective Treatments for PTSD*. New York: Guilford Press.

Frueh, B.C., Grubaugh, A.L., Cusack, K.J. *et al.* (2009) Exposure-based cognitive behavioural treatment of PTSD in adults with schizophrenia or schizoaffective disorder: A pilot study. *Journal of Anxiety Disorders, 23(5),* 665–675.

Garety, P., Kuipers, E., Fowler, D. *et al.* (2001) A cognitive model of the positive symptoms of psychosis. *Psychological Medicine, 31,* 189–195.

Gearon, J.S., Bellack, Alan, S. *et al.* (2004) Preliminary reliability and validity of the clinician-administered PTSD scale for schizophrenia. *Journal of Consulting and Clinical Psychology, 72(1),* 121–125.

Grey, N., Young, K. and Holmes, E. (2002) Cognitive restructuring within reliving: A treatment for peritraumatic emotional 'hotspots' in posttraumatic stress disorder. *Behavioural and Cognitive Psychotherapy, 30(1),* 37–56.

Grubaugh, A.L., Zinzow, H.M., Paul, L. *et al.* (2011) Trauma exposure and posttraumatic stress disorder in adults with severe mental illness: A critical review. *Clinical Psychology Review, 31*, 883–899.

Lysaker, P.H. and LaRocco, V.A. (2008) The prevalence and correlates of trauma-related symptoms in schizophrenia spectrum disorder. *Comprehensive Psychiatry, 49(4)*, 330–334.

Marks, I., Lovell, K., Noshirvani, H. *et al.* (1998) Treatment of posttraumatic stress disorder by exposure and/or cognitive restructuring. *Archives of General Psychiatry, 55*, 317–325.

McGovern, M.P., Lambert-Harris, C., Alterman, A.I. *et al.* (2011) A randomized controlled trial comparing integrated cognitive behavioral therapy versus individual addiction counseling or co-occurring substance use and posttraumatic stress disorders. *Journal of Dual Diagnosis, 7*, 207–227.

Morrison, A.P. (2001) The interpretation of intrusions in psychosis: An integrative cognitive approach to hallucinations and delusions. *Behavioural and Cognitive Psychotherapy, 29*, 257–276.

Mueser, K.T., Rosenberg, S.D., Goodman, L.A. *et al.* (2002) Trauma, PTSD, and the course of schizophrenia: An interactive model. *Schizophrenia Research, 53*, 123–143.

Mueser, K.T., Rosenberg, S.D., Jankowski, M.K. *et al.* (2004a) A cognitive-behavioural treatment program for post-traumatic stress disorder in severe mental illness. *American Journal of Psychiatric Rehabilitation, 7*, 107–146.

Mueser, K.T., Rosenberg, S.D. and Rosenberg, H. (2009) *Treatment of Posttraumatic Stress Disorder in Special Populations: A Cognitive Restructuring Program.* Washington, DC: American Psychological Association.

Mueser, K.T., Rosenberg, S.D., Xie, H. *et al.* (2008) A randomised controlled trial of cognitive-behavioural treatment of posttraumatic stress disorder in severe mental illness. *Journal of Consulting and Clinical Psychology, 76*, 259–271.

Mueser, K.T., Salyers, M.P., Rosenberg, S. D. *et al.* (2004b) Interpersonal trauma and post-traumatic stress disorder in patients with severe mental illness: Demographic, clinical and health correlates. *Schizophrenia Bulletin, 30*, 45–57.

National Institute for Clinical Excellence (NICE) (2005) *Post-traumatic Stress Disorder: The Management of PTSD in Adults and Children in Primary and Secondary Care. National Clinical Practice Guideline 26.* London: Royal College of Psychiatrists and British Psychological Society.

Pitman, R.K., Altman, B., Greenwald, E. *et al.* (1991) Psychiatric complications during flooding therapy for posttraumatic stress disorder. *Journal of Clinical Psychiatry, 52*, 17–20.

Resnick, S.G., Bond, G.R. and Mueser, K.T. (2003) Trauma and posttraumatic stress disorder in people with schizophrenia. *Journal of Abnormal Psychology, 112*, 415–423.

Resick, P.A., Nishith, P., Weaver, T.L. *et al.* (2002) A comparison of cognitive processing therapy with prolonged exposure and a waiting condition for the treatment of posttraumatic stress disorder in female rape victims. *Journal of Consulting and Clinical Psychology, 61*, 384–991.

Rosenberg, S.D., Mueser, K.T., Jankowski, M.K. *et al.* (2004) Cognitive-behavioral treatment of posttraumatic stress disorder in severe mental illness: Results of a pilot study. *American Journal of Psychiatric Rehabilitation, 7*, 171–186.

Smucker, M.R., Grunert, B.K. and Weis, J.M. (2003) Posttraumatic stress disorder: A new algorithm treatment model. In R. L. Leahy (ed.), *Roadblocks in Cognitive-Behavioral Therapy: Transforming Challenges into Opportunities for Change* (pp. 175–194). New York: Guilford Press.

Tarrier, N., Pilgrim, H., Sommerfield, C. *et al.* (1999) Cognitive and exposure therapy in the treatment of PTSD. *Journal of Consulting and Clinical Psychology, 67*, 13–18.

Van den Berg, D.P.G. and Van der Gaag, M. (2012) Treating trauma in psychosis with EMDR: A pilot study. *Journal of Behaviour Therapy & Experimental Psychiatry, 43*, 664–671.

Weathers, F.W., Ruscio, A.M., and Keane, T.M. (1999) Psychometric properties of nine scoring rules for the Clinician-Administered Posttraumatic Stress Disorder Scale. *Psychological Assessment, 11(2)*, 124–133.

4

CBT for Individuals at High Risk of Developing Psychosis

Nicola Smethurst, Paul French
and Anthony P. Morrison

This chapter aims to outline the use of cognitive therapy for people at high risk of developing psychosis. We begin by defining who is considered to be 'at-high risk' of developing psychosis, and provide a brief summary of our clinical trials for this population and our treatment protocol. Cognitive therapy intervention strategies are then described and illustrated with a case example.

Who is at Ultra-High Risk of Developing Psychosis?

Early detection and prevention of psychosis has become a topic of growing interest, since Yung and colleagues' influential work (1998) led to the development of operational criteria that identify at-risk mental states (ARMS). Using these criteria, they found that 40 percent of individuals identified as ultra-high risk made transition to psychosis over a 9-month period (Yung *et al.*, 1998).

The criteria identify four groups who are at ultra-high risk, and are associated with a combination of state and trait risk factors. State factors include both 1) attenuated or sub-threshold psychotic symptoms and 2) brief limited intermittent psychotic symptoms (BLIPS) which remit without treatment within a week. Trait factors are 1) experiencing a recent

CBT for Schizophrenia: Evidence-Based Interventions and Future Directions,
First Edition. Edited by Craig Steel.
© 2013 John Wiley & Sons, Ltd. Published 2013 by John Wiley & Sons, Ltd.

deterioration in functioning and having a family history (first degree relative) of psychosis, and 2) a diagnosis of schizotypal personality disorder also coupled with the experience of a recent deterioration in functioning. For the purposes of this chapter, our focus will be on a group defined by the presence of attenuated symptoms, as they make up approximately 80 percent of 'at-risk' clients seen by early detection services and within clinical trials (Morrison *et al.*, 2004). There are several assessments that can be used to identify people that meet criteria for at risk mental states, including the comprehensive assessment of at-risk mental states (CAARMS: Yung *et al.*, 2005) and the structured interview for prodromal syndromes and the scale of prodromal symptoms (Miller *et al.*, 2003).

What are Attenuated Psychotic Symptoms?

Attenuated psychotic symptoms refer to psychotic-like experiences that are below the clinical threshold for clinically diagnosable psychotic symptoms. They differ from frank psychotic symptoms in their intensity, frequency and/or duration (Yung *et al.*, 2005). For example, a persecutory idea that is held with less than delusional conviction is attenuated as it has less intensity than a persecutory delusion, being held with less conviction and having less impact on behaviour and emotion. If an individual fleetingly holds a persecutory belief with delusional conviction (100 percent conviction) but only for 1 hour, this does not meet clinical criteria for a diagnosable psychotic symptom on the basis of duration. Similarly, if an individual had paranoid ideas only twice within a month, these would be considered attenuated psychotic symptoms as the frequency is below the threshold for frank psychosis (at least 1 month duration).

Clinical Interventions for Individuals at Ultra-High Risk

Advances in the identification of individuals considered 'at-risk' have raised the possibility of preventing transition to psychosis. The efficacy of interventions for this group has been evaluated in a number of randomized controlled trials: a combination of psychological and pharmacotherapy (McGorry *et al.*, 2002); cognitive therapy alone (Morrison *et al.*, 2004); pharmacotherapy alone (McGlashan *et al.*, 2006); cognitive therapy compared with supportive therapy (Addington *et al.*, 2011); and omega-3 polyunsaturated fatty acids (Amminger *et al.*, 2010).

A further randomized control trial (RCT) investigated the use of amisulpride as an addition to supportive needs-focused intervention

(Ruhrmann *et al.*, 2007). This study differs from the other studies in that the German clinical staging approach of the at-risk state differentiates between an early- and a late-risk syndrome, in the early part of the syndrome psychological interventions are offered but if clients make the transition to the late stage then they utilize antipsychotic medication. The psychological intervention for early stage syndromal clients was a group intervention using CBT. This treatment found significant results in terms of reducing transition to the late syndromal stage and to full stage psychosis (Bechdolf *et al.*, 2005).

McGorry *et al.* (2002) found that, in comparison with supportive therapy and case management (i.e. needs-based intervention (NBI)) a combination of psychological therapy and specific pharmacotherapy (specific preventative intervention (SPI)) reduced the risk of transition to psychosis (10 percent transition rate compared with 36 percent in the NBI group). However, results were not maintained at 6-month follow up. Thus, it was concluded that it might be possible to delay transition to psychosis rather than prevent it. McGlashan *et al.* (2006), compared olanzapine to placebo in a RCT (n=60), and did not find a significant difference in the numbers of transitions to psychosis at 12 months (16.1 percent transition rate in the olanzapine group compared with 37.9 percent in the placebo group), suggesting that antipsychotic medication does not delay or prevent transition to psychosis in 'at-risk' individuals. McGlashan and colleagues (2006) reported a trend towards significance and acknowledged deficient power as a potential cause for the lack of statistical significance. In addition to the lack of supporting evidence, there are also ethical issues to consider (e.g. side effects, stigma) in relation to using antipsychotic medication with this clinical group (Bentall and Morrison, 2002). A study in Vienna, Austria, found that the use of omega-3 fatty acids was successful in reducing both transition to psychosis and psychotic symptoms over 12 months, without any adverse side effects (Amminger *et al.*, 2010). Most recently a study comparing the effects of CBT to supportive therapy has been published (Addington *et al.*, 2011). This utilized the treatment manual developed by French and Morrison (2004) as the basis of their CBT intervention. The randomized test used a sample of 51 individuals assessing them at 6, 12 and 18 months. Conversions to psychosis only occurred in the supportive therapy group although this was found to be non-significant due to the low level of conversions across the sample. They also found a more rapid improvement in attenuated positive symptoms in the CBT group.

Our Trials

Morrison *et al.* (2004) carried out an RCT (n=58), the EDIE (Early Detection, Intervention and Evaluation) study, comparing cognitive therapy with monitoring alone (no treatment). Cognitive therapy significantly

Table 4.1 Entry routes based on CAARMS criteria

Route	CAARMS criteria
BLIPS	1. A Global Rating Scale score of 6 on Unusual Thought Content, Non-Bizarre Ideas, or Disorganized Speech; or 5–6 on Perceptual Abnormalities 2. A Frequency Scale score of 4–6 on the relevant symptom scale 3. Symptoms are present for less than one week 4. Symptoms resolve without medication 5. Symptoms occurred during the past year
Attenuated symptoms	A. Subthreshold intensity: 1. A Global Rating Scale score of 3–5 on Unusual Thought Content or Non-Bizarre Ideas; or 3–4 on Perceptual Abnormalities; or 4–5 on Disorganized Speech 2. A Frequency Scale score of 3–6 on the relevant symptom scale 3. Symptoms are present for more than one week 4. Symptoms occurred during the past year B. Subthreshold frequency: 1. A Global Rating Scale score of 6 on Unusual Thought Content, Non-Bizarre Ideas, or Disorganized Speech; 5–6 on Perceptual Abnormalities 2. A Frequency Scale score of 3 on the relevant symptom scale 3. Symptoms occurred during the past year
State-plus-trait	1. History of psychosis in a first-degree relative OR identification of Schizotypal Personality Disorder 2. 30% drop in Global Assessment of Functioning (GAF; APA, 2000) score from pre-morbid level, sustained for at least one month, within the past year OR a GAF score of 50 or less for at least past year

reduced transition to psychosis at the end of treatment (6 percent transition rate compared with 22 percent in the treatment as usual group) and this result was maintained at 12-month follow up. Consequently, it was concluded that it may be possible to prevent transition to psychosis (currently a large multisite RCT based on EDIE is ongoing to test this proposition further). This significant difference remained at 3-year follow-up when cognitive factors are controlled for in the analysis. In July 2010 we completed recruitment (n=288) for a larger multisite trial evaluating CT for ARMS (the EDIE-2 trial: Morrison *et al.*, 2011), which is based on the same treatment protocol (French and Morrison, 2004) and cognitive model (Morrison, 2001) as our initial trial; the final results of this trial were being analyzed in late 2011.

Our entry criteria have been operationalized using the CAARMS (Yung *et al.*, 2005), along with age (14–35) and being help-seeking; see Table 4.1 for our specific CAARMS-based criteria. Our exclusion criteria were current or previous receipt of antipsychotic medication for more than 2 days, moderate to severe learning disability, organic impairment, and insufficient fluency in English. We did not exclude anyone because of substance misuse or other Axis I disorders, thus enhancing the generalizability of our findings.

The Cognitive Model of Psychosis

A cognitive model that accounts for the formation and maintenance of psychotic experiences, including paranoia, has been proposed (Morrison, 2001) and is shown in Figure 4.1. The EDIE trial has provided preliminary evidence that cognitive therapy based upon this model can prevent or delay psychosis in those at high risk (Morrison *et al.*, 2004). The model implies that it is the interpretation of intrusions (e.g. mood states, external perceptions or intrusive thoughts) that is important. Essentially, a person

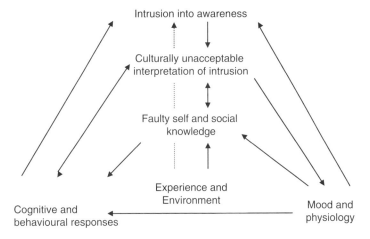

Figure 4.1 Morrison's (2001) cognitive model of the formation and maintenance of psychotic experiences

is seen to be psychotic if they endorse a culturally unacceptable interpretation of intrusions (e.g. assuming hearing one's first name on TV is evidence that everyone is talking about you). Morrison (2001) also states that similar processes are involved in the development of psychotic and non-psychotic disorders. Consequently, the model encompasses key aspects of the S-REF (self-regulatory executive function) model of emotional dysfunction (Wells and Matthews, 1994).

Morrison (2001) proposes that culturally unacceptable interpretations of intrusions are maintained by safety behaviours (e.g. watching people from window), procedural beliefs (beliefs about information processing strategies; e.g. paranoia keeps me safe), faulty self and social knowledge (such as negative beliefs about self and others), mood and physiology. The model implies unhelpful cognitive responses (e.g. selective attention/ thought control strategies/perseverative processing), behavioural responses (e.g. avoidance/safety behaviours) and emotion (e.g. anxiety, low mood and anger) maintain distress and psychotic symptoms. There is considerable overlap between this model and other cognitive behavioural approaches to understanding psychosis (see Chapter 1).

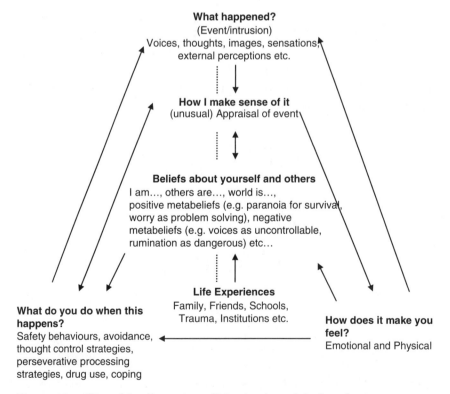

Figure 4.2   Client-friendly version of Morrison's model of psychosis

The purpose of this model is to facilitate the collaborative development of idiosyncratic case formulations, from which intervention strategies can be derived. Within our trials, we utilize a more user-friendly version of this formulation template (Morrison *et al.*, 2008) in order to collaboratively develop case conceptualizations. This version is presented in Figure 4.2, which is also populated with suggestions as to the content of each section. The key elements of this model are the normalizing of intrusions, the emphasis on promoting less distressing (and more normalizing) appraisals of unusual experiences, the evaluation and modification of beliefs regarding the uncontrollability and danger of psychotic experiences and the emphasis on using behavioural experiments to test out beliefs and evaluate the utility of control strategies.

The Treatment Protocol Used in the Trial

Our treatment protocol is based on a published manual (French and Morrison, 2004), and incorporates guidelines that were intended to represent the default assumptions of what would occur throughout the course of treatment. All clients are allocated up to a maximum of 26 sessions over the first 6 months (plus up to four boosters over the subsequent 6 months). They were to be used flexibly, and could change in response to client characteristics. The content of sessions and expected milestones are outlined below. When training our trial therapists, some have commented that the pace of sessions moves very quickly; however, we have found that this is important in order to maintain people's engagement in the therapy and progress towards quick successes, which is particularly important given that most transitions to psychosis are likely to occur in the first few months (Yung *et al.*, 2008).

First session

During the first session it is important to explain the limits of confidentiality to clients. An explanation of cognitive therapy, the trial and number of sessions (e.g. window of 6 months and optional booster sessions) would follow. Initially, a brief (6–10 sessions) contract would be agreed. It is important to conduct a cognitive behavioural assessment of presenting problems and life experiences, based on the cognitive model. This assessment might take place over the first two sessions; however, initially in the first session it is important to begin to formulate the client's current difficulties using a basic event, thought, feeling, behaviour cycle. An assessment of risk to self and others should also take place during this first session, and information gathered about their current resilience and protective factors to aid the therapist during any potential times in the future when risk may be increased.

By session 3

By session 3, a problem list should have been developed and a list of SMART goals (specific, measurable, achievable, realistic and time-limited) that the therapist and client will be working towards in the contracted sessions (i.e. if 6 sessions were agreed initially, then goals should be appropriate to that timeframe). Further, at this point, simple formulations (event-thought-feeling-behaviour cycles) focusing on recent events should have been developed to aid socialization of the client to the specific cognitive model. In addition, a shared longitudinal formulation of the client's difficulties, based on the specific cognitive model, should either be a work in progress or nearing completion.

Subsequent sessions

With a formulation in place, the choice of intervention strategies should easily follow, being negotiated collaboratively with the client in relation to their goals, their existing skills repertoire, the suggested relationships between factors within the formulation and the likelihood of success. The agenda for each session should include a target, for example, behaviour or appraisal, related to the goal list and formulation, providing both the therapist and client with a focus for the work during the session. All cognitive and/or behavioural change strategies should be selected on the basis of negotiation with the client (for acceptability) and based on the formulation (suggesting a likelihood of success). The strategies chosen should be selected from those summarized in Figure 4.3. More detailed illustrations of these strategies are available in our treatment manual (French and Morrison, 2004).

Final two sessions

The final two sessions are reserved for both therapist and client to focus on relapse prevention and maintenance of gains made so far. In building a blueprint with the client, it can be useful to provide a copy of the longitudinal formulation, and the simpler formulations followed by a summary of the strategies they have found most useful. The blueprint must also contain

---

Treatment strategies

Work on problem and goals

Normalisation

Coping strategies

Role play/skills practice

Examining advantages and disadvantages

Evidential analysis

Generating alternative explanations

Survey planning / review

Safety Behaviours / behavioural experiments-in session/therapist-assisted

Metacognitive beliefs (e.g. positive/negative beliefs about paranoia/rumination/worry)

Metacognitive strategies (e.g. postponing perseverative processing)

Attentional strategies (e.g. external focus)

Core beliefs / schema change (e.g. historical tests, positive data logs, continuum)

Reducing social isolation / increasing activity

Relapse prevention

Figure 4.3 A list of treatment strategies from the treatment manual used in the tria

early, middle and late warning signs and how these will be monitored and a plan of action should they feel they need future help.

It is important to recognize that while this approach described was designed for use in a clinical trial, this treatment strategy is also used routinely as the intervention of choice in our clinical service for at risk individuals. This process is described using the case example below.

Case Example: 'At-Risk' Client with Attenuated Paranoia and Thought Broadcasting

Background and assessment information

Jacob was a 19-year-old male who was currently unemployed and living with his parents. Over the past 2 years he had begun to feel more suspicious about people, and described a feeling of being watched especially by other men and reported that his experiences had significantly increased in the previous few months. At times, he had experienced thoughts that the people looking at him were 'eyeing him up' as they wanted to beat him up to teach him a lesson. On these occasions, Jacob also believed his thoughts, often sexual in nature, are being broadcast so that others can hear them. He believed that when people hear his thoughts they will realize he is gay and will beat him up due to his sexuality. He reported that this only seemed to happen in busy places such as on the bus or in the local supermarket. Understandably he was very distressed and confused by this experience. He reported that his conviction in these beliefs varied considerably which seemed to add to his confusion. He rated his conviction in the belief 'Other people can hear my thoughts' at 70 percent, increasing to 100 percent when he is directly in the situation, sometimes dropping to 40 percent. He rated his conviction in his belief that 'Others are watching me and will attack me' at 60 percent, increasing to 99 percent when he is directly in the situation. Jacob reported he felt in turmoil about his current thinking and whether his beliefs were realistic or not, was 'all in his mind'? Understandably, the alternative explanation induced further anxiety as it would mean he 'was going insane' or 'losing his grip'. Jacob engaged in several behaviours to keep himself safe and prevent his thoughts from being heard. These included trying not to think/have any sexual thoughts or force thoughts out of his head while paying very close attention to other people around him for any signs that they may have heard his thoughts (although he was not sure of the exact signals) and always trying to keep his head down so he did not draw attention to himself. He had one close friend, Matthew, who he had told about these experiences, he had tried to persuade Jacob that it was not true but without success. In the weeks prior to using the service, Jacob became increasingly low in mood, isolating himself in his bedroom and refusing to spend time with the family which sparked concern from his mother and resulted in him attending the GP practice.

Jacob described himself as a creative person, passionate about photography and art. He described growing up in a very strict religious family environment and reported his father as being extremely homophobic and very vocal about his opinions. Jacob reported that he had known for a long time he was gay and had only recently told his mother and sister who were very supportive of him and they agreed it would be best to keep it from his father as they worried his father may disown him. He had recently completed two 'A' levels at college with lower than expected grades. Jacob reported that he was a loner at secondary school and bullied daily by his peers; the bullying had begun as verbal teasing although prior to his GSCEs it had escalated with a recent fight occurring outside school. Consequently, he did not achieve very good grades in his GCSEs and was therefore not able to continue to complete his 'A' levels at that school. Jacob reported that his father constantly reminded him how disappointed he was that he would not be going to university. Jacob has not been able to secure any employment since leaving college, adding to his father's disappointment in him.

Risk assessment

Jacob reported that he did have suicidal thoughts, and experienced these thoughts for about half an hour every other day. He explained that he had thought about the method and would consider hanging himself as it would be over quickly but had not considered the, how, where, or when and had no current intention of carrying anything out. He reported that his mother and sister were strong protective factors who he would miss and did not want to leave them behind. He reported no risk to others. It was agreed that we would review his level of risk as an agenda item throughout therapy.

As a therapist, it can often be anxiety provoking to ask about risk to self and others for fear of what might be revealed and therefore what you might have to deal with. However, Jacob noted that no one had ever asked him about it before, especially in so much detail and even though his level of risk did not increase throughout therapy, he welcomed knowing he had the opportunity to talk about it.

Problem list and goals of therapy

Jacob attended his first few sessions regularly and during these initial sessions identified the following difficulties for his problem list:

i   thinking that other people could hear his thoughts,
ii   thinking that other people were out to attack him,
iii feeling low in mood, and
iv   not wanting to spend time with family.

These problems were translated into goals, which were:

i   To feel less suspicious that others were out to attack him, which would mean he would be able to get the bus all the way home.
ii   To understand why this was happening.
iii To feel better in mood rated at 7/10 (where 0=the worst it could be, 10=the best it could be), currently 3/10.
iv   To feel comfortable being around others especially his family, for example, to be able to watch television with them for half an hour.
v   To feel more confident in himself, which he operationalized as being able to have one drink in a 'gay bar'.

Formulation

As described, early in the therapy process it is important to begin to build idiosyncratic case conceptualizations to help Jacob understand how his thoughts, feelings and behaviours were connected, this also facilitates engagement and guides intervention strategies. He had already identified that he only believed others could hear his thoughts and would be attacked as a consequence when he was on the bus or in a supermarket. Further discussion highlighted that it seemed to occur in any situation without an immediate escape route. Initially, the case conceptualizations were basic event-thought-feeling-behaviour chains. By making use of a simple formulation to begin with, Jacob noted he felt more able to make use of this following incidents occurring between sessions (see Box 4.1).

As sessions progressed, a more complex formulation began to build, which included Jacob's early experiences, schemas and assumptions, critical incidents and current environmental factors (see Figure 4.4). A longitudinal formulation is not always developed so early, sometimes it can be prior to or become part of the intervention; the development of a more complex and historical formulation needs to be clinically judged on an individual basis. Throughout the trial, all formulations were based on the most appropriate cognitive model of the difficulties highlighted by the client. The model of psychosis outlined above was used with Jacob to explain the development and maintenance of his current difficulties, one of his identified goals.

Throughout his life, Jacob had experienced a number of events that had influenced how he viewed himself, other people and the world around him. He had grown up in a strict religious household, which had prevented him from doing certain activities with his peers and having to conform to

---

Box 4.1   A basic event-thought-feeling-behaviour chain for Jacob

What happened: In supermarket, check out man is rude to me
↓
What did I think: He has heard my thoughts and knows I'm gay; he might be after me
↓
How did I feel: Anxious, sick in stomach, tense
↓
What did I do: Head down, didn't look at him; didn't talk to him; tried to control thoughts, push out sexual thoughts; ran out of shop quickly

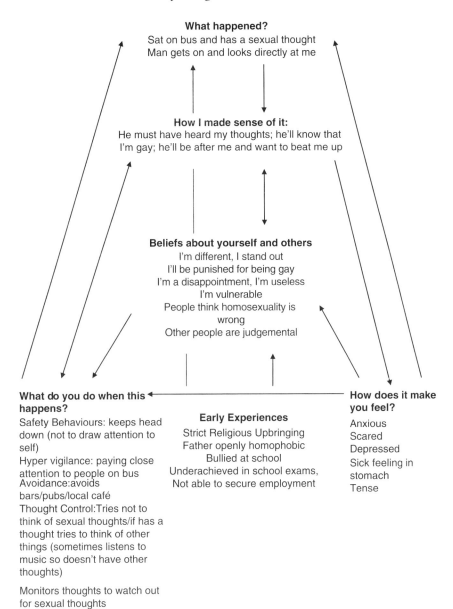

What happened?
Sat on bus and has a sexual thought
Man gets on and looks directly at me

How I made sense of it:
He must have heard my thoughts; he'll know that
I'm gay; he'll be after me and want to beat me up

Beliefs about yourself and others
I'm different, I stand out
I'll be punished for being gay
I'm a disappointment, I'm useless
I'm vulnerable
People think homosexuality is
wrong
Other people are judgemental

What do you do when this happens?
Safety Behaviours: keeps head down (not to draw attention to self)
Hyper vigilance: paying close attention to people on bus
Avoidance:avoids bars/pubs/local café
Thought Control:Tries not to think of sexual thoughts/if has a thought tries to think of other things (sometimes listens to music so doesn't have other thoughts)

Monitors thoughts to watch out for sexual thoughts

Early Experiences
Strict Religious Upbringing
Father openly homophobic
Bullied at school
Underachieved in school exams,
Not able to secure employment

How does it make you feel?
Anxious
Scared
Depressed
Sick feeling in stomach
Tense

Figure 4.4   Longitudinal Case Formulation of attenuated paranoia and thought broadcasting in a client at high risk of developing psychosis

several household rules which he felt had made him easily stand out as someone very different to his peers. Jacob strongly felt this was the reason why he was constantly bullied at school, and reported he didn't seem to ever fit in no matter how hard he tried. This had lead him to feel very alone and vulnerable. Further, the outcome of his school exams, his lack of employment and his father's disappointment in him had led him to believe 'I'm a disappointment; I'm useless'. In addition, Jacob reported that his father had longstanding beliefs about the downfall of society, of which he believed homosexuality was one reason, and that homosexuals would be punished by God. This had led Jacob to believe that 'other people think homosexuality is wrong', 'other people are judgemental', and 'I'll be punished for being gay'.

Following assessment, the therapist will often have hypotheses about what the formulation may look like and how a client's difficulties have arisen. However, it is important that this is developed collaboratively with the client rather than presented to the client as a definitive version of their problems. The therapist should utilize Socratic dialogue to enable the client to develop understanding of their difficulties and also leads to greater ownership of the formulation.

Interventions

After deciding on a problem list and goals and developing an understanding with Jacob about his difficulties and maintaining factors, intervention strategies were discussed and chosen based on what would achieve a quick success and impact on quality of life. This is often important with 'at-risk' clients who may be ambivalent about engaging with therapy (especially as some clients view this as confirmation that they are 'going mad/losing it' if they need therapy) to help them see the changes they can make over a short period of time if they continue with therapy on a regular basis. On this basis, it can often be the therapist that chooses the initial intervention strategies, for example, providing normalizing information, particularly as the aim is to move quickly in the first few sessions.

Normalizing information

At the beginning of therapy, often while establishing goals, providing a client with normalizing information can be vital to reducing distress, reducing self-stigma and aiding engagement. Jacob felt confused about his experiences. At times when his belief rating dropped, he believed that these thoughts meant 'this is the start of going insane/crazy' (see Box 4.2).

Jacob did not know anyone else who had similar thoughts, and his friend's evident concern about him had led him to think 'there must be something wrong; I'm the only one; I must be crazy'. Further Jacob believed he stood out from the crowd and that he appeared mad to others. He believed that if you put him in a group of people, he would easily stand out as different

---

Box 4.2   A more specific event-thought-feeling-behaviour chain for Jacob

What happened: Sometimes I think people have heard my thoughts and are after me

↓

What I thought: 'This is the start of me going insane and crazy'; 'There must be something wrong; I'm the only one; I must be crazy'; 'I look mad to other people'

↓

How I felt: Tense, worried, frightened, scared, anxious, sick in stomach

↓

What I do: Only tell people close to me about these thoughts; Don't go out; Looking around me to see if people are looking at me (to see if they have guessed I'm crazy); Spend lots of time thinking about what to wear; Try to push thoughts out of my head

---

from other people and others would be able to pick him out as the 'mad one' because of how he dressed and that he believed he looked weak and vulnerable. This led to two intervention strategies around normalization.

The first intervention strategy was to provide Jacob with information about suspicious thoughts (see Morrison *et al.*, 2008 and Freeman *et al.*, 2006) such as how common suspicious thoughts are, the diverse forms these thoughts can take and hence varying levels of anxiety that result and the difference in frequency for people. Prior to receiving this information, Jacob rated his belief 'I'm going crazy/insane' at 90 percent. Following this information, Jacob expressed his surprise at how many other people had similar experiences and rated his belief at 30 percent explaining that even though he didn't feel alone in his experiences as before, if he was not going crazy what else could it be and why was it happening. This gave rise to a discussion about recent experiences such as exams at college and thus it was possible to begin to generate alternative explanations with Jacob, and help him to conduct evidential analysis.

The second intervention strategy used video feedback of Jacob walking along a busy street. Although initially sceptical about this strategy, Jacob realized that he had never seen himself before and so did not actually have any evidence for his beliefs. He believed he would look different to others because of how he was dressed and his stance as he walked (80 percent). He also consented for the video to be shown to four of the therapists' colleagues to ask them if they could see anyone they thought may be experiencing mental health difficulties. He predicted that all four therapists would choose him. At first sight of the video being played back, Jacob laughed and said 'I can't see where I am'. He realized that he dressed very similarly to other young people and that everyone has different stances and walking style to each other, especially across the generations of people in the video. Of the four therapists, no one could pick any one in the video that looked very different or weak or vulnerable, with most therapists saying 'it just looks like a busy street with lots of people rushing around'. Jacob reported that he no longer believed he 'appeared mad' to other people (0 percent), in fact he looked very similar to other people his age.

Further normalizing strategies can include the development of the formulation, whether at a basic maintenance or complex historical level to help clients to begin to understand how past experiences can affect their core beliefs and assumptions they hold and hence begin to provide reasons for their experiences, thereby lowering distress. In addition, the therapists can provide the client with a normalizing experience by being warm, empathic, non-judgemental and not challenging of their beliefs but accepting and curious about what, why, when and how. Jacob reported that when he told his GP what he was experiencing he was told how thoughts cannot be transmitted to other people. This Jacob had interpreted as 'I'm definitely crazy even the doctor thinks so' and found her approach challenging.

Thought broadcasting

Jacob rated his belief that other people could hear his thoughts at 70 percent most of the time, rising to 100 percent in the situation after he believes it has happened (see Box 4.3).

Box 4.3   A further event-thought-feeling-behaviour chain for Jacob

What happened: On bus, man looks directly at me
↓
What I thought: He has heard my thoughts and knows I'm gay; he might be after me
↓
How I felt: Anxious, sick in stomach
↓
What I do: Head down, don't look at him; Try to control thoughts, push out sexual thoughts; Get off bus quickly

The above formulation suggests a number of intervention strategies. Initially, it was useful to draw on a quick exercise looking at Jacob's current thought suppression strategy to show the counter-productive nature of his current control strategy. Jacob rated his belief in this strategy at 90 percent. Jacob was asked for his favourite animal and favourite football team (an owl and Manchester City), and then asked to not think about an owl in a Manchester City t-shirt for one minute. Jacob reported, as expected, that the more he tried not to think about the owl the more it popped back into his head and he found it very hard to get rid of the owl image. In relating this to his thoughts, he was able to understand that the more he tried to force the thoughts out of his head, the more the thoughts rebounded, making them more frequent and therefore harder to eliminate. Following this, Jacob was asked to have the image of the owl in the Manchester City t-shirt but to not interact with it by forcing it out of his head, but to just leave it alone for 1 minute. Jacob reported that after a few seconds the image faded out and he began to think about what he had planned for the rest of the day. In relating this to his thoughts, Jacob could see how a change in strategy may decrease the frequency of his thoughts and lessen his distress. As Jacob wanted to try this during the week, this was set as a homework task.

A subsequent task was to generate a number of alternatives with Jacob as to 'Why people might look at you on the bus?'. To make this a more visual exercise for Jacob, a pie chart, as shown in Figure 4.5, was created, where each alternative explanation was given a proportion of 100 percent making sure his explanation 'He has heard my thoughts' is rated last. Jacob reported he found this exercise helpful as he had not considered how many reasons there were for why someone might look at you on a bus.

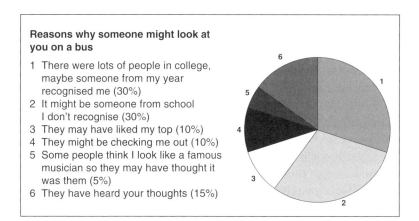

Reasons why someone might look at you on a bus

1 There were lots of people in college, maybe someone from my year recognised me (30%)
2 It might be someone from school I don't recognise (30%)
3 They may have liked my top (10%)
4 They might be checking me out (10%)
5 Some people think I look like a famous musician so they may have thought it was them (5%)
6 They have heard your thoughts (15%)

Figure 4.5   A pie chart to show all of the alternative explanations generated

> **Box 4.4**   An example of an evidence for and against sheet
>
> *Belief to be examined*: It might be someone from school I don't recognize
> *Associated mood*: Relaxed
> *Belief rating*: 30
>
> | Evidence for | Evidence against |
> | --- | --- |
> | There were lots of people in school | It felt like he had heard my thoughts |
> | I didn't know everyone in the whole school | |
> | I kept myself to myself in school so I didn't even know everyone in my class | |
> | I only stay in touch with one person from school | |
> | Everybody that went to my school lived in the area | |
>
> *Belief re-rating*: 60
> *Alterative thought*: Maybe the person looked at me because he recognized me from school, he may still live in the area and I didn't know everyone at school so I wouldn't be able to recognize them

When a number of alternatives have been generated, it is possible to take these explanations in turn and begin to consider the evidence that may or may not support them (see Box 4.4)

After this exercise, Jacob rated his belief that other people could read his thoughts at 15 percent yet stated that in the situation this increases to 50 percent (dropped from 100 percent). At this point, it was important to question (not challenge) the mechanism with Jacob, how do they hear your thoughts? Are they aloud? Does everyone hear them or just certain people? If your thoughts are broadcast aloud, why do only certain people hear them?

One in-session experiment conducted with Jacob involved using a Dictaphone to record these thoughts. Jacob reported that he believed that his thoughts weren't spoken aloud but a person or technological device would pick them up. Jacob was asked to think certain thoughts (neutral and emotive) repeatedly for one minute while a Dictaphone recorded the session. Jacob requested that he held the Dictaphone close to his head so that it could pick up any broadcasting. It is important that it is clear that the experiment is not about whether the therapist heard the thought as some clients may not fully trust that a therapist would give them the correct answer. The Dictaphone was played back to Jacob and he reported how shocked he was that it had not

> **Box 4.5** A formulation for Jacob
>
> **What happened**: Walk past a house on estate, see movement in lounge of house
>
> **What I thought**: The people in that house are watching me to see where I go, they are after me to beat me up because I'm gay
>
> **How I felt**: Frightened, scared, anxious, sick in stomach, tense
>
> **What I do**: Already dressed in black, hood up; Kept head down; Don't make eye contact with anyone Make way home instantly, constantly changing route home; Walk very fast; Lock self in house

picked up any of his thoughts. He re-rated his belief that other people can hear his thoughts at 0 percent, however in the following session he reported this increased to 30 percent in the situation and then decreased back down to 0 percent after he had employed the techniques we had discussed.

Another in-session experiment investigated the results of deliberately broadcasting thoughts and observing others reactions. Jacob was asked to think of a thought that would provoke a reaction in others. He decided that he could get on a bus, with the therapist, and deliberately have the thought 'there is a bomb on this bus'. He reported that if people could hear his thoughts, people would tell the bus driver to stop and all want to get off. This experiment was carried out with Jacob. He observed a few people on the bus looking at him over a period of 5 minutes, and only a few people got off the bus at a bus stop. Jacob reported that this confirmed no one could hear his thoughts.

Suspiciousness and paranoia

Jacob reported that sometimes when he is walking around the housing estate near his home he feels he is being watched by someone who is waiting to beat him up. Jacob rated his belief that 'people are watching me to beat me up because I'm gay' as fluctuating from 60 percent outside of the situation to 99 percent in the situation. In relation to his goals, Jacob wanted to lower his conviction in this belief, and so we began to investigate this belief by developing a formulation (see Box 4.5).

Initially, it was useful to look at the evidence for and against this belief, an example of these are seen Table 4.2. Jacob's answers show some cognitive dissonance in his thoughts, for example, he knew he felt like he stood out as different to others, but also had the evidence of the video feedback completed earlier in therapy to draw on.

Table 4.2 Evidential analysis of Jacob's persecutory belief

Evidence for	Evidence against
I have heard of other people being attacked on the estate	Walked on the estate all my life, never been attacked before
Other people don't like homosexuals, they think they deserve to be punished	I know lots of people on the estate and everyone is friendly towards me when I see them e.g. say hello.
I sometimes feel that I stand out from other people on the estate, and people will know I am a homosexual	Other people that have been attacked are known drug dealers; I am not a drug dealer The video showed me I look the same as other young people, I don't stand out as different in any way, how would they know. There are lots of events worldwide e.g. festivals and marches, for gay people and attacks are very rare.
	Throughout the year, there are very few publicized assaults on gay people in the media; I have heard of 1 in the last year, out of 60 million people in the UK.

Following this, Jacob re-rated his belief 'People are watching me to beat me up because I'm gay' at 45 percent, later reporting that in the situation it rose to 80 percent.

A further intervention strategy used with Jacob was a survey around his deservedness to be attacked given his sexuality. A survey is a useful technique to gather information about a range of people's opinions and beliefs. The survey was not about disproving anybody's religious beliefs but providing Jacob with a wider viewpoint. The questions Jacob wished to asked are outlined in Table 4.3, and were anonymously sent to a bank of therapists (all colleagues of the therapist, of which 25 replied). The table also shows Jacob's predicted percentages and the actual percentages. Jacob also decided that he felt able to ask his mothers' and sisters' opinion and his best friend, Matthew. This was quite a bold move by Jacob, perhaps a sign of his increasing mood and self-esteem.

Jacob expressed his surprise at the results of the survey. Jacob had predicted that everybody would have strong homophobic opinions. This clearly conflicted with his father's beliefs and those he had been surrounded with as a child. His mother, sister and friend had given similar opinions to those shown in Table 4.3, of particular importance Jacob was able to see others felt that people who are gay should not be punished.

Table 4.3 An example of a survey conducted

Question		Predicted %	Actual %
Do you have a friend, or know someone, that is gay?	Yes	20	80
	No	80	20
Do those people keep it a secret from others in their family?	Yes	90	5
	No	10	95
Do you think that people who are gay should be punished e.g. be attacked?	Yes	100	0
	No	0	100
Do you think people who are gay deserve anything bad that happens to them?	Yes	90	0
	No	10	100
Do you think people who are gay should be accepted in society?	Yes	100	95
	No	0	5 'due to religion'

Jacob had not realized that people did not believe people that are gay should be punished or deserve bad things to happen to them, and began to question why he would be beaten up because he was gay. In bringing forward the evidential analysis, he added that the majority of attacks, on his estate, were not purposefully directed at people that are gay, but mainly local drug dealers. He began to make a small shift in his belief around his deservedness of being punished due to his sexuality, which resulted in a shift in his conviction in his belief that he would be attacked (30 percent outside the situation, rising to 65 percent in the situation).

Behavioural experiment

Due to Jacob's belief of being watched and attacked he had understand-ably begun to employ a number of in-situational safety behaviours when he ventured outside. These included putting up his hood, dressing all in black, looking at the ground and never making eye contact with passers-by, and constantly changing his route across the estate. Therefore, to complete this section of work, it was important to carry out a behav-ioural experiment to help Jacob see the counterproductive nature of his safety behaviours.

When conducting a behavioural experiment it is important to make sure the formulation is as detailed as possible; 'the devil is in the detail'. If you have not ascertained all of the safety behaviours the client carries out in their feared situation, at the end of the experiment the client may have experienced less distress but they will attribute this to the unidentified safety behaviour(s) and the experiment will need to be repeated. As clients can sometimes be unaware of all their safety behaviours it can be useful to ask if they carry out behaviours you know other people do, for example, walking very fast, wearing sunglasses or a hat. In addition, following socialization and prior to the experiment, it can be useful for the client to enter their feared situation with the task of discovering all their safety behaviours. By carrying this out with Jacob, he discovered that he kept his hands in his pockets because he has a distinctive scar across his hand, and that although he kept his head down he was hypervigilant for sounds of other people around him. He also reported that he constantly focused on his thoughts and feelings (internal focus of attention). It is important to consider the therapist's role in the experiment, some male clients will only venture out when they are with a female friend as they believe this prevents them being attacked. Therefore, it is important to check with the client what they believe your role is, if it is one of safety then other options need to be considered, for example, the therapist remaining behind and using a mobile telephone to communicate (although beware, being on the phone is a common safety behaviour). Generally, the feedback has been that therapists tend to stand out and can make the person feel more obvious to others.

Jacob reported it would be good to 'see what happens; try it out' and agreed he would enter his feared situation twice for ten minutes each time; initially carrying out all of his safety behaviours and then dropping them all. We agreed that we would monitor his distress and conviction in his belief ratings at 3, 6 and 9 minutes throughout each experiment. Further, Jacob agreed to be videoed throughout each experiment to observe others reactions and himself. We agreed that there would be no break or discussion between the two halves of the experiment, just a quick check to make sure he was able to continue, as at times a break can discredit any change in distress ratings. The experiment is summarized in Box 4.6.

Of interest, Jacob reported that he held certain beliefs about his safety behaviours such as 'wearing all black makes me invisible to others' 'putting my hood up makes me unrecognizable'. Clearly some clients do not agree so readily to take part in a behavioural experiment. At times like these, it can be helpful to make use of metaphors, for example, villagers and vampires. It can also be advantageous to conduct evidential analysis on the beliefs about how the safety behaviour keeps them safe. Following a discussion of advantages and disadvantages of being videoed, Jacob agreed that it would also provide us with richer information towards his beliefs about his safety behaviours.

Box 4.6 An example of the detail and construction of a behavioural experiment

Aim	Activity/thoughts
Experiment to test thought	To walk around the estate on a pre-determined route for 20 minutes in total
Belief(s) to be tested and belief rating:	'I need to keep my guard up; I am being watched and may be attacked' (65% in situation)
Associated feeling	Anxious (80%), scared
Beliefs in safety behaviours and belief rating:	'Wearing all black/hood up/hands in pockets/head down makes me invisible' (95%)
	'Never making eye contact with anyone keeps me safe' (100%)
	'Carrying out all of my behaviours will keep me extra safe'
Prediction about what will happen:	'Not doing anything will mean someone will recognise me, walk past me and say something derogatory to start a fight'
Likely problems	'I'll no longer feel safe and my anxiety will go through the roof, I won't be able to cope and will want to go home'
Strategies to deal with problems	Tell myself that this will help me to find out if my behaviours keep me safe AND this may feel worse at first but it might help me feel better

1st experiment: carrying out all safety behaviours

	0	3	6	9
Distress rating	80	95	90	85
Belief rating	90	80	75	75

Box 4.6 (continued)

2nd experiment: dropping all safety behaviours

	0	3	6	9
Distress rating	90	75	55	50
Belief rating	95	75	60	55

Belief in safety behaviours

Before 1st experiment	95–100
After 1st experiment	85
After 2nd experiment	40

| 'I think they might make me more anxious, I'm not sure if they actually work' |
| 'I felt very anxious at first but this soon decreased, unlike before, I'm not sure they keep me safe at all, when I carry them out I can't concentrate on anything else, I'm so focused on myself, I don't see what is happening around me' |

Re-rating of original belief 45%

Alternative explanations and learning outcomes

Not carrying out any of my safety behaviours did not result in me being attacked as I thought. I actually look more inconspicuous when I don't do my safety behaviours than when I do them.

If I was being watched and going to be attacked, carrying out these behaviours will not help keep me safe.

Having the thought and feelings doesn't mean it is going to come true, it might just be a thought.

The things I do make me believe my thoughts even more and make me more anxious; when I don't do them I am much less distressed.

Moving my attention from my thoughts and feelings to what is going on around me makes me feel less anxious

Table 4.4   An example of some of Jacob's counter evidence for his core belief: 'I'm a useless and worthless person'

	Evidence or experiences suggesting this is not 100% true all the time
Past evidence	Matthew and I have been very close friends for a long time, I have managed to maintain this friendship.
	I did complete two A levels.
	I have received compliments for my photography.
Current evidence (collected daily)	My sister asked me if I could help her with homework
	I helped my mum with her dishes
	Matthew phoned to ask if I could go around to his for dinner, he has said that he enjoys spending time with me.
	I completed a form at the employment centre, they think I have a good CV and can get a job soon
	My neighbour asked me if I could help her with her shopping and then made me a cup of tea and we talked for a long time.
	I did the food shopping for my family
	I showed Matthew some photographs I had taken, he told me he was really impressed and thinks I should try to sell them.
	Another man at the job centre started a conversation with me today, and invited me to play football with a group of men at a local park.
	My sister invited me for a drink
	My dad made me a sandwich for lunch and said he had enjoyed having lunch together.

Evaluation of core beliefs

During the last few sessions Jacob wanted to focus on some of his core beliefs. As Jacob had done well so far throughout therapy and made significant progress, it was important to stress to him that a change in core beliefs is a gradual process that takes time. To begin this process we took a recent event which Jacob had found distressing and then used the downward arrow technique, using the question 'What does X say about you?'

'What does X mean to you?' Initially, Jacob could identify one main core belief, 'I'm useless/ worthless' that seemed to arise in many situations. The process of looking at this belief began by Jacob collating evidence that the belief 'I'm useless/worthless' is not 100 percent true all the time. Jacob began by thinking of any possible evidence from the past that was counter to this core belief. Obviously, this was a hard task to complete; Jacob had held this view for a long time. Following this and outside of the session, he collected one piece of evidence every day for the week in between sessions. Following this, he began to gather two or three pieces of evidence every day over the following week. Table 4.4 illustrates an example of the evidence Jacob managed to collate. In beginning this exercise with Jacob in session, it opened up a discussion about the biases that existed for him and his automatic tendency to discount evidence challenging his core belief but his ability to recall with great clarity even small negative experiences both past and present that supported his core belief. As a result, he felt able to include all evidence however small or irrelevant it seemed at the time. In conclusion, Jacob was able to rerate his belief that 'I am a useful and worthwhile person', from 0 percent to 25 percent and he also recognized his own biases in disregarding evidence in support of this belief and was prepared to continue to work on this belief. More importantly, he felt able to apply this technique to other core beliefs he held about himself. More information regarding re-evaluation of core beliefs can be found in Chapter 1.

Homework

It cannot be expressed in words how integral homework is to outcome of therapy. In his original manual, Beck (1976) states that homework is an 'integral, vital component of treatment', 'unless patients can apply the concepts learned in therapy sessions to their lives outside, there will be no progress'. To convince you further, we see clients for 1 hour per week (if you are lucky), that works out to be 1 hour out of 168 hours, roughly 0.6 percent of their week. Homework provides the therapist with an opportunity to make a huge impact outside the therapy session. The homework set can range from information gathering (e.g. diaries, surveys, reading), to practising a change in behaviour or trying new experiences to gather information in the context of their own environment to aid the reappraisal of beliefs.

For Jacob, homework started out as a chore. He related the word 'homework' with school, a place he did not like and did not think of himself as academic. As such, it was replaced with 'work through the week'. After explaining the rationale to Jacob of the importance of work between sessions and the collaborative nature of setting the work, he was over

90 percent compliant with homework. On the one occasion when home-work wasn't completed, Jacob reported that he had not understood the rationale for the homework and how it related to his difficulties. This was important feedback information for the therapist as it helped to address these issues in therapy so that therapy could progress.

Engagement

Although it could be argued the therapy was in the context of a trial and hence engagement was key for completion of therapy and follow ups, trying to put in place as many strategies as possible to maintain an 'at-risk' client is essential due to their often chaotic lives. Initially, with Jacob this involved giving him a quick call the day before an appointment to check on timings and a text in the morning of the appointment to remind him (often by request of the client). In addition, as Jacob was unemployed, a meeting was arranged for him with a local job centre designed specifically for people Jacob's age and his benefit forms were completed with a letter of support from the therapist. Jacob was seen in a non-stigmatizing venue, his GP practice, which was his choice and while Jacob did not wish for a recording of the sessions on CD, he often requested a summary of the session to have to look over throughout the week and found the blueprint invaluable at the end of therapy.

Other clients require liaison with other members of the wider care team while others request for information on medication or to be accompanied to their GP to help them explain their symptoms and the help they want. The engagement process is idiosyncratic to the client and can be extremely varied; what is important is that the client maintains their engagement with you and begins to form a therapeutic relationship they can trust in.

Relapse prevention: The development of a blueprint

The development of a blueprint is a collaborative process, and represents all the skills the client has learnt throughout cognitive therapy, how they will apply them in the future and a chance to discuss how they may handle any future obstacles. Jacob was worried about the end of therapy and reported that although he had made a marked improvement, he imagined there would be many obstacles in the future to overcome and understandably was anxious about managing these. However, developing the blueprint gave us an opportunity to discuss what plans he might put in place for these predicted future obstacles. Jacob was able to identify early warning signs, even asking his mother if she had noticed any signs, and together an action plan of what he would need to do and who he would need to contact in this situation was developed. Jacob reported that he had found many strategies helpful so the therapist began the blueprint with a simple formulation used during therapy, and then followed this with generating alternative interpretations and evidential analysis, providing a summary on any related behavioural experiments were appropriate.

It is important to reiterate that while this case and the therapy discussed in this chapter took place as part of a clinical trial there are two clinical teams within our mental health trust (Greater Manchester West Mental Health NHS Foundation Trust) that offer these interventions for individuals considered to be at risk of psychosis. These teams have been in operation for a number of years and have attracted national and international visitors to learn about this approach to managing this client group. They continue to have high rates of acceptability, low drop-out rates and low transition to psychosis.

References

Addington, J., Epstein, I., Liu, L. *et al.* (2011) A randomized controlled trial of cognitive behavioral therapy for individuals at clinical high risk of psychosis. *Schizophrenia Research, 125(1)*, 54–61.

Amminger, G.P., Schafer, M.R., Papageorgiou, K. *et al.* (2010) Long-chain omega-3 fatty acids for indicated prevention of psychotic disorders: A Randomized, placebo-controlled trial. *Archives of General Psychiatry, 67(2)*, 146–154.

Bechdolf, A., Köhn, D., Knost, B. *et al.* (2005) A randomized comparison of group cognitive-behavioural therapy and group psychoeducation in acute patients with schizophrenia: Outcome at 24 months. *Acta Psychiatrica Scandinavica, 112(3)*, 173–179.

Beck, A.T. (1976) *Cognitive Therapy and the Emotional Disorders*. New York: International Universities Press.

Bentall, R.P. and Morrison, A.P. (2002) More harm than good: The case against using antipsychotic drugs to prevent severe mental illness. *Journal of Mental Health, 11*, 351–365.

Freeman, D., Freeman, J. and Garety, P.A. (2006) *Overcoming Paranoid and Suspicious Thoughts*. London: Robinson.

French, P. and Morrison, A.P. (2004) *Early Detection and Cognitive Therapy for People at High Risk of Developing Psychosis: A Treatment Approach*. London: Wiley.

McGlashan, T.H., Zipursky, R.B., Perkins, D. *et al.* (2006) Randomized, double-blind trial of Olanzapine versus placebo in patients prodromally symptomatic for psychosis. *American Journal of Psychiatry, 163(5)*, 790–799.

McGorry, P.D., Yung, A.R., Phillips, L.J. *et al.* (2002) Randomized controlled trial of interventions designed to reduce the risk of progression to first-episode psychosis in a clinical sample with subthreshold symptoms. *Archives of General Psychiatry, 59*, 921–928.

Miller, T.J., McGlashan, T.H., Rosen, J.L. *et al.* (2003) Prodromal assessment with the structured interview for prodromal syndromes and the scale of prodromal symptoms: predictive validity, interrater reliability, and training to reliability. *Schizophrenia Bulletin, 29(4),* 703–715.

Morrison, A.P. (2001) The interpretation of intrusions in psychosis: An integrative cognitive approach to hallucinations and delusions. *Behavioural and Cognitive Psychotherapy, 29,* 257–276.

Morrison, A.P., French, P., Walford, L. *et al.* (2004) Cognitive therapy for the prevention of psychosis in people at ultra-high risk: Randomised controlled trial. *British Journal of Psychiatry, 185(4),* 291–297.

Morrison, A.P., Renton, J.C., French, P. *et al.* (2008) *Think You're Crazy? Think Again: A Resource Book for Cognitive Therapy for Psychosis.* London: Routledge.

Morrison, A.P., Stewart, S., French, P. *et al.* (2011) Early Detection and Intervention Evaluation for people at high-risk of psychosis-2 (EDIE-2): Trial rationale, design and baseline characteristics. *Early Intervention in Psychiatry, 5,* 24–32.

Ruhrmann, S., Bechdolf, A., Kühn, K.-U. *et al.* (2007) Acute effects of treatment for prodromal symptoms for people putatively in a late initial prodromal state of psychosis. *The British Journal of Psychiatry, 191(51),* s88–s95.

Wells, A. and Matthews, G. (1994) *Attention and Emotion: A Clinical Perspective.* London: LEA.

Yung, A., Phillips, L.J., McGorry, P.D. *et al.* (1998) A step towards indicated prevention of schizophrenia. *British Journal of Psychiatry, 172,* Supplement 33, 14–20.

Yung, A.R., Yuen, H.P., McGorry, P.D. *et al.* (2005) Mapping the onset of psychosis – the Comprehensive Assessment of At Risk Mental States (CAARMS). *Australian and New Zealand Journal of Psychiatry, 39(11–12),* 964–971.

5

CBT for Medication-Resistant Psychosis: Targeting the Negative Symptoms

Neil A. Rector*

In the past two decades considerable progress has been made in the development and delivery of effective CBT interventions for persistent symptoms of psychosis (CBTp), such as delusions and hallucinations. Randomized controlled trial studies have demonstrated the ability of CBTp to produce significant and sustainable gains in the reduction of distress caused by the experience of positive symptoms (Rector and Beck, 2001; Pilling *et al.*, 2002; Tarrier and Wykes, 2004; Wykes *et al.*, 2008; Gould *et al.* 2010). However, much less attention has been given to understanding and treating the negative symptoms of psychosis. The current diagnostic description of negative symptoms include: restrictions in the range and intensity of emotional expression (affective flattening), in the fluency and productivity of thought and speech (alogia), and in the initiation of goal-directed behaviour (avolition) (American Psychiatric Association (APA), 2000). The loss of ability to enjoy pleasure (anhedonia) has also been identified as an associated feature (APA, 2000). Patients experiencing flat effect speak in monotone, stare vacantly, and appear unresponsive. Alogia, meaning 'a (without) logos (speech)' (poverty of speech) is reflected in brief and empty replies. Avolition is characterized by reductions in the pursuit of goal-directed activities. The psychological understanding and management of these

* The author would like to thank Alex Daros and Vincent Man for their editorial assistance.

negative symptoms of psychosis is especially important given their comparative refractoriness to medications and association with poor long-term functioning (e.g. McGlashan and Fenton, 1993).

A number of studies have found that CBTp also leads to clinically significant reductions in negative symptoms (see Rector and Beck, 2001; Tarrier and Wykes, 2004; Wykes *et al.*, 2008 for quantitative reviews). Although recent effect size estimates in the treatment of negative symptoms point to small-to-moderate effects, they emerge as the most malleable symptom dimension with CBTp (Wykes *et al.*, 2008). This is of particular interest given that they have not represented a specific treatment target in the majority of RCTs conducted to date. Our clinical CBTp trial work commencing in Toronto in the late 1990s, explicitly aimed at treating patients experiencing persistent *positive* and *negative* symptoms. Through this work, we formulated a new conceptualization of the negative symptoms and outlined novel intervention approaches that were found to be efficacious in our study.

Toronto Clinical Trial for CBTp

The aim of the Toronto study was to assess whether patients with a DSM-IV diagnosis of schizophrenia and experiencing persistent positive and negative symptoms improve with the addition of CBT to enriched standard treatment within specialty services. A controlled study was completed with 42 patients randomized to either CBT plus enriched treatment-as-usual (CBT-ETAU) (n = 24) or enriched treatment-as-usual only (ETAU) (n = 18). ETAU comprised comprehensive psychiatric management with medication optimization and clinical case management. The stated goals of ETAU were to optimize medication effectiveness and adherence; improve patient empowerment and choice; and increase social and occupational functioning.

CBTp was delivered on an individual basis for 6 months as an augmentation to ETAU. The CBTp approach in this study was guided by the principles and strategies developed by Beck in the treatment of the emotional disorders and tailored to treat the specific symptoms of schizophrenia within a diathesis-stress framework and in keeping with the generic CBTp approach outlined in the first chapter. The clinical approach employed in our trial work was reported earlier (Beck and Rector, 2000, 2002a, 2002b) and elaborated in full more recently (Beck *et al.*, 2009). Unlike the step-by-step manualization of the cognitive therapy treatment of the emotional disorders, the preferred approach in CBTp, given its broad symptom heterogeneity, has been to develop specific modules that can be flexibly employed to treat selective symptoms of psychosis depending on the patient's presentation. Prior to the initiation of the study, modules on assessment and engagement; socialization to the cognitive model and normalizing of psychotic symptoms; the treatment of positive symptoms, negative symptoms, and co-morbid anxiety and depression; and finally relapse prevention, were developed and each of the therapists received formal training and supervision in their delivery.

The first phase of therapy focused on engagement and assessment. The initial sessions were relatively unstructured and consisted of empathic listening and gentle questioning which then progressed to a structured assessment and the development of a problem list. The second phase of therapy aimed to socialize the patient to the cognitive model and to impart cognitive and behavioural coping skills, including self-monitoring with a thought record and the completion of homework tasks. Overlapping with the first two phases of treatment, a third aspect of treatment focused on providing psychoeducation with a normalizing rationale (Kingdon and Turkington, 1994). Based on an idiosyncratically derived cognitive conceptualization, specific techniques were then used to target positive and negative symptoms. Guided discovery was employed to identify delusions as well as the cognitive and behavioural patterns that serve to maintain them. Through gentle questioning, patients were led to question and then test the extent to which their life experiences support their delusional beliefs and to begin to develop alternative appraisals. The treatment of hallucinations aimed to identify, test, and correct cognitive distortions in the content of voices and then, following Chadwick and Birchwood (1994), identify, question, and begin to test the beliefs the person has about the origins and nature of the voices. The approach to negative symptoms included standard behavioural strategies such as behavioural self-monitoring, activity scheduling, mastery and pleasure ratings, graded task assignments, and assertiveness training methods within an elaborated cognitive conceptualization of the negative symptoms (Rector *et al.*, 2005) and with newly defined cognitive intervention strategies (Beck *et al.*, 2009) that will be detailed below. Patients completed homework assignments between each session following a CBTp tailored homework program (Rector, 2007). Homework tasks included the completion of: bibliotherapy, dysfunctional thought records, modified dysfunctional thought records for voices and delusions, activity schedules, core belief approaches, and a range of behavioural tasks and experiments to target positive and negative symptoms. Therapists assessed adherence to homework in each weekly session although not formally tabulated on standardized homework rating forms.

Clinical assessments were conducted at pre-treatment, post-treatment and at 6-month follow up by raters blind to group allocation. Significant clinical effects were observed for positive, negative and overall symptom

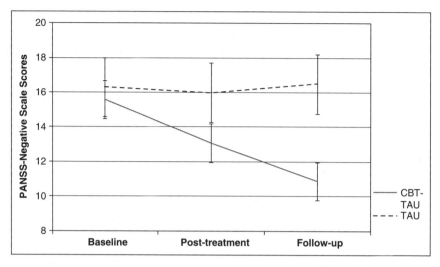

Figure 5.1   Cognitive expectancies in the production of negative symptom
Source: Rector *et al.*, 2003

severity for patients treated in CBT-ETAU, although there were no statistically significant differences between the treatment groups at post-treatment. The most pronounced effect of CBT-ETAU in comparison to ETAU in this study was in the reduction of negative symptoms at follow-up as seen in Figure 5.1. Further, on the PANSS-Negative scale, 67 percent of those in CBT-ETAU condition experienced clinically significant gain whereas only 31 percent of those in ETAU did so, and this difference was statistically significant.

Implications of the Toronto CBTp Trial

Our study (Rector *et al.*, 2003) provided the context for determining the efficacy of CBT for both positive and negative symptoms when both symptom domains are explicitly targeted in treatment. CBT was shown to significantly reduce both positive and negative symptoms and the changes in these symptoms were relatively independent: changes in negative symptoms were not simply a secondary consequence of change in positive symptoms (or of depression or medication). The most pronounced effect of CBT-ETAU in comparison to ETAU in this study was in the reduction of negative symptoms at follow-up thus showing promise for the positive impact of CBTp on negative symptoms when explicitly targeted in treatment. The management of negative symptoms is especially important as these represent the most debilitating aspect of psychosis and predict an overall poor prognosis (e.g. McGlashan and Fenton, 1993).

The evolution of cognitive-behavioural theory and treatment has followed a coherent conceptual framework, first early systematic clinical observations and definition and psychometric operationalization of key disorder-specific cognitive, emotional and behavioural constructs, to later progression from early non-controlled clinical outcome studies to the development of sophisticated, large-scale randomized controlled trials comparing the disorder-specific CBT treatment to waiting list conditions, comparative psychotherapy conditions, and medication-based interventions. In the context of our trial work in Toronto (Rector *et al.*, 2003) through careful systematic clinical observations and the development of negative symptom specific cognitive interventions, we subsequently defined and operationalized key cognitive constructs that are hypothesized to contribute to the development and maintenance of the negative symptoms. The general thrust of this new conceptualization was to reframe some negative symptoms as reflecting cognitive, emotional and behavioural *dysfunction* rather than stable *deficits*, which are therefore amenable to change via strategies that have proven effective in harnessing motivation and social and emotional re-engagement in those with severe emotional disorders.

The Cognitive Model of Negative Symptoms

Research has shown that negative symptoms are associated not only with aversive attitudes toward social relations but also toward goal directed activity in general. Barrowclough and colleagues (2003) found a significant negative correlation between patients' evaluation of their own positive attributes and role functioning, on the one hand, and their manifest negative symptom levels, on the other. A cross-sectional examination of patients' beliefs and attitudes as assessed by the Dysfunctional Attitude Scale (DAS) found that endorsement of items on the DAS such as 'Taking even a small risk is foolish because the loss is likely to be a disaster' and 'If a person avoids problems, the problem tends to go away' were significantly correlated with negative symptoms but not positive symptoms (Rector, 2004; Rector *et al.*, 2005). The association between these defeatist beliefs and negative symptoms held after controlling for depression. Attitudes such as 'If I fail partly, it is as bad as being a complete failure', 'If you cannot do something well, there is little point in doing it at all', and 'If I fail at work, I'm a failure as a person', feed into avoidance, apathy and passivity. Follow-up work has found that defeatist performance beliefs mediate the relationship between neurocognitive impairment and both negative symptoms and functional outcomes (Grant and Beck, 2010; Horan *et al.*, 2010; Quinlan and Granholm, 2009). Further, our hypothesis (Rector *et al.*, 2005) that defeatist

Table 5.1 Negative expectancy appraisals associated with DSM-IV negative symptoms

Symptoms	Appraisals			
	Low self-efficacy (success)	*Low satisfaction (pleasure)*	*Low acceptance*	*Low available resources*
Affective flattening	If I show my feelings, others will see my inadequacy	I don't feel the way I used to	My face appears stiff and contorted to others	I don't have the ability to express my feelings
Alogia	I'm not going to find the right words to express myself	I take so long to get my point across that it's boring	I'm going to sound weird, stupid, or strange	It takes so much effort to talk
Avolition	Why bother, I'm just going to fail	It's more trouble than it's worth	It's best not to get involved	It takes too much effort to try

Source: Rector *et al.*, 2005

performance beliefs precede the onset of psychosis has recently been substantiated empirically through the finding that high-risk individuals report elevated defeatist beliefs relative to controls, and these beliefs correlate with greater negative symptom severity (Perivoliotis *et al.*, 2009).

We also first outlined (Rector *et al.*, 2005) the cognitive factors that contribute to negative symptoms independent of positive symptoms and which reflect an exacerbation of negative attitudes toward social affiliation. Specifically, an outlook characterized by low expectancies for pleasure, success, acceptance, and the perception of limited resources is pivotal to the production and maintenance of negative symptoms. We outlined that distinct negative expectancy appraisals contribute to the development and particular expression of negative symptoms as seen in Table 5.1. Patients with prominent negative symptoms often think (and sometimes state), 'What's the point?', 'Why should I bother?', 'It's too much work' when prompted to participate in an activity. They expect to derive little satisfaction for their efforts. Research has also demonstrated that when patients with schizophrenia, including those with prominent and severe negative symptoms, are presented with pleasurable stimuli, they can and do derive pleasure from these experiences. As such, there is an observable disconnect between appetitive pleasure (i.e. anticipating that something will bring pleasure) and consummatory pleasure (i.e. the actual level of pleasure experienced from participating in an activity). This is similarly reflected in clinical observations where, despite their initial low expectancy for pleasure, patients demonstrate some enjoyment once engaged in a task.

Patients also demonstrate low expectancies for *success* in their day-to-day experiences. They expect to fail to meet goals and if they meet the goals, they tend to perceive substandard performance in comparison to their expected performance. This negative outlook affects their motivation to initiate and sustain goal-directed behaviour, especially when under stress. In addition to the real limitations produced by the symptoms of schizophrenia, patients with prominent negative symptoms incorporate *stigmatizing* views into their self-construals. These have a negative influence on their perceived self-efficacy when they are faced with life challenges. It is very common for patients to state, 'What do you expect, I'm mentally ill,' or 'It doesn't matter what I do, it's not going to change the fact that I'm just a schizophrenic,' or 'There's no hope for me since I've got schizophrenia.' Also contributing to a pattern of disengagement are beliefs pertaining to the perceived personal costs of *expending energy in making an effort*. When presented with the opportunity to participate in a putative pleasant activity, patients will state, 'It's too much' or 'I can't handle it' or 'Why bother?' The subjective accounts of limited resources by patients are likely to reflect, in part, an accurate perception of diminished resources. However, we have also proposed that patients with prominent negative symptoms exaggerate the limited availability of resources as a result of a fixed defeatist cognitive set. Evidence that they have more available resources than they believe they have is apparent in their increased productivity when these negative attitudes are addressed in treatment.

The CBT Approach to Negative Symptoms

The cognitive behavioural approach to treating negative symptoms that emerged from our trial work in Toronto (Rector *et al.*, 2003; Rector *et al.*, 2005) has been elaborated in our recent text (Beck *et al.*, 2009). A brief outline of the treatment approach is provided below with a brief description of a case.

John[1] is a single 24-year-old male living in a group home in a large metropolitan city. He experienced his first onset of psychotic symptoms approximately 5 years prior to the referral for CBT that focused on delusions with persecutory themes. Within the past 5 years, he has experienced persistent and severe paranoid delusions that include members of his family, former friends, and strangers, and worsening negative symptoms focusing on severe affective flattening, avolitioin, anhedonia and moderate alogia. John was referred by a community psychiatrist working with a special service for people with long-term psychiatric difficulties to assist in the CBT treatment of his paranoia and negative symptoms with the downstream goal of improving his functioning and engagement. He had no past experience of psychotherapy or CBT. At the time of referral, he was compliant with medication treatments of Seroquel (500 mg/day) and Celexa 40 mg/day. He was receiving case management, which included biweekly meetings with a community team specialist and psychiatric follow-up. John was assessed with the Structured Clinical Interview for Axis 1 Disorders (SCID-1/P version 2.0; First *et al.*, 1996), and the assessment of symptoms of psychosis with the Positive and Negative Syndrome Scale (PANSS; Kay *et al.*, 1987). He also completed the Dysfunctional Attitude Scale (DAS; Weissman and Beck, 1978). Diagnostically, John's primary Axis I condition was Schizoaffective Disorder, Depressive Type and his General Assessment of Functioning (GAF) score was 28. At the time of first assessment, John described a pervasive fear of being monitored and persecuted by former high school students and their associates that prevented him from leaving his home without anxiety. He described infrequent contact with his family and having no close friendships or past or present romantic partners, reflecting social and emotional withdrawal. He demonstrated severe blunted affect with an attendant lack of spontaneity and flow of conversation. He had limited insight into his difficulties and there was suggestion of compromised executive functions with an inflexible, rigid and concrete cognitive style with noticeable difficulties with planning and execution, attention and memory. He also reported a range of dysfunctional performance beliefs that have been previously associated with negative symptoms (Rector, 2004).

The *cognitive conceptualization* provides the framework for understanding how past and present factors contribute to the development and persistence of the person's current problems. It is important to assess the role of early learning experiences, critical incidents, the timing and nature of formation of dysfunctional beliefs and assumptions, and coping behaviours developed over time to cope with stressors, and the illness in particular. The case conceptualization should lead to initial hypotheses about the role of distal environmental factors that contribute to a vulnerability for avoidance and disengagement (e.g. rejection, few friends, early academic failures) as well as consolidating negative attitudes toward social affiliation and negative dysfunctional performance beliefs. For example, John described a long history of feeling disliked by his peer group and there was a period of significant bullying through middle school (grades 7–9) that resulted in a 6-month depressive episode. From an early age, he had come to see people as 'mean and untrustworthy' and felt that he had to be continuously vigilant for his safety. He also had a number of academic problems starting from early childhood that led to streaming into special education and low achievement striving. He was fired from two of his summer jobs in his teen years and he failed to complete high school. This was particularly difficult as he grew up in a successful and affluent family. In short, John described early experiences that led him to develop dysfunctional beliefs pertaining to interpersonal vulnerability and inadequacy and a lack of perceived competency in goal directed pursuits. His responses on the DAS also reflected heightened dysfunctional interpersonal and performance beliefs. He had also established a behavioural pattern of social and emotional avoidance and limited striving toward goals before the first onset of psychosis.

Following a careful detailed assessment of the negative symptoms and the development of a provisional case conceptualization, the first step in addressing the negative symptoms in treatment is to help normalize these symptoms for patients. Patients often perceive their difficulties with motivation as signs of laziness and weakness. The aim of the normalizing approach is to impart to the patients that their problems are familiar to most people at some time in their life but for a variety of reasons they have experienced these problems for a longer period of time. It is important to provide a multidimensional view of the development and maintenance of the negative symptoms including a biological (e.g. automatic resetting of the thermostat) and psychological (e.g. reducing activity to prevent being overwhelmed) explanations. Additional points that should be discussed include the problems of approaching goals under pressure with links to areas in their life where they perceive themselves to be under pressure. Kingdon and Turkington (1998) use the analogy of the patients requiring a period of recovery or 'convalescence' to heal from the effects of a serious illness.

Importantly, the focus on improving motivation in CBT is about trying to help the patient generate meaningful goals and then to stay engaged with these goals. For patients whose negative symptoms are secondary to delusions and hallucinations, the socialization to the cognitive model for negative symptoms may be introduced as a component of the cognitive model for these positive symptoms. Similar to the cognitive conceptualization of avoidance and safety behaviours in the anxiety disorders, escape and avoidance behaviours are framed as adaptive short-term solutions for reducing distress but treatment will aim to gradually reduce these behaviours. John's psychosis developed in the final year of high school following an incident that involved the police at a local mall. Over the course of several weeks, he made daily visits to a store in the mall to see one of the store attendants whom he found to be pleasant and attractive. He misinterpreted her friendliness as sign of romantic interest. He began to make phone calls to the store, asking for the attendant, then hanging up due to anxiety. The day before the incident, he called the store and spoke to her, and at the time made a sexually inappropriate comment. The attendant, in turn, spoke with him and then invited him to come and speak with her at the store the next day. When John arrived to the store the next day he was apprehended by the police and given a warning regarding the inappropriate phone calls and taken home to his parents in the police car. John was confused and upset over the incident and described mounting feelings of worthlessness and guilt over his actions. Over a 4–5 week period, he began to suspect that he was being watched, followed, and undermined by the police, staff at the store, and friends of the woman that he had approached and that he was going to be 'punished' and 'physically harmed' for his actions. He began to suspect that people were being 'nice to his face' but ridiculing and mocking him behind his back. Soon, he began to see 'signs' all around him – family members speaking quietly, people on the street laughing, cryptic messages in TV commercials and his CDs referring to his behaviour, and so forth. His delusional fear and guilt mounted until he could no longer cope and it culminated in a serious suicide attempt and subsequent protracted hospitalization. At the time of assessment for CBT, his persecutory symptoms remained virtually unchanged since onset 5 years earlier, with daily preoccupation with being watched and followed by people in the shared environment. To manage, John avoided social contact as much as possible and spent most of his time alone in his room providing the context for the worsening of his negative symptoms.

Treating Secondary Negative Symptoms

As previously noted, we have found that the negative symptoms which are secondary to delusions and the delusional beliefs about the voices (e.g. agency, control, meaning etc.), are either *coping* strategies to reduce the threat associated with having these symptoms or represent behaviours that have meaning within the delusional system (Rector *et al.*, 2005). As in the treatment of anxiety and depression, an important aim of treatment is to help the patient learn strategies to resist getting 'stuck' in the downward spirals. Irrespective of the particular content of the delusions, patients report escaping or avoiding situations where they anticipate having fear-related (delusional) thoughts, which, for some, can extend to nearly all interpersonal contexts, including minimal contact with family and healthcare workers. Similarly, patients who hear voices report a wide range of behavioural avoidance and safety behaviours to reduce: a) their activation, b) their persistence or c) the distressing delusional beliefs about the voices. When negative symptoms are coping strategies to deal with the positive symptoms, they can be tackled in conjunction with the cognitive behavioural approach for positive symptoms. The early phase of John's treatment focused on targeting the persecutory delusions so as to reduce ongoing distress but also the likelihood that subsequent efforts to enhance behavioural activation and engagement around targeting the negative symptoms, would not lead to a broader range of delusional triggers and distress. In short, treatment focused on normalizing the delusional distress, socializing John to the CBT, and working to create change in delusional interpretations pertaining to perceived persecution. Treatment further focused on the nature of belief formation and how beliefs can sometimes be held with great emotional investment even though they may turn out to be false. Next, the therapeutic approach involved a number of cognitive and behavioural strategies aimed at undermining the rigid conviction and centrality of the delusion(s). Once the therapist has a thorough understanding of the patient's delusional beliefs and the past and current events that are interpreted as supporting the belief, gentle questioning of the evidence is undertaken. During this phase of treatment, questioning continued to identify different sources of evidence for John's delusional beliefs both past and current. For instance, common triggers included passing police cars, policemen on the streets, identification of unmarked police cars, white and black vans outside his residence, people smiling or laughing, and especially any person in the environment with hands in their pocket. John believed that people put their hands in their pocket to communicate to him that they knew of his masturbation following visits and calls to the attendant at the store. As one example, John passed a bakery and a group of five teenagers were standing out front with hands in their pockets. His automatic thought (i.e. delusional interpretation) was 'they're following me . . . they're going to punish me.' His emotional response was fear (80%). Questioning the delusional interpretation led to evidence that was seen to support the initial interpretation: they seemed to be looking over at him while putting their hands in their pockets. However, John was also able to stand back and evaluate evidence that did not support his interpretations, recognizing that some of them appeared to be looking for change in their pockets, that some people put their hands in their pockets as a habit, and that hands in their pocket continued even when he appeared out of their sight (although within his), and that over 5 years of believing this, no person with hands in their pockets had ever approached or confronted him. This consideration of this evidence led to the alternative conclusion, 'they're just hanging around and don't know me.' John completed dysfunctional thought records for delusional triggers between sessions and began to make progress in identifying, testing and correcting these types of delusional interpretations. The overall quality of the thought records was quite low, but John was developing the habit of identifying, questioning and finding less threatening alternative explanations for other's behavior.

The treatment of secondary negative symptoms to delusions and voices is analogous to the treatment of panic disorder. The patient with panic disorder would be typically exposed to *in vivo* exposures to overcome avoidance and safety behaviours after they had made progress in conceptualizing their panic attacks within the cognitive framework, and developed at least some preliminary skills to deal with elevated distress in difficult situations. Similarly, patients with secondary negative symptoms who are experiencing threatening delusions and hallucinations can make the most out of their exposure exercises after they have made progress in identifying, testing, and creating alternative interpretations of their delusions and voices outside 'hot' situations. Then the reduction of secondary negative symptoms can proceed with the development of a graded hierarchy listing situations that are feared and avoided. As in the treatment of anxiety disorders, exposure to situations proceeds from least to most distressing. The main goal is for the patient to gradually reduce emotional, social and behavioural avoidance strategies. John's hierarchy for triggers for his paranoid fears exceeded 30 different contexts, and included comparatively mild to moderate subjective distress (SUDS) items such as watching TV in shared group room (SUDS:30); going for a walk close to the group home (SUDS:35); going for a walk downtown (SUDS:50); sitting in a nearby café (SUDS: 60), up to high distress triggers such as walking in a shopping centre (SUDS:85) and walking close to the store where he was apprehended (SUDS:95). He completed weekly exposure exercises, working through the hierarchy. He also completed behavioural experiments including going to a range of places where he could remain out of view while observing the frequency of people putting hands in their pockets. The data generated by the behavioural experiment was reviewed (i.e. the frequency of the behaviour was the same when he was present or absent). At the end of this phase of treatment, John's belief rating in feeling persecuted by others had fallen dramatically with the ability to reduce catastrophizing and delusional cycles in the presence of familiar triggers. As a result, he was now able to go out to the shopping centre, coffee shops, the cinema and spend time with people in his residence without experiencing significant delusional fear. He also appeared to enjoy attending the weekly CBT meetings and was becoming increasingly communicative in sessions. While there was noted improvement in his social and emotional withdrawal as a result of this progress, the second phase of treatment required direct targeting of his primary negative symptoms.

Treating Primary Negative Symptoms

The central feature of the cognitive approach to negative symptoms is the attempt to enhance behavioural activation toward changing the negative expectancies and performance beliefs that represent the more enduring vulnerability for chronic disengagement (Beck *et al.*, 2009; Rector *et al.*, 2003; Rector *et al.*, 2005).

Targeting Low Expectancies for Pleasure

Patients with prominent negative symptoms typically report that they find little enjoyment in their lives and, in turn, expect to receive minimal enjoyment when presented with the opportunity to participate in activities. We know from clinical experience and experimental research (Gard *et al.*, 2003) that patients, once engaged in activities, derive pleasure in the same way that others do. As such, the major treatment goal is to create a list of idiosyncratically-defined pleasurable activities, increase the scheduling of these activities day-to-day, and to reduce the negative expectancy for pleasure so that it does not become a barrier to participation. The steps in the treatment approach follow the sequence: 1) Identifying cognitive distortions in low pleasure expectancies; 2) Working with disconfirming evidence pertaining to low expectancies; 3) Schedule meaningful activity; 4) Record online pleasure, ratings *in vivo*; and 5) Use feedback to shift low expectations.

Through the years, John had come to spend the entire day at home sleeping and watching television. As noted, part of this was due to delusional fear but when asked about why he had had come to stop something that had previously been enjoyable, he stated: 'What's the point.' In response, the therapist tries to reharness motivation to pursue something that was of moderate pleasure in the past by targeting low expectancies for pleasure:

THERAPIST: So, you used to enjoy riding the bus?

PATIENT: Ya, every day for years.

THERAPIST: What did you like about it?

PATIENT: I felt like there was something to get up for. I got to know the bus drivers. I had a coffee schedule and took my breaks with the drivers.

THERAPIST: I'm sure you also got to know the city well?

PATIENT: Ya, I got to know the streets, the different neighbourhoods, including places you shouldn't go.

THERAPIST: Do you ever think about doing this still?

PATIENT: Not really, or maybe once in a blue moon, but what's the point.

THERAPIST: So when you think about how it was in the past in contrast to what you expect now, it just doesn't seem worth it?

PATIENT: Pretty much

THERAPIST: I wonder, do you think it's possible that it could still be at least a little enjoyable even though maybe not as enjoyable as it was in the past?

PATIENT: Ya, but still worth it – I don't know.
THERAPIST: Ok, but would you be willing to test out whether it's still somewhat enjoyable – still worth it?
PATIENT: I'm not sure . . . I don't even know how much it costs to get on the bus now.
THERAPIST: I think it's still around 2 dollars . . . just one coin or a token . . . what do you think?
PATIENT: But I won't know the drivers or the routes like I used to?
THERAPIST: How about if I came with you to keep you the company the first time?
PATIENT: Ok, there's not much to lose.
THERAPIST: What if you found through our bus ride together that it wasn't too bad, maybe even a little enjoyable, would that be worthwhile?
PATIENT: I'd have a reason to leave the house again, I guess.

This *in vivo* task provided the opportunity to help John not only schedule the activity but also to address any barriers that might get in the way of its completion. It also allowed the therapist to obtain pleasure ratings from John (0–10) throughout the bus ride (which ranged from 4–6) so as to minimize any subsequent minimization or disqualification by him when discussing its pleasure at a later time. John began to increase outings for bus rides and kept track of his pleasure ratings until there was enough consolidated data that he had come to expect the bus rides to be pleasurable and worth it again.

Targeting Low Expectancies for Success

A factor that contributes to the pattern of withdrawal and low motivation are patients' expectations that if they push themselves to meet goals they are likely to fail or to achieve some substandard level of performance. The first step in this process is helping patients to identify areas where they feel pressure to perform beyond what they feel they can handle. This may involve working with the perceived sources of pressure. For instance, family-based cognitive therapy for helping patients' family members establish and maintain realistic expectations around motivation and not construing negative symptoms as signs of laziness has been well illustrated in clinical case material (Pelton, 2002). There is also some preliminary evidence to support the benefit of reducing familial demands toward improving negative symptom functioning. Once external pressures are reduced, the treatment focus is on helping patients work on establishing and pursuing realistic and meaningful goals. The therapist's aim is to socialize the patient to the importance of setting goals, breaking down broader goals in to small manageable steps, structuring and scheduling the steps to be completed and dealing with barriers to engagement, as well as negotiating setbacks.

Similar to the cognitive distortions involved in minimizing expected pleasure, patients often pass on opportunities to gain mastery because they expect to fail, seeing themselves as 'useless,' and 'incompetent'. The minimization of successes can be reduced by having patients monitor activities throughout the week on an activity schedule with applied mastery ratings on a continuous scale (as described by Beck *et al.*, 1979). Other cognitive distortions that fuel negative expectancies for success such as overgeneralization, mental filter, and disqualifying the positive, can be similarly addressed as patients report on weekly updates. Finally, while the initial work focuses on helping the patient learn to identify and question his/her negative expectancies for success to enhance engagement, successful treatment requires some attention to the deeper dysfunctional attitudes and beliefs the person has about performance.

For example, John had once considered learning more about computers at the local community centre. In reviewing the barriers that had prevented him from pursuing this further, he stated, 'I'll make mistakes and embarrass myself' and 'I won't be able to learn and remember things'. The first step was to explore the evidence around his current knowledge of computers and the probability and consequences around making mistakes in front of others. John had access to a computer and used it daily to surf the Internet and play games. The therapist also discussed the probability and consequences of making mistakes and the likelihood that the instructor would be patient, given that it would be an introductory course. Finally, the therapist questioned and helped to generate alternative evidence around the appraisal, 'I won't be able to learn and remember things'. Here the therapist was able to use evidence directly obtained from the treatment process thus far to help John recognize that he was able to learn and remember important sources of information. With the help of the therapist John started and completed a 4-week introductory training course. Over the weeks of training, John completed thought records between sessions to identify and collect evidence for negative appraisals related to 'failing' and fears of not being able to complete the course.

As the therapist attempted to reduce John's negative expectancies around failing at the computer course, and its eventual completion, John and the therapist began to discuss the possibility of taking up a part-time volunteer position to enrich his life and allow him much needed breaks from his residence. John acknowledged that he did not know where to begin in coordinating the volunteer work. The therapist and John reviewed his past and current interests and it was determined that among his remaining interests, he still liked watching hockey and might be interested in volunteering in this area somehow. Together, the therapist and John thought of three possible opportunities – volunteering at: a) the hockey hall of fame, b) with the local professional hockey team, and c) a more local community hockey arena. John and the therapist next worked to identify the different steps that would be involved in finding out more about volunteering possibilities at these venues, including: a) finding out information about who the name and contact of the volunteer coordinator at each site, b) learning more about volunteer possibilities at each site, c) identifying the top choice of activity, d) helping him to develop a cover letter or introductory statement when calling the volunteer coordinator, e) and finally scheduling when these different activities would take place. Given the lack of guarantee that he would secure a volunteer position at any of the three sites, the therapist also helped John to anticipate this and to consider other volunteer possibilities in this area. As it turned out, the first two options did not have coordinated volunteer activities but John was able to pursue the local arena where he ended up assisting the skate sharpener twice weekly.

In order to help patients achieve their goals, the initial work focuses on the identification and questioning of negative expectancies for success. However, as noted, given that patients with negative symptoms often hold deeper dysfunctional attitudes and beliefs regarding performance, such as 'If I fail partly, it is as bad as being a complete failure' or 'Taking even a small risk is foolish, because the loss is likely to be a disaster' or 'If a person asks for help, it is a sign of weakness' (Rector, 2004; Rector *et al.*, 2005), these beliefs require targeting with standard core belief treatment strategies (e.g. see Beck *et al.*, 2009) for elaboration.

Targeting the Impact of Stigma

The demoralization due to the stigma of schizophrenia contributes to the development and persistence of emotional and social disengagement. Because schizophrenia is frequently presented in the broader culture as reflecting 'craziness' or 'dangerousness', patients unfortunately have con-siderable evidence to support their perceptions. While it may be difficult to fully reduce the experience of stigma, there are a number of strategies that therapists can take to help with this problem. First, stigma can be reduced by normalizing the symptoms of psychosis. Second, the dysfunctional beliefs that patients hold about themselves often emerge in response to adverse life experiences and circumstances and can be normalized. Third, another strategy for reducing stigma and enhancing self-esteem is to have patients make personal connection with other patients who have similar experiences. There are numerous links to peer support groups for patients with psychosis throughout the world. Fourth, in addition to addressing the 'real world' problems of living with a stigmatizing illness, cognitive therapy aims to help patients identify and reduce exaggerated negative expectancies pertaining to stigma. When prompted to participate in activities, patients think, 'Why bother, I'm just a schizophrenic' and the like which fuel avoidance and withdrawal behaviours. Common to these expectancy statements is a range of cognitive distortions such as all-or-nothing and overgeneralization that can be identified, questioned and reframed. Finally, part of the therapeutic aim is to identify 'high risk' situations where the experience of stigma may be more likely to occur and to develop and rehearse coping responses. For instance, John had to learn how to cope with perceived and on two occasions, actual, taunting from teenagers in his volunteer role at the hockey arena. While these led to temporary distress and withdrawal, the therapist and John were able to defuse the impact of these events by examining cognitive distortions, normalizing teenage behaviour as sometimes insensitive, and meeting to discuss the events with the owner of the skate sharpening outlet to provide on-site support for John in the event of a similar circumstance in the future.

Targeting Perception of Low Resources

Patients exhibit a range of difficulties pertaining to attention, memorial functioning and skills associated with planning and organization (Nuechterlein and Dawson, 1984), all of which probably contribute to limitations in effortful task involvement. Research has demonstrated that when patients are given encouragement and support it converts into improved task performance on experimental tasks. The goal in therapy, then, is to break this self-perpetuating cycle of perceived limited resources, reduced effort and withdrawal, and subsequent perceived resourcelessness. The use of the graded task assignment can aid in helping patients more realistically assess what resources are required to complete a task, once the goal has broken down into more manageable parts. Patients frequently state, 'I'm too tired', 'It's not worth the work', 'It's too hard' and the like. Therapists are attentive to cognitive distortions in these expectancy appraisals, aiming to help the patient identify and correct all-or-nothing thinking and minimization of resources. The therapist and John addressed cognitive distortions as they emerged across the behavioural activation strategies (e.g. bus trips, computer course, volunteer position). One strategy that we have discussed previously is the use of the continuum perspective that can be introduced through the metaphor of a gasoline tank ranging from near-empty, to quarter-full, all the way to full tank. The patient identifies activities that are completely easy to do on a full tank, still relatively easy but somewhat harder at three-quarters full and so on down to tasks, activities, situations and so on that are perceived as too overwhelming (Beck *et al.*, 2009). It was important for John to start with a volunteer position that would provide the flexibility for him not to attend on days when his gas tank was too low without threat of judgement or embarrassment. However, he was still able to achieve more on these days than in the past by setting, small manageable goals rather than relinquishing all goals on difficult days.

Overall, John made progress in his CBT treatment across the 20 sessions, both in terms of secondary negative symptoms, following the successful reduction of his 5-year persecutory delusion and attendant avoidance and social withdrawal. Across the treatment, there was also steady advancement in his primary negative symptoms; avolition, affective flattening, alogia and anhedonia. He demonstrated better self-care and interpersonal relations at his residence. He reported more enjoyment in his activities, from watching television in his residence to taking walks. He was doing well in his volunteer position and had a good relationship with the owner of the skate sharpening outlet. There were also new plans to take an introductory computer course at a community college that offered special programs and support for people with long-term illness. While beyond the scope of this brief discussion of John's case, there was also a family component to the treatment that focused on exposure to family members to reduce delusional distress in the early phase of treatment which, in turn, led to more regular and supportive visits by his parents in the second phase of treatment that served to encourage and reinforce John in his progress with goal-directed activities. His parents were outspoken about the noted improvements in his communicativeness by the end of treatment.

Summary

The CBTp approach developed in Toronto provided the context to develop an integrated cognitive-behavioural to the negative symptoms of psychosis. The approach to the treatment of negative symptoms highlights the role of beliefs and appraisals that contribute to patterns of disengagement following internal and external triggers of stress, as well as cognitive-behavioural strategies to harness hope, enthusiasm and resources to achieve meaningful goals. The framing these symptoms in cognitive-behavioural terms provides a roadmap for how patients can overcome the pattern of passivity and withdrawal in their day-to-day lives. Since completing our trial, other studies have shown promise in reducing negative symptoms when using behavioural activation patterns for secondary depression (Peters *et al.*, 2010) and Turkington and colleagues

(2008) demonstrated that improvements in negative symptom functioning that occur following CBTp have excellent medium-term durability of up to 5 years. A number of studies are currently underway to further evaluate the cognitive formulation and treatment of negative symptoms.

Note

1   In addition to name-change, aspects of John's clinical presentation and treatment have been modified to protect his anonymity.

References

American Psychiatric Association (APA) (2000) *Diagnostic and Statistical Manual of Mental Disorder*, 4th edn Washington, DC: APA.

Barrowclough, C., Tarrier, N., Humphreys, L. *et al.* (2003) Self-esteem in schizophrenia: Relationships between self-evaluation, family attitudes, and symptomatology. *Journal of Abnormal Psychology, 112*, 92–99.

Beck, A.T. and Rector, N.A. (2000) Cognitive therapy of schizophrenia: A new therapy for the new millennium. *American Journal of Psychotherapy, 54*, 291–300.

Beck, A.T., Rector, N.A., Stolar, N. *et al.* (2009) *Schizophrenia: Cognitive Theory, Research, and Therapy*. New York: Guilford Press.

Beck, A.T., Rush, A.J., Shaw, B.F. *et al.* (1979) *Cognitive Therapy of Depression*. New York: Guilford Press.

Chadwick, P.D. and Birchwood, M.J. (1994) The omnipotence of voices: I. a cognitive approach to auditory hallucinations. *British Journal of Psychiatry, 164*, 190–201.

First, M.B., Spitzer, R.L., Gibbon, M. *et al.* (1996) *Structured Clinical Interview for DSM-IV Axis I Disorders, Clinician Version (SCID-CV)*. Washington, D.C.: American Psychiatric Press, Inc.

Gard, D.E., Germans Gard, M.K., Horan, W.P. *et al.* (2003) *Anticipatory and consummatory pleasure in schizophrenia: A scale development study*. Paper presented at the annual meeting of the Society for Research in Psychopathology, October, Toronto, CA.

Gould, R.A., Meuser, K.T., Bolton, E. *et al.* (2001) Cognitive therapy for psychosis in schizophrenia: An effect size analysis. *Schizophrenia Research, 48*, 335–342.

Grant, P.M. and Beck, A.T. (2010) Asocial beliefs as predictors of asocial behavior in schizophrenia. *Psychiatry Research, 177*, 65–70.

Horan, W.P., Rassovsky, Y., Kern, R.S. *et al.* (20 (2010) Further support for the role of dysfunctional attitudes in models of real-world functioning in schizophrenia. *Journal of Psychiatric Research, 44*, 499–505.

Kay, S., Fizbein, A. and Opler, L. (1987) The Positive and Negative Syndrome Scale (PANSS) for Schizophrenia. *Schizophrenia Bulletin, 13*, 261–275.

Kingdon, D.G. and Tukington, D. (1994) *Cognitive-Behavioral Therapy of Schizophrenia*. New York: Guilford Press.

Kingdon, D.G. and Turkington, D. (1998) Cognitive behavioural therapy of schizo-phrenia: Styles and methods. In T. Wykes, N. Tarrier and S.F. Lewis (eds), *Outcome and Innovation in Psychological Treatment of Schizophrenia* (pp. 59–79). Chichester: Wiley.

McGlashan, T.H. and Fenton, W.S. (1993) Subtype progression and pathophysiologic deterioration in early schizophrenia. *Schizophrenis Bulletin, 19,* 71–74.

Nuechterlein, K.H. and Dawson, M.E. (1984) Information processing and attentional functioning in the developmental course of schizophrenic disorders. *Schizophrenia Bulletin, 10,* 160–203.

Pelton, J. (2002) Managing expectations. In D. Kingdon and D. Turkington (eds) *A Case Study Guide to Cognitive Behavior Therapy of Psychosis* (pp.137–157). Chichester: Wiley.

Perivoliotis, D., Morrison, A., Grant, P. *et al.* (2009) Negative performance beliefs and negative symptoms in individuals at ultra-high risk of psychosis: A preliminary study. *Psychopathology, 42,* 375–379.

Peters, E., Landau, S., McCrone, P. *et al.* (2010) A randomized controlled trial of cognitive behaviour therapy for psychosis in a routine clinical service. *Acta Psychiatrica Scandinavica, 122,* 302–318.

Piling, S. , Bebbington, P., Kuipers, E. *et al.* (2002) Psychological treatments in schizophrenia: I. Meta-analysis of family intervention and cognitive behavior therapy. *Psychological Medicine, 32,* 763–782.

Quinlan, T. and Granholm, E. (2009) *Defeatist performance attitudes mediate relationships between neurocognition and negative symptoms and functioning in schizophrenia.* Paper presented at the Society for Research in Psychopathology, Minneapolis, MN, September.

Rector, N.A. (2004) Dysfunctional attitudes and symptom expression in schizophrenia: Differential associations with paranoid delusions and negative symptoms. *Journal of Cognitive Psychotherapy, 18,* 163–174.

Rector, N.A. (2007) Optimizing homework completion with patients with psychosis. *Cognitive and Behavioural Practice, 14,* 303–316.

Rector, N.A. and Beck, A.T. (2001) Cognitive behavioural therapy for schizophrenia: An empirical review. *Journal of Nervous and Mental Disease, 189,* 278–287.

Rector, N.A. and Beck, A.T. (2002a) Cognitive therapy for schizophrenia: From conceptualization to intervention. *Canadian Journal of Psychiatry, 47,* 39–48.

Rector, N.A. and Beck, A.T. (2002b) A clinical review of cognitive therapy for schizophrenia. *Current Psychiatry Reports, 4,* 284–292.

Rector, N.A., Beck, A.T. and Stolar, N. (2005) The negative symptoms of schizophrenia: A cognitive perspective. *Canadian Journal of Psychiatry, 50,* 247–257.

Rector, N.A., Seeman, M.V. and Segal, Z.V. (2003) Cognitive therapy for schizophrenia: A preliminary randomized controlled trial. *Schizophrenia Research, 63,* 1–11.

Tarrier, N. and Wykes, T. (2004) Is there evidence that cognitive behaviour therapy is an effective treatment for schizophrenia? A cautious or cautionary tale? *Behaviour Research and Therapy, 42,* 1377–1401.

Turkington, D., Sensky, T., Scott, J. *et al.* (2008) A randomized controlled trial of cognitive-behavior therapy for persistent symptoms in schizophrenia: A five-year follow-up. *Schizophrenia Research, 98,* 1–7.

Weissman. A. and Beck, A.T. (1978) *Development and validation of the Dysfunctional Attitudes Scale: A preliminary investigation.* Paper presented at the meeting of the American Educational Research Association, Toronto, Ontario, Canada, November.

Wykes, T., Steel, C., Everitt, B. *et al.* (2008) Cognitive behavior therapy for schizophrenia: Effect sizes, clinical models, and methodological rigor. *Schizophrenia Bulletin, 34,* 523–537.

6

The Challenge of Anger, Aggression and Violence when Delivering CBT for Psychosis: Clinical and Service Considerations

Gillian Haddock

Introduction

There are a number of factors that have been considered in relation to the occurrence of violence and aggression in schizophrenia and these have been widely studied. However, research has not produced consistent findings and the relationship is not well understood despite the media portrayal of schizophrenia being associated with increased frequency of violence or aggression. There have been some studies that have shown that the frequency of violence and aggression within populations of people with schizophrenia may be slightly higher than other clinical and non-clinical populations (Arseneault *et al.*, 2000). However, this has varied depending on the population studied and the type of violence investigated (Walsh *et al.*, 2004). Methodological considerations make much of the research findings difficult to interpret as researchers have varied in the way they have measured aggression and violence in the samples studied and in their methods used to assess schizophrenia symptoms. This lack of clarity has led some researchers to examine whether other factors in addition to the diagnosis of schizophrenia may contribute to the relationship between schizophrenia and violence and findings suggest that multiple factors may be important in determining whether someone who has a diagnosis of schizophrenia may be likely to engage in aggressive or violent behaviour.

CBT for Schizophrenia: Evidence-Based Interventions and Future Directions, First Edition. Edited by Craig Steel.
© 2013 John Wiley & Sons, Ltd. Published 2013 by John Wiley & Sons, Ltd.

Particular areas which have been explored are: historical factors, such as past history of engaging in aggression or violence; dispositional or predisposing factors, such as personality or impulsiveness, environmental and contextual factors; and clinical factors such as severity and content of psychotic symptoms, substance misuse and emotional factors such as anger. Many of these factors have been shown to contribute to a higher incidence of violence in non-clinical populations as well as clinical populations suggesting that it may not be the diagnosis per se that is important in determining the occurrence of violence. However, for people with schizophrenia, these factors may be exacerbated and may make this group of people more vulnerable to becoming aggressive or violent.

Substance Use, Schizophrenia and Violence

For example, one consistent finding is the link between substance abuse, schizophrenia and violence. People with a diagnosis of schizophrenia show higher rates of substance misuse than non-clinical populations. Those with schizophrenia who misuse substances show consistently higher rates of violence than non-substance using clients (Monahan *et al.*, 2001; Wallace *et al.*, 2004). One reason for this might be that substance use interferes with clients' ability to engage in treatment, resulting in more persistent psychotic symptoms. This is consistent with findings that higher rates of violence have also been shown to be associated with particular delusional symptoms. Specific psychotic symptoms that have been highlighted are symptoms where the individual feels threatened or controlled by external forces or people, such as paranoid beliefs of voices that imply control over the individual (sometimes referred to as threat control over-ride symptoms; Link and Steuve, 1994).

Anger, Schizophrenia and Violence

In addition to these clinical factors, which may be specific to schizophrenia, research has also highlighted the importance of anger in relation to the occurrence of violence and aggression. This has been clearly demonstrated in both non-clinical and clinical samples although the link between anger and violence is not a simple one, as anger may not always lead to aggression and violence. Similarly, aggression and violence can occur without the obvious presence of anger. Anger may be particularly pertinent for people who have psychosis; they may live in impoverished environments where there is high potential for anger provocation and may experience psychotic symptoms that are anger inducing, such as paranoia or unwanted hallucinations. Hence, the experience and response to anger provoking events of people with psychosis may be partly influenced by their delusional thinking, but also by their day-to-day life within adverse, controlling, disrespectful and unempathetic environments. This combination of factors may be particularly toxic for people with psychosis and, together, with specific environmental provocation, either intended or not, they may be particularly vulnerable to reacting in an aggressive or violent way, which may be expressed in relation to self directed harm to themselves, others or property.

Implications for Interventions

As a result, the clinical intervention must consider the key roles of historical and personality factors and the current clinical and environmental concerns that may contribute to the occurrence of violence and aggression. Psychological treatments for this group of people have not been widely described in the literature, however, cognitive behavioural treatments have been shown to be effective at reducing the severity and frequency of psychotic symptoms in people with treatment resistant psychosis (Wykes *et al.*, 2008), anger (Novaco, 2002) and substance use related problems in clients with severe mental health problems (Barrowclough *et al.*, 2010). However, there has been little evaluation of combining these approaches to address the specific problems in people with a history of aggression and violence. This has been addressed however, in the development of a new clinical intervention for people with schizophrenia who have persistent psychotic symptoms and a history of violence and aggression; the PICASSO programme (Haddock *et al.*, 2009). The programme is a formulation-based CBT oriented intervention that considers the unique role of psychotic symptoms, anger, substance misuse and the environmental determinants of anger. The intervention was evaluated in a small randomized controlled trial that indicated that the intervention was superior to a control treatment (Social Activity Therapy; an intervention matched for therapist contact time but focusing wholly on engaging the individual in activities they enjoyed rather than a psychological therapy) on improving delusions, reducing violence and reducing risk. The intervention was delivered over 6 months with an average of 17 sessions delivered, although up to 30 were offered. The majority of people who took part in the trial were inpatients (some lived in secure settings) with a history of violence and aggression. There were few drop outs from treatment, suggesting that the approach was suitable for clients who may, traditionally, be considered to be difficult to engage in psychological therapies.

The emphasis of the intervention is on viewing any aggression or violence as something that is not wholly located within the individual but something that is a product of a complex system of constantly changing variables. The occurrence of violence is seen as a product of a dynamic interaction between psychosis, anger, environment and substance use. These key factors contribute to the likelihood of violence, which will occur once the threshold for the person being unable/or not wishing to restrain from violence is reached. These factors should also be considered in the context of the specific challenges faced by this group. They often reside on inpatient or secure units and present with a range of complex needs when compared to those living within the community. For example, although there is some variation, they are likely to have a history of prior challenges to services in terms of anger and violence, often occurring within the context of a history of chronic substance use. They are more likely to be 'resistant' to traditional treatment approaches; persistent psychotic symptoms or beliefs may have interfered with traditional assessments and treatments. Their typical symptom profile could include specific types of command hallucinations, delusional beliefs that interfere with interpersonal relationships and engagement in services and intense paranoia. In addition, it is not uncommon for clients to be socially unsupported outside their current living situation due to a history of gradual deterioration in interpersonal and family relationships.

These particular factors may have contributed to previous difficulties in engaging the individual in treatment and are likely to influence engagement in a psychological treatment. As a result, CBT needs to be modified in order to help the individual to engage in the approach. The PICASSO programme incorporates motivational interviewing approaches (Miller and Rollnick, 2002) with CBT to enhance engagement. This is based on the assumption, at least for some clients, that their current situation requires them to be aggressive and violent and that, in order for therapy to proceed, it is necessary to gain their collaboration in identifying that their behaviour is problematic and that change would benefit them.

Engagement

Clients may be difficult to engage in treatment and attention needs to be paid to this before attempting to proceed with complex psychological interventions. CBT is a collaborative intervention and should not be delivered unless the individual wishes to make changes, and proceeding when the client is not motivated for change may be, at least unhelpful and, at worst, extremely detrimental to the relationship between the client and the mental health services. The individual may not wish to engage in treatment for a range of reasons. Common reasons are that the individual does not agree that they have mental health problems, they disagree with their diagnosis, they may believe the treatment they have been given is incorrect or not required, hence that there is no need to accept the treatment offered. In addition, medical treatment or restraint may have been used to manage aggressive incidents in the past and this may have interfered with a client's willingness to engage in further dialogue about their treatment with mental health staff who they do not perceive as being helpful. Psychotic beliefs may also make clients suspicious of the intentions of clinicians and this can lead to unwillingness to discuss symptoms or problems.

It is essential to work collaboratively with the client to overcome the above issues and to identify what issues are most important for the client to work on. Motivational interviewing approaches can be extremely helpful in engaging people in treatment where there is resistance to do so (Miller and Rollnick, 2002). This approach was originally developed to help people with substance use problems engage in treatment, however, this has been shown to work very well to help people with psychosis engage in CBT (Barrowclough *et al.*, 2010, Haddock *et al.*, 2009). Motivational interviewing is an interview style that aims to help the client collaboratively identify what their key goals and aspirations are and what factors or behaviours in which they are engaging are preventing them for working towards those goals. For example, for many people in the PICASSO programme, key goals were about getting out of hospital, leading a normal life, getting a girlfriend and so forth. The focus of the initial engagement phase was to help the client identify what was most important for them and what was interfering with them achieving their goals. For many, it was the continued aggression and disengagement with treatment that was contributing to their lack of progress in the service. By providing a supportive, empathic and collaborative therapeutic environment within which to explore this, clients were able to explore their current situation and behaviour and to identify what they may be able to do to achieve their goals. If they identified that they would like to make changes, this provided a focus for further CBT assessment, formulation and intervention. It was not until the client had identified that they wished to make changes that the intervention developed into a more traditional CBT approach. Once key areas or goals were agreed, the therapist's aim was to build up a good understanding and formulation to direct the application of CBT intervention strategies. Further assessment and exploration of the areas around which change was focused was carried out to build up a clear understanding of the interaction between psychosis, anger, substance use and the environment. If required, structured assessment can also be helpful to build a fuller picture of the client's difficulties.

Useful Assessments

1   *Psychosis*: the impact and severity of psychotic and non-psychotic symptoms can be assessed using structured interviews, such as The

Positive and Negative Syndrome Schedule (PANSS) to allow detailed exploration of the individual's experiences. The Psychotic Symptom Rating Scales (PSYRATS) are more in-depth interviews that help the individual explore their hallucinations and delusional beliefs in a detailed way. They ask about the content of the experiences and about the individual's beliefs and distress in response to their experiences. These symptom-based assessments can be extremely useful in gaining a comprehensive picture of the individual's psychotic and non-psychotic experiences that can be used to guide treatment and monitor progress. Other useful assessments include, the Maudsley Assessment of Delusions Scale (Buchanan *et al.*, 1993) that explores delusional beliefs and their emotional, cognitive and behavioural correlates in detail, and service user self-report questionnaires report on aspects of their psychotic experience, for example, the Service User Experience of Psychosis Scale (Haddock *et al.*, 2011) and the Beliefs about Voices Questionnaire (Chadwick *et al.*, 2000).

These instruments can aid a cognitive behavioural assessment and will help build up a clear picture of the nature of the experiences, their impact on the individual's life, interpersonal experiences, their cognition, affect and behaviour with the ultimate aim of identifying how specific aspects of the individual's experiences may, or may not, be contributing to their lack of progress towards their goals and how the psychosis, anger, interpersonal environment and substance use interact.

2 *Assessing anger*: individuals' experience of anger can be very comprehensively assessed using self-report scales. The Novaco Anger Scale (Novaco, 2003; NAS) is widely used in forensic and non-forensic psychosis populations. It is a self-report scale that asks the individual to describe what they are like when they feel angry in terms of the way if affects their thinking their levels of arousal and their behaviour (e.g. do they argue, shout, hit, keep it to themselves). It can also be helpful to have an external account of an individual's anger and aggression. A good assessment scale that is rated by ward staff is the Ward Anger Rating Scale (Novaco and Renwick, 2002; WARS). This is designed to record staff's observations of the individual being angry, threatening or violent and how they relate to the presence of specific hallucination and delusional driven behaviour. These instruments, in conjunction with careful and sensitive exploration of the individual's anger and the situations in which they feel provoked, can be extremely useful in engaging clients in discussion about their current situation and how their anger or aggression is interfering with their goals.

3 *Substance misuse*: Substance use has been consistently linked with the occurrence of violence and, even if the individual is living in a facility where there is little or no access to illicit substances, substance use may still play a part in the likelihood of future aggression or violence. Many

people may have only had violent incidents when under the influence of substances and they may believe that simply avoiding substances is the key to not being violent in the future. While this may be true, this may lead to the problems relating to violence being discounted until there is a greater likelihood of substances being encountered resulting in persistent problems of substance use if the client moves to an environment where substances are readily available. Alternatively, clients may not conceal the fact that they desire substances, and would seek out substances if they were able, possibly leading staff to prevent or limit the client's freedom in order to prevent their access to substances – often resulting in increased acrimony between clients and staff. As a result, it is important to understand what role, if any, substance misuse may have played in the individual's problems to ensure that this is addressed if necessary. How this is addressed will depend on the individual's attitude towards their substance using and their motivation to change.

4   *Environmental factors*: as highlighted, the context in which aggression or violence takes place is extremely important and should form a major part of the assessment process. A good understanding can be gained from examining the circumstances under which previous acts took place for example, were certain places, certain people and certain times of day significant? Circumstances may not be immediately obvious but can be informed by other assessments and discussions with the individual and carers. For example, an individual's delusional beliefs can be important in determining the situations where they may feel uncomfortable or start to become aroused. People with paranoid beliefs about others may become more distressed when in situations involving other people for example, around mealtimes, in the TV room. People who feel that they are controlled by external agents may feel more threatened when faced with controlling situations such as when being given medication or when faced with routines which they don't like. Items from the NAS and the WARS can give clues as to the most likely situations when an individual may become provoked or feel angry. Information can be gathered from case notes and by questioning key staff who witnessed, or were involved in, the aggression or violence. If there appears to be no particular pattern contributing to the occurrence of violence then some detailed prospective observational assessment may be helpful.

Formulation in Preparation for Intervention

The strategies described above together with other appropriate assessments will result in a thorough and comprehensive view of the individual's experiences and key problems (including psychotic symptoms) and how they relate to aggression and violence. The assessment should be 'individually tailored' to the specific difficulties the person is experiencing with the aim of gaining a thorough history of the client's experiences, a history of their illness and an understanding of the range of current problems. Personal history is likely to include; early experiences, significant experiences throughout life to date, the client's present situation, a history of the client's use of coping strategies and how any aggression or violence fits into this. Cultural beliefs about anger and aggression may be extremely important. For example, cultural stereotypes may be important motivators for some people to act aggressively and may be linked closely to their self-esteem. Staff or therapists can use the assessment material collected to stimulate discussion of anger and aggression or other issues to help elicit these types of beliefs. This can be useful if there is ambivalence or denial of issues relating to these areas.

Problems are likely to be identified in a range of areas, including; psychosis, negative symptoms, depression, anxiety, financial problems, social, interpersonal and familial problems, anger, and disagreements with treatment and diagnosis. The therapist and client should negotiate priorities for formulation and assessment to address one or two key areas. However, whatever the agreed priorities, the therapist should ensure that the aggression and psychosis are incorporated into the assessment and formulation in some way. Even when anger or aggression is not acknowledged to be problematic, they can still be formulated in the context of 'normal' responses to difficult or intolerable situations. A clear and succinct clinical formulation of psychosis and aggression as described earlier can be used as a focus for assessment and intervention and a collaborative plan for intervention should be devised.

Intervention

Areas with potential for change should be considered collaboratively and idiosyncratic action plans devised together. The plans may involve action required by the individual client, therapist, care coordinator, social worker or other involved carer or relative. Where help with dealing with psychosis, substance use and anger problems are identified as priorities, individual cognitive behaviour interventions for psychotic symptoms, anger and substance use are likely to be helpful and can be applied similarly to the way they are applied in other populations. As motivation and maintaining the engagement is particularly important for this group, ensuring that the approach is extremely collaborative is important. Traditionally, CBT is usually delivered by a therapist meeting weekly with the client for about an hour. However, for many clients this typical approach may not be suitable and flexibility is required depending on the individual client. Problems with concentration, anxiety, agitation and negative symptoms can sometimes mean that more frequent shorter sessions are more acceptable and this should be acknowledged and negotiated with the client.

Identifying the Focus for Therapy

The assessments should provide a good overview of the areas of concern that the individual has. However, where there are multiple problems it is sometimes difficult to decide what should be prioritized. Ensuring that the key factors interfering with the person's goals are identified as the primary targets should help maintain motivation to engage and should form the focus for intervention, at least initially. This may change as therapy progresses and this should be reviewed throughout. Using the formulation to assimilate information and feedback to the client can assist with focusing the intervention. The case description below illustrates this.

Case example: Paul

Paul was 42 and had a 20-year history of schizophrenia. He had experienced many inpatient admissions over this time period. He had a history of substance misuse and a number of aggressive and violent attacks with people where he had lived. He had a short spell in prison about 15 years ago as a result of a conviction for assault on a former flat-mate. He had also been extremely difficult to manage within his inpatient admissions and had been recently admitted to a medium secure facility after an incident where he took a member of staff hostage, threatening them with a knife. He was extremely hostile and angry with staff and felt that he was wrongly detained in the unit. He felt the staff had provoked him prior to his admission, which was why he had reacted by taking the staff member hostage. He felt that he had to demonstrate that his treatment was not acceptable and this was his only way he could do this. He believed that the staff were wrong about what his problems were and that they didn't listen to what he had to say and didn't try to help him. He disliked being treated with medication, he felt that he became sluggish and lethargic. He didn't like this as he believed that he needed to stay alert at all times to make sure that 'no-one was on his back'. He believed that he was being monitored by staff and people in government and that they had put microphones in his room and in the TV to monitor his movements. He believed they did this because he possessed a 'secret' that they needed, one he had acquired during his late teens when he was living in Israel. He was very scared about what he thought the government might do to capture him and as a result he was constantly highly aroused and vigilant in his environment. He felt trapped on the unit and that he was being made vulnerable by the staff who kept him there. He felt highly frustrated and angry about his situation and wanted staff to help him by recognizing that the government was after him and making his situation 'public' in the press. He didn't feel that staff took him seriously and was angry with them for not taking any notice. He was angry that they discounted his experiences as being due to 'schizophrenia' when his experiences were real and threatening. Staff would not listen to him and they continued to give him treatment he didn't need so he couldn't help hitting out at them sometimes. The hostage incident was the last straw – the staff member had provoked him by repeatedly telling him that the government had no interest in him. He had become angry and grabbed the staff member and dragged him into a room. He didn't really intend to hurt him but wanted to frighten him and to get his point over.

As Paul was extremely angry with all the staff on his unit, it was thought necessary to bring in a more 'neutral' therapist who was not part of the core ward team to attempt to engage him. This was presented to Paul as a way of trying to mediate between him and the staff to try to identify a way forward. Several sessions were spent listening to Paul's side of the story and trying to identify what the real problems were that were preventing him from achieving his goals of getting out of hospital and living a more normal life without living in fear of the government harming him. Although, initially he was not keen to engage, he decided to have some time to talk the issues through. He was keen to tell his side of the story and it was necessary to let him clearly express his point of view to gain his trust to continue. After a number of sessions it was identified that, despite his problems, he had some key goals. These were to get out of hospital, to try to live a normal life without feeling constantly monitored and in fear of his life, and to contact a daughter who he had not seen for 10 years (she was now aged 15 and living with a former girlfriend). It was agreed that the therapy would focus on how he might be helped to achieve these goals by identifying what was preventing these from being achieved, as follow.

a   The disagreement between him and staff about his diagnosis and treatment was preventing him moving on (he wanted them to see his point of view; they wanted him to acknowledge he had schizophrenia).
b   His frustration and anger which he found difficult to control especially when he was thinking about the government and when the staff ignored him or made him do something he didn't want e.g. take medication.
c   His desire to get back to using alcohol and cannabis as soon as he was discharged. This latter was significant in that he had been told that he would not be discharged unless he promised not to use alcohol or drugs.

Paul had always used alcohol and cannabis, and didn't see anything wrong with it. All his friends and family used it and he felt it was good for getting him to 'chill out'. He didn't know why the staff were so opposed to it so didn't see why he should say he wouldn't do this.

Clarifying these issues allowed a clear plan of intervention to be developed between therapist and Paul, and with the ward staff. This started initially with a review of his medication to see whether there was any possibility of identifying something he was happier with, embarking on a one-to-one discussion and assessment around his diagnosis, anger, frustration and delusional beliefs with a view to identifying a CBT that he might find helpful and identifying someone on the unit who could help him start proceedings to have some contact with his daughter. Substance use wasn't addressed explicitly; however, exploration of whether substance misuse might have exacerbated his problems in the past (and potentially in the future) was addressed during the CBT sessions. Paul was happy with this approach as it appeared to have a clear focus on helping him to achieve his goals. The assessment and intervention was carried out over 28 weekly sessions, with additional sessions jointly with staff to facilitate information sharing and to ensure that all staff were taking a common approach to his care. This, in part, was also aimed at reframing Paul's difficulties in order that the staff attributions about his behaviour could become more understandable to them, that is, that his delusional beliefs played a significant part in his anger and aggression. This was facilitated by sharing of a detailed formulation drawn up with Paul during the sessions. This included Paul identifying that some of his beliefs about the government might not be entirely true and that he may be able to live a partly normal life despite the government inter-ference. Exploration of his beliefs and some testing out using experiments helped him to acknowledge that his thinking resulted in him misinterpreting some situations, and that, at times, he was wrong about the government. This allowed him to acknowledge that mental health problems could be contributing to some of his beliefs and this meant that it was alright to take medication. This had a considerable impact on his anger towards staff as he could acknowledge that they may be useful in helping him control some of his symptoms. In addition, staff helped him to arrange a meeting with his daughter. This resulted in a significant reduction in his anger and frustration. With some further help around managing anger using CBT strategies (such as self-monitoring to help him identify when he was becoming aroused, hierarchies to identify situations that were particularly provoking for him, cognitive reframing to help him reappraise 'angry situations' and learning arousal reduction strategies that he could employ in difficult situations), he was able to interact more easily with staff and his peers and was hopeful that he would be able to have some regular contact with his daughter.

Paul illustrates a key issue when working with people with this type of problem and highlights why motivation has to be considered as an important part of the engagement process. Individuals often need to believe that there is something in it for them in order to make it worth changing their behaviour. It is common for their anger and aggression to be playing an important role for them and giving this up may involve considerable effort. Having an important goal that provides some intrinsic motivation can be essential and without this change efforts and CBT are likely to be unsuccessful and possibly unhelpful. However, once goals are clarified, identifying how psychosis, anger substance misuse and so on are interfering with achieving these goals highlights the priorities for intervention. The intervention can be focused on a wide range of problems or needs and may not always relate to intervening with psychotic symptoms or anger. However, CBT interventions documented elsewhere in this volume can be applied similarly with this group and no specific modifications are required over and above those highlighted above. Where managing anger is identified, the following approaches can be helpful.

Strategies for Working with Anger

Comprehensive interventions for working with anger have been described fully by Novaco and colleagues (Novaco, 2002; Novaco, Ramm and Black, 2000; also see Haddock and Shaw, 2008) and have been adapted to apply to people with psychosis with problems of aggression and substance misuse in the PICASSO programme (Haddock *et al.*, 2009) The approach includes:

- *Psychoeducation and self monitoring to assist with identifying areas for potential change*: helping people to gain an understanding of their anger, its cognitive, behavioural and affective components and its functions is a useful starting point when someone identifies that anger may be an important area of concern for them or for others. This also should include identifying the positive role of anger in stimulating action or attempts to resolve conflict as well as the potential negative consequences that can arise if anger results in aggression or violence. Conceptualizing anger in CBT terms can also be extremely useful in helping people to recognize their own anger and to identify strategies to overcome aspects of this. An important component of this can be to help people to self-monitor situations when they become angry. This can help them identify the environmental and other triggers to anger and to identify how this impacts on their thinking, emotions and behaviour. Some people wish to keep a diary or recording sheet similar to those used to record negative thinking patterns for depression, which can be used to identify potential areas for change. For example, an individual who notices that they become upset and angry whenever they have interactions with a particular person may become aware that there is something about the interaction that is distressing. This may be due to numerous reasons, for example, psychotically driven delusional beliefs or paranoia, or may be due to justifiable provocation from that individual. Understanding the reason for anger determines the correct source for intervention. In the former, the intervention may involve exploring and testing out delusional beliefs, whereas for the latter, the intervention may involve changing the way the individual interacts with the person who is provoking them. The individual and therapist can examine the cognitions that may be contributing to their feelings of provocation and anger and use CBT techniques to help modify and reduce the impact of these. An awareness of how physiological arousal serves to exacerbate anger inducing situations can also be helpful to ensure that this is dealt with in therapy too.

- *Using anger hierarchies*: hierarchy systems that help individuals identify specific situations where anger is particularly problematic are extremely useful. They can help to identify anger provoking situations in a graded fashion, those with the lowest to the highest provocation and anger inducing properties. This can be used to identify the most problematic situations, to identify appropriate strategies to cope with these and provide a graded platform for introducing change in the situations that are least provoking initially and then building up to those that are most provoking. This allows the individual to practice skills in less challenging situations and to receive feedback for coping in those situations in preparation for using those skills in more challenging situations and helping the individual to inoculate themselves to more severe challenges.
- *Working with cognitions and beliefs*: anger hierarchies can be used to identify key thoughts and beliefs in relation to anger and can facilitate the identification of alternative appraisals and coping strategies. Cognitive strategies can be used to elicit alternative thoughts and to question conclusions in relation to inaccurate or distorted thinking. Behavioural experiments can be used to test out alternatives and to practice coping.

It is also important to discuss, identify and explore key beliefs in relation to the function and meaning of anger and aggression. Common beliefs relating to the expression of anger necessitating violence and aggression to demonstrate assertion or dominance may need to be explored. Examining how changes to aggression and violence in the light of such beliefs may be needed to find alternative ways for the individual to demonstrate these characteristics. This might involve assertion training or self-esteem building strategies.

Working with Environmental Issues

Ensuring that the intervention takes account of the role of environmental factors and their relation to anger and aggression is essential to ensure the maximum generalization of the intervention. Some people are unwilling or find it difficult to engage in face-to-face therapy and, in these cases, focusing the intervention on the environment may be the main focus for therapeutic work rather than individual CBT. The PICASSO programme highlights the importance of identifying a particular staff member or carer who can act as a co-worker or facilitator of the CBT therapy. As a minimum, even for people who are well engaged in individual work, joint meetings between a staff member or carer, the client and the CBT therapist should be carried out early in therapy, mid-therapy and towards the end of therapy to consolidate generalization and share the key therapy goals and interventions. This ensures that the therapy is generalized to other team members, helps to identify how staff attitudes and behaviour interact with the individual's concerns and problems, helps facilitate attitude and behaviour change with staff if required and helps to ensure that changes implemented by both the client and staff are collaboratively agreed. This approach is especially important with individuals who have been aggressive within services and are living within inpatient and secure environments where a common feeling is of having little control or influence over their treatment and their future plans for discharge or progression. For many people, moving on from hospital is a key goal and this type of joint meeting can be extremely powerful in helping to gain a shared understanding between the mental health care team and the individual.

This can also be important in facilitating good working relationships between staff and individuals. Staff on inpatient and secure units work in challenging environments and are sometimes expected to take on conflicting roles. For example, they are expected to act as 'carers' where they may be required to provide therapeutic input, support and psycho-social care and, on the other hand, they may be expected to carry out restraint procedures and report on risk and other areas of concern, which may impact on the individuals potential for discharge. This type of 'dual' role can hinder the development of a therapeutic relationship and joint sessions can focus on trying to address this potential conflict for the staff and service users. This may be empowering for both parties and helps to ensure that staff who are inadvertently behaving in ways that are exacerbating clients' behaviour with treatment regimes that are inappropriate or unhelpful can be identified. Individual sessions with staff can also help them to develop alternative ways of responding to aggression and violence by becoming aware of the cognitive behavioural formulation of the client's difficulties.

Consolidating Progress and Use of the 'Staying Well Manual'

CBT is a short-term approach, however, individuals with psychosis who have been aggressive or violent often have long histories of mental health problems and will continue to receive services over a long period. As a result, it should be acknowledged that, even though the CBT intervention is relatively short-lived (often over 9 months or a year), the impact of the intervention should continue beyond the end of the intervention. In order to facilitate this, 'staying well' strategies to ensure the treatment gains are consolidated and generalized should be incorporated into each client's treatment package, usually towards the end of therapy.

The amount of detail and complexity will depend on the progress made during therapy. Typical things to include are: a description of the key needs/problems identified during treatment; a summary of the individual's understanding and formulation of their problems incorporating, where appropriate, the key areas of anger, substance use, environment and aggression/violence; and a summary of the approaches that have been used to help address these problems, who has carried them out and how they will be continued to ensure the continued benefit of any helpful approaches. This should also involve identifying key people who can be assigned to undertake certain tasks beyond the end of the initial, intensive treatment period. Often this is a key worker or care coordinator who will take responsibility for meeting with the client regularly to monitor salient issues or needs and to help implement CBT strategies when needed. Plans for monitoring lapse/relapse and danger times should also be incorporated. The individual might be encouraged to use a 'traffic light' system to help them to monitor their staying well plan (Haddock and Shaw, 2008). This helps the individual to identify how they are by relating it to the colours on traffic lights. This can be represented in pictorial form. Green depicts the state where the individual feels relatively okay, feels in control of key problem areas and feels as though they are able to cope with everyday stresses. Strategies that help the individual to remain in the 'green' phase can be described here. Amber depicts the state where the individual has started to experience some exacerbation of the thoughts and feelings that contribute to a worsening of their experiences or problems. This is considered to be the 'warning' phase that stimulates some action by the individual and/or others to prevent further exacerbation and to facilitate return to the green phase. Red is considered to be the 'danger' state. Identifying these signs can help to ensure that appropriate, collaboratively agreed actions can take place. This will vary depending on the unique needs of the individual but may involve a change in treatment regime, living accommodation and/or involve actions for staff and families and so forth. Having plans for this stage firmly in place and agreed with the individual and the care staff prior to entering the 'red' stage reduces the potential for conflict.

The complexity of the above system can vary from simple descriptions to very detailed accounts. It is helpful to describe each stage in terms of the way the individual is experiencing their feelings, cognitions and behaviours in line with a CBT model with accompanying strategies to address these. These will be extremely idiosyncratic and will be based on the strategies identified during the intensive intervention period. The staying well manual can also include useful information that has been acquired during therapy such as handouts or psychoeducation materials. Useful telephone numbers and contacts can be included to ensure the individual has all the resources they might require together in one individualized and personalized package. Ideally, the staying well manual will be cerated collaboratively and shared with key personnel. Even if an individual is unwilling to work on a staying well plan individually, a manual for staff to refer to can be helpful. It is essential that the manual is agreed and shared with other people where appropriate. The client's collaboration and permission in this is important.

References

Arseneault, L., Moffitt, T.E., Caspi, A. *et al.* (2000) Mental disorders and violence in a total birth cohort: results from the Dunedin Study. *Archives of General Psychiatry, 57(10)*, 979–986.

Barrowclough, C., Haddock, G., Wykes, T. *et al.* (2010) A randomised controlled trial of integrated motivational interviewing and cognitive behaviour therapy for people with psychosis and co-morbid substance misuse – the MIDAS trial. *British Medical Journal, 341*, c6325.

Buchanan, A., Reed, A., Wessley, S. *et al.* (1993) Acting on delusions (2): The phenomenological correlates of acting on delusions. *British Journal of Psychiatry, 163*, 77–81.

Chadwick, P., Lees, S. and Birchwood, M. (2000) The revised beliefs about voices questionnaire (BAVQ-R). *British Journal of Psychiatry, 177*, 229–232.

Haddock, G., Barrowclough, C., Shaw. J. *et al.* (2009) Randomised controlled trial of cognitive behaviour therapy versus a social activity controlled treatment for people with psychosis and a history of violence. *British Journal of Psychiatry, 194(2)*, 152–157.

Haddock, G. and Shaw, J. (2008) Understanding and working with aggression, violence and psychosis. In Mueser, K.T. and Veste, D.V. (eds) *The Clinical Handbook of Schizophrenia* (pp. 398–410). New York: Guilford Press.

Haddock, G., Wood, L., Watts, R. *et al.* (2011) Service User Experience of Psychosis Scale (SEPS): Psychometric evaluation of a scale to develop assess outcome in psychosis. *Schizophrenia Research, 133*, 244–249.

Link, B.G. and Steuve, A. (1994) Psychotic symptoms and the violent/illegal behavior of mental patients compared to community controls. In J. Monahan and H.J. Steadman (eds) *Violence and Mental Disorders* (pp. 137–159). Chicago, Chicago University Press.

Miller, W. and Rollnick. (2002) *Motivational Interviewing*, 2nd edn. New York: Guilford Press.

Monahan, J., Steadman, H. J., Silver, E. *et al.* (2001). *Rethinking Risk Assessment: The MacArthur Study of Mental Disorder and Violence.* Oxford: Oxford University Press.

Novaco, R.W. (2002) Anger control treatment. In G. Zimmar (ed.) *Encyclopaedia of Psychotherapy Volume 1* (pp. 41–48). New York: Academic Press.

Novaco, R.W. (2003) *The Novaco Anger Scale and Provocation Inventory.* Los Angeles: Western Psychological Association.

Novaco, R.W., Ramm, M. and Black, L. (2000) Anger treatment with offenders. In C. Hollin (ed.) *Handbook of Offender Assessment and Treatment* (pp. 281–296). London: Wiley.

Novaco, R.W. and Renwick, S.J. (2002) Anger predictors of assaultiveness and the validation of a ward behaviour scale for anger and aggression. Unpublished manuscript.

Wallace, C., Mullen, P. and Burgess, P. (2004) Criminal offending in schizophrenia over a 25-year period marked by deinstitutionalization and increasing prevalence of comorbid substance use disorders. *American Journal of Psychiatry, 161,* 716–727.

Walsh, E., Gilvarry, C., Samele, C. *et al.* (2004) Predicting violence in schizophrenia: A prospective study. *Schizophrenia Research, 67,* 247–252.

Wykes, T., Steel, C., Everitt, B. *et al.* (2008) Cognitive behaviour therapy for schizophrenia: Effect sizes, clinical models and methodological rigour. *Schizophrenia Bulletin, 34(1),* 523–537.

7

CBT for Relapse in Schizophrenia: A Treatment Protocol

Andrew I. Gumley

Introduction

There is now robust evidence showing that cognitive behaviour therapy for psychosis (CBTp) is effective in alleviating positive symptoms, negative symptoms and in improving mood and functioning (Wykes *et al.*, 2008). Even though the methodological quality of clinical trials of CBTp have been criticized by some investigators (Lynch *et al.*, 2009), adequate control for methodological quality demonstrates that outcomes for positive symptoms are robust (Wykes *et al.*, 2008). However, these consistent gains in terms of positive symptoms do not translate to the prevention of relapse (Kuipers *et al.*, 1997; Tarrier *et al.*, 1998; Lewis *et al.*, 2002; Bechdolf *et al.*, 2004; Startup *et al.*, 2004; Valmaggia *et al.*, 2005; Barrowclough *et al.*, 2006; Garety *et al.*, 2008; Gleeson *et al.*, 2009). In an analysis of Garety and colleagues important study of CBTp for the prevention of relapse (2008), Dunn and colleagues (2012) have shown that when CBTp includes the active ingredients of specific cognitive and behavioural change strategies, CBTp promotes increased time spent in remission but it does not protect against relapse. So why does the prevention of relapse remain an elusive target?

In this chapter I describe our original approach taken to CBT for relapse prevention (Gumley *et al.*, 2003), identifying that two of the key

CBT for Schizophrenia: Evidence-Based Interventions and Future Directions,
First Edition. Edited by Craig Steel.
© 2013 John Wiley & Sons, Ltd. Published 2013 by John Wiley & Sons, Ltd.

aspects of this approach were that (a) relapse was prioritized as the key primary outcome and (b) that the approach to relapse prevention was not to target psychotic experiences themselves but the cognitive and affective processes underpinning relapse. This position is consistent with others. For example, in a recent meta-analysis, Alvarez-Jimenez and colleagues (2011) have argued that for CBTp to be effective in the prevention of relapse it requires that it is delivered in a context where relapse prevention is relevant to the individual and that CBTp be tailored to the prevention of relapse. We have argued previously that targeting positive symptoms (e.g. paranoia) and their associated underlying mechanisms (e.g. jumping to conclusions) are insufficient for the prevention of relapse (Gumley, 2007). We have argued that psychotic experiences (and by extension relapse) emerge in the context of *affect dysregulation*. Therefore, the key targets of CBTp, which is tailored to the prevention of relapse, should be the psychological processes and mechanisms linked to the dysregulation of affect and not the maintenance of psychotic symptoms *per se*. In this chapter, I will show how this has been a central argument in our approach to relapse prevention as well as describing our original approach to relapse prevention (see also Gumley *et al.*, 2003, 2006). I will then describe developments in our approach as informed by interpersonal and developmentally based models of affect (dys)regulation (Gumley and Schwannauer, 2006).

Relapse as a Manifestation of Affect Dysregulation

Emotional recovery and relapse prevention are two sides of the same coin (Gumley, 2007). Relapse occurs at the rate of 20–35 percent at 1 year, 50–65 percent at 2 years and 80 percent at 5 years (Robinson *et al.*, 1999). Relapse provides a basis for the development of feelings of demoralization and entrapment and has been linked to problematic emotional adjustment following psychosis. Feeling unable to prevent relapse is linked to the development of depression (Birchwood *et al.*, 1993) and anxiety (Gumley *et al.*, 2004; Karatzias *et al.*, 2007). Such negative feelings about psychosis are grounded in the reality of individuals' experiences and are associated with persisting psychotic experiences, more involuntary admissions, greater awareness of negative consequences, the stigma of psychosis, being out of work and loss of social status and friendships (Rooke and Birchwood 1998).

Feelings of fear, depression, helplessness, hopelessness, embarrassment and shame are common emotional experiences prior to relapse. These emotional responses arise from the development of low-level psychotic-like experiences such as cognitive perceptual anomalies, hearing voices, suspiciousness and interpersonal sensitivity. The combination of these experiences is sensitive but not specific to relapse (Jørgensen, 1998). This means that while most relapses are preceded by these experiences, the occurrence of low-level psychotic experiences in combination with affective distress does not necessarily lead to a relapse.

The person's cognitive, behavioural and interpersonal coping reactions and resources moderate the intensity of emotional distress. For many individuals the threat of relapse is likely to lead to catastrophic expectations and disorientation. The experience of psychosis is traumatic and is often linked to the experience of intrusive memories, hypervigilance and fear, and sealing over and avoidance. The threat of relapse is therefore likely to generate competing and disorientating reactions such as catastrophic appraisals of relapse, fear, vigilance and interpersonal threat sensitivity on the one hand, and cognitive, emotional and behavioural avoidance, and delayed help seeking on the other (Gumley and Macbeth, 2006). Fear of relapse has been previously identified in retrospective studies of the phenomenology of early relapse (e.g. Herz and Melville, 1980). Catastrophic expectations of relapse (reflected in painful autobiographical memories) can then drive delayed help seeking – an understandable defensive response to the threat of relapse. The unintended consequence of this is an increased likelihood of more severe psychotic experiences, admission to hospital and use of involuntary procedures thus confirming catastrophic expectations.

CBTp and Relapse Prevention

In our study of CBT for relapse prevention (CBTrp; Gumley *et al.*, 2003) we randomized 144 people with a diagnosis of schizophrenia to CBTrp (n=72) or treatment as usual (TAU; n=72). CBTrp was delivered in two phases. The initial engagement phase focussed on the development of an individualized formulation of relapse risk, which was then used to devise an idiosyncratic early signs monitoring measure. This measure was then sent to participants on a fortnightly basis by post and returned by participants in a sealed envelope. Individuals were eligible for the second phase of CBTrp (targeted CBTrp) if they had an increase in early signs or did not return their early signs for two or more occasions. Of those randomized to CBTrp (n=72), 66 (92 percent) engaged in the treatment. Of those who either relapsed or were deemed at risk of relapse (n=34), 28 (82 percent) engaged in targeted CBTrp. The study found a significant reduction in relapse. In addition, those participants receiving CBTrp showed greater improvement in PBIQ (Personal Beliefs about Illness Questionnaire) loss and Rosenberg self-esteem (Gumley *et al.*, 2006).

Overview of CBT for Relapse

CBTrp was divided into two phases: an engagement and formulation phase and a targeted phase were delivered at the appearance of early signs of relapse. Phase one of CBTrp for relapse focused on engagement and formulation of the key psychological factors and early signs that might be associated with initiation or acceleration of early relapse. Phase one began with an explanation of the cognitive model of relapse, which emphasized the occurrence of early signs of relapse, and the triggering of negative beliefs concerning relapse. An explanation of the potential role of these beliefs in accelerating relapse was given, similar to the description of a 'panic cycle'. This did not exclude conceptualizing the acceleration of relapse via beliefs generating feelings of hopelessness, demoralization, shame and fear of rejection and disappointment. Individuals were encouraged to make sense of this model of relapse through the exploration of previous experiences of relapse. This enabled the identification of negative beliefs relating to the self, to others or to illness. This also necessitated the careful exploration of the historical antecedents of these beliefs. This enabled the development of an individualized case formulation of the individuals' beliefs and the link between these beliefs and the early signs of relapse. This was important in helping individuals make sense of their early signs, reattribute early signs to more internal and controllable factors and it created opportunities to explore mastery and coping. At the end of this phase, an idiosyncratic early signs monitoring questionnaire was constructed and used to monitor early signs on a fortnightly basis (see Tait *et al.*, 2002). Every 2 weeks individuals' questionnaires were dispatched by post. Individuals are asked to complete and return their questionnaires using a stamped addressed envelope.

There were two main routes to targeted CBTrp. First, an assessment for targeted CBT was initiated if there were increases in individuals' self-reported early signs. Second, if an individuals' key worker reported symptom changes or circumstances/stressors, which were suggestive of an increase in relapse risk, an assessment for targeting was initiated. Session one of targeted CBT involved a detailed assessment of the evidence for and against emerging relapse. The purpose of this assessment was twofold: to identify potential false alarms, and to provide a test of the case formulation developed during the engagement phase. The therapist collaboratively elicited any negative beliefs concerning relapse including negative beliefs about mental health services. These beliefs were prioritized according to their importance and associated distress as rated by the participant. In order to reduce individuals' fear or helplessness associated with early relapse, early signs were reframed as an opportunity to develop mastery over an apparently uncontrollable and inevitable process.

Alternative beliefs of relapse as a controllable process were developed in collaboration with the individual. These alternative beliefs were tested using within and between session behavioural experiments. Behavioural experiments tended to involve strengthening existing coping skills or developing novel coping strategies. The outcomes of experiments were then used as evidence for and against alternative beliefs concerning relapse. Emphasis was given to developing strategies to counter withdrawal, avoidance, and the use of alcohol and non-prescription drugs. In addition, cognitive and behavioural strategies were employed to help reduce intrusive cognitive phenomena such as flashbacks to previous episodes.

Therapist Style

A key assumption of CBTrp was that the development of beliefs concerning relapse have arisen from traumatic or distressing experiences, and individuals' beliefs about their illness were adaptive and understandable in the context of that experience. The therapist therefore adopted a supportive, empathic and validating approach. The therapist made frequent summaries to check for accuracy of understanding. Careful assessment of negative treatment experiences was made; in particular negative experiences concerning relapse, emergency or compulsory admissions to hospital were elicited. The therapist adopted a non-judgemental role, balancing validation of the individual's experience without making evaluative statements regarding other service providers.

Assessment and Engagement

Assessment and engagement was conducted over five sessions. The aim of the assessment and engagement phase was the development of a therapeutic alliance, the identification of barriers to early intervention, the development of an early signs hypothesis informed by cognitive behavioural formulation, and the engagement in early signs monitoring. The initial session was crucial to the identification of individual's principal concerns and problems related to relapse, and potential barriers to engagement as described below. The therapist made a careful assessment of the individual's view of their experiences, their attitude to their diagnosis and their readiness to discuss their experience and symptoms.

Early in the process of engagement, it was important to consider a number of specific potential barriers. These possible barriers included the individual's style of coping (for example, minimizing or denying significant aspects of experience), the presence of traumatic reactions to psychosis, and the development of shame and self-blaming attributions. Clearly, while these factors might act as barriers to engagement, they were also relevant to the development of an individualized formulation of relapse, including the identification of factors, which may act against early and prompt intervention.

Formulation

Formulation provided a guide to the key cognitive, affective and behavioural/coping factors involved in vulnerability to relapse, and was used to make sense of the pattern of early signs experienced during the early stages. The experience of acute psychosis as a critical incident was an important aspect of case formulation. It was proposed that the beliefs and assumptions, which arise from this experience, represent the individual's attempts to make sense of their experience, and that these beliefs may represent an enduring cognitive vulnerability to relapse. During the process of formulation the therapist's skills in pacing and being alert to subtle changes in mood, eye contact and behaviour was important. This was because the individual was being asked to recollect previous episodes of acute psychosis and hospitalization. In the original study we utilized Gumley *et al*.'s (1999) model of relapse, which predicted that the activation of negative beliefs about self and illness serve to accelerate the transition into acute psychosis. Therefore it is possible to identify important beliefs and assumptions, which may be relevant to relapse, by identifying specific memories associated with previous episodes. This is usually in relation to the most salient previous episode.

A key aspect was the co-construction of a time line between the onset of early signs and the initiation of acute psychosis upon which relevant and personally significant events are 'pegged' to the process of relapse. The therapist collaboratively elicits and prioritizes, in terms of personal significance, events that the individual considered critical in the development and evolution of relapse. That is those events, which defined the meanings that they attach to becoming unwell. Guided discovery is used to uncover the significance that the individual attached to these memories, for example, 'I have lost control' or 'I've let others down'. These beliefs were then linked to their associated cognitive, emotional, behavioural and physiological sequelae, for example fearfulness, shame, avoidance, increased tension and sleeplessness. The pattern of symptoms elicited associated with personal meanings was then used as a basis for the early signs hypothesis. An historical test of this hypothesis can be carried out by comparing the configuration and timing of symptoms in relation to previous episodes of relapse. The information gathered by the therapist and individual is then used to develop an idiosyncratic early signs questionnaire. Relevant beliefs and assumptions are included in this scale in order to help 'bind' the apparent variance in symptoms.

Explaining Beliefs

Beliefs are regarded as arising from the individual's attempts to either assimilate or accommodate their experience of psychosis with their pre-existing beliefs and assumptions. These beliefs act like rules, which contain predictions about the significance and consequences of internal or external events. Accordingly, the occurrence of experiences reminiscent of previous episodes of psychosis will have implicational meaning for the personal relevance of those experiences. For example, during the early stages of relapse, Sarah experienced physiological changes including increased tension in the head, neck and shoulders, as if her head was growing out of proportion to her body. Sarah's beliefs about this experience were 'I'm losing control', 'people will start staring at me', 'I'm vulnerable', 'People will attack folk who look vulnerable'. The impact of these beliefs on relapse can be explored with reference to systematically identifying the advantages and disadvantages or negative consequences of these beliefs. Sarah felt that her beliefs about losing control were protective in that she would avoid situations where she felt conspicuous or self-conscious. She had painful and difficult experiences at school related to bullying and these experiences were particularly linked to being teased about her appearance. On the other hand, Sarah felt that her avoidance of others increased her fear of others, and in particular made her feel weak and inadequate. This feeling of being weak and inadequate thus confirmed her expectation that others would harm her – 'People attack folk who look vulnerable'.

Early Signs Monitoring

The case formulation allows the development of an early signs hypothesis and this in turn informs the development of an individualized early signs questionnaire, which integrates the cognitive, emotional, behavioural and physiological factors that characterize the evolution of relapse. The use of a formulation driven early signs questionnaire enables the person to make sense of the particular way in which experiences combine.

Targeted CBT

Targeted CBTrp was delivered during the early phase of relapse. Given the nature of relapse, the opportunity for intervention is limited. Therefore the strategies employed during treatment are designed to minimize the risk of, and reduce the speed of, the relapse process, thereby increasing the window of opportunity to prevent the occurrence of a relapse. Treatment tasks are prioritized at the beginning of targeted CBT according to the careful assessment and identification of: evidence of risk of harm to self and/or harm to others; barriers to collaboration and risk of disengagement; building coping and resilience.

The initial session for targeted CBT

The initial session began with a brief review of the individual's early signs, and the identification of any other problems or symptoms, including checks for risk. The therapist and individual prioritized problems identified in the review for the session's agenda. Problems and symptoms identified in the review were examined in relation to concerns regarding relapse. The evidence for and against relapse was considered in relation to the formulation developed during the assessment and engagement phase. In addition, given that relapse was likely to be associated with heightened arousal, high levels of fear and anxiety, and catastrophic thoughts, the therapist needed to take particular care in pacing the initial and subsequent targeted sessions. The pace of the session was deliberately slowed in order to identify salient beliefs, and indeed to provide a model of a non-catastrophic reaction to emerging relapse.

Testing the formulation
An important task was the identification of evidence for and against emerging relapse. This had three functions including (a) the careful assessment of relapse risk, (b) assisting the individual in taking a reflective stance on their experiences, and (c) clarification of the relapse hypothesis. This process also provided an opportunity for the therapist and individual to critically evaluate the accuracy of their formulation. This could be undertaken using a number of strategies. First the accuracy of the formulation could be evaluated by comparing the nature and pattern of current early signs, with those predicted by the formulation itself. Second, variations between expected and current experience were examined in terms of the individual's appraisal of their early signs, their current beliefs about relapse, and their recollections of previous relapses. Third similarities between current and prior experience could also be evaluated.

Decatastrophizing relapse
An important task was to prioritize any catastrophic beliefs concerning relapse. This was an important clinical priority, as catastrophic beliefs

increase physiological arousal and fear, thereby accelerating the speed at which a potential relapse progresses. A number of techniques were useful in decatastrophizing relapse. First, relapse could be reframed as an opportunity for new learning. In particular, historical evidence concerning delayed intervention for relapse can be employed to underline the current opportunities, which may arise from early intervention. On the other hand, previous experiences of failed early intervention could be examined in terms of identifying additional procedures, which may have been helpful. Second, the therapist could further work with the individual to highlight the advantages and disadvantages of early intervention. The results of this could be compared to previous experiences. Third, the therapist could elicit experiences where individuals had sought help and/or employed coping skills, which had prevented or reduced the severity of relapse. Evidence of this could be discovered by asking the individual to recall previous experiences where early signs have been experienced without a subsequent relapse. While this procedure allowed the therapist to evaluate the probability of the current episode being a false positive, it also enabled the identification of particular coping skills employed by the individual, which have been helpful. Fourth, the therapist remained vigilant throughout for evidence of increased affect. Evidence of increased affect within session was explored by the therapist in order to elicit other negative beliefs concerning self, illness, others and future that may be relevant to relapse, or acting as barriers to reframing relapse itself. Finally, use of a normalizing rationale was also important to reduce feelings of fear and shame around psychotic experiences. Indeed, experiences such as paranoia could be interpreted as understandable reactions to feeling under threat.

Contracting intervention
At the end of the initial session, targeted CBTrp was contracted on the basis of the evidence collected concerning relapse probability. The rationale for CBTrp was made on the basis of the accuracy of the original or adapted formulation, which provided a focus for targeting key beliefs and behaviours that seemed to be relevant to the relapse process. For example, in explaining the rationale, it could be useful to feedback the relationship between the catastrophic thoughts, which had arisen from negative experiences, and the acceleration of increased fear, arousal, and sleeplessness. The use of metaphor could be helpful, where the relapse process is compared to an engine, which becomes engaged by frightening thoughts, memories, and beliefs, that increases the speed of unpleasant emotions and feelings. By learning new or strengthening existing coping strategies, this engine can be slowed down, or disengaged. The purpose of the metaphor also enables the introduction of hope, optimism and increased control over relapse.

Subsequent sessions

Identifying the most emotionally salient beliefs
It was important to remain vigilant for any changes in affect, and follow changes in emotion as signals that a particular belief is active. Changes in emotion provided an opportunity to gently enquire about any thought and/or images that the individual was experiencing. Ascertaining the meaning of events was a crucial procedure. While increased emotion and distress was an obvious consequence of early relapse, the meaning of the event needed to be established.

Making specific enquiries about the nature and presence of imagery could also be helpful in ascertaining the meaning and psychological significance of early relapse. Given that relapse experience can be traumatic, the therapist needed to be aware of evidence of intrusive imagery in relation to previous events, and that individuals' may describe images or memories in an over general manner (cognitive avoidance).

The therapist was careful and supportive in eliciting key thoughts, beliefs and images, which occur during relapse. It is important for the therapist to ensure that they have a reasonable sample of cognitions in order not to miss any salient concerns. However, the vast number of thoughts and images, which occurred during early relapse can, understandably, be overwhelming to both individual and therapist. This difficulty can be addressed by identifying the most salient cognition. Most simply this could be achieved by asking which thought or image was most upsetting. On the other hand careful documentation of thoughts, beliefs and images could then enable the therapist to invite the individual to systematically rate the distress associated with each. By this means the most salient cognition or cognitions could be identified. Furthermore, the therapist could undertake reliability checks by verifying the relationship between specific thoughts and the principal emotions, physiological reactions, and behaviours associated with the relapse process.

Introducing flexibility into beliefs

Beliefs during early relapse could be absolute, acting like unconditional core beliefs, for example, 'I have no control', and 'I am bad'. Critical to the process of decelerating relapse was the introduction of flexibility into such beliefs through identifying situations where that belief is true or untrue. However, if the individual states that it was true in all situations, then eliciting the evidence for the belief could be used as a means of introducing flexibility. This evidence was then utilized to create conditions where the belief was true for the individual, thereby creating a conditional belief. An example of this process is given below.

THERAPIST:	You say that you have no control. Can you tell me what makes that true for you?
PATIENT:	My thoughts are going too fast, I can't think. I can't talk to people properly. There's nothing I can do.
THERAPIST:	Are there other things that make you feel that you've no control?
PATIENT:	Yes. Thoughts keep coming into my head (looks away), they're awful. It's like I've harmed someone. I can see my sister lying dead.
THERAPIST:	How does that make you feel?
PATIENT:	I'm doing something wrong, something bad is going to happen if I don't stop it.
THERAPIST:	Let me see if I've got this right. Because your thoughts are going too fast, you can't think right, and awful thoughts keep coming into your mind, this makes you feel that you have no control. Is that right?
PATIENT:	Yes I can't stop what is happening in my head.
THERAPIST:	So 'If you can't stop what is happening in your head, then you have no control'. Does that feel right to you?
PATIENT:	Yes, that's it. It's what's going on inside my head that is so bad.

Here the therapist balanced validation of the belief, with an enquiry into the conditions that activated the belief and make it 'feel' true. Creating conditions attached to the belief facilitates the implementation of strategies to transform the belief. These beliefs bind the personal experiences of relapse (e.g. changes in thought, emotion, physiology, cognition and behaviour) to consequences for self (e.g. loss of control, failure), world/others (e.g. anger, punishment), and future (e.g. hospital admission).

Transforming beliefs

A key principle underpinning targeted CBTrp was that the beliefs concerning relapse emerge as a result of negative experiences, and therefore these beliefs should be seen as contextually adaptive. During this process the therapist identified a number of conditional beliefs. This was dealt with by identifying which belief was associated with the strongest emotion, for example by rating each belief for the amount of distress associated with it. The therapist explored the evidence supporting these beliefs in order to establish their function for the individual. For example, the belief 'If I do not control my thoughts, then I will become unwell' is likely to result in a number of safety behaviours such as avoidance of situations that trigger intrusive thoughts, vigilance for changes in thinking, cognitive avoidance, or other thought control strategies. The function of these safety behaviours was the control of thinking. Transforming beliefs involved establishing alternative assumptions that achieve similar functions (in this case 'control'), without the costs associated with the former conditional belief. The therapist established the meaning of 'control' and the parameters which determined control, for example, whether perceived control is governed by the individual's cognitive experience alone, whether there were other factors which influenced perceived control, and importantly, whether there are alternative behaviours that can enhance the individual's sense of control. By identifying alternative, or existing coping strategies that enhanced a sense of control, this alternative coping could be used to bind a new belief. The importance of using behaviour to transform and develop alternative beliefs was related to the subsequent use of behavioural experiments to test transformed beliefs. In this way the therapist did not challenge the logic or truth of the former belief, but worked with the individual to develop alternative beliefs. An example of this process is given below.

THERAPIST: You say, 'If I do not control my thoughts, then I will become unwell'. Could you tell me how that belief is helpful to you?

PATIENT: It means I won't get unwell.

THERAPIST: Are there other ways this belief is helpful to you?

PATIENT: Well . . . I suppose it means that I feel better, I feel more in control of my head.

THERAPIST: OK, so this way of looking at your thoughts means that you're less likely to get unwell, you feel better and feel more in control. Is there anything else that is helpful about this belief?

PATIENT: I don't think so, but I never seem to feel better, and I get unwell anyway.

THERAPIST: OK, while this belief can be helpful for you, it doesn't work all the time. Are there disadvantages to having to control your thoughts?

PATIENT: It's really hard, the harder I try the harder it gets. I worry about what I'm thinking, and I can't go outside because I might start getting upsetting thoughts, other people might notice. I get really depressed about it.

THERAPIST: So this is really hard for you, it leads you to worry about what you're thinking, worry about whether other people will notice, so you don't go outside, and you get really depressed. So rather than avoiding upsetting thoughts altogether, what if you felt as if you could cope better with upsetting thoughts? How would that be?

PATIENT: I'm not sure. I don't like getting these thoughts.

THERAPIST: (therapist checks parameters of control) All right so when you say that you would like to control these thoughts what do you mean by that?

PATIENT: Well I mean not get them at all, I should be able to control my thoughts all of the time.

In this example the therapist decided to address the belief that all thoughts should be controlled and provides some explanation of the difference between voluntary (e.g. planning a shopping list) and involuntary thoughts (e.g. negative automatic thoughts or intrusive thoughts in reaction to stress). Information could be provided and discussed on the frequency of intrusive thoughts in the general population, and the role of thought suppression in producing rebound. A behavioural experiment investigating the effects of thought suppression was conducted within the session by asking the individual construct an image of a banana in their imagination and then to avoid thinking about bananas. Once the belief that all thoughts should be controllable is addressed, the belief that 'If I do not control my thoughts, then I will become unwell' can be addressed. At this point the therapist offered an alternative transformed belief, and as with the former belief (If I do not control my thoughts, I will become unwell), the therapist works with the individual to identify the advantages and disadvantages of this belief with respect to self and relapse.

Testing transformed beliefs

During the process of relapse individuals adopt a range of behavioural strategies aimed at increasing safety, preventing relapse or increasing control. For example common signs associated with early relapse include suspiciousness and vigilance, withdrawal and avoidance, use of alcohol and drugs. However, these 'safety behaviours' may result in the acceleration of relapse, thus confirming individuals' beliefs concerning their helplessness, or the inevitability of relapse.

Behavioural experiments provided an ideal methodology of intervention during this process. Behavioural experiments enable the individual to achieve a behavioural change (e.g. implementing a coping skill), which results in a cognitive change (beliefs concerning self or illness). Behavioural experiments can be conducted within session and between sessions. Furthermore behavioural experiments can also be graded according to difficulty. During CBTrp behavioural experiments are targeted on the development of alternative behaviours practised across a number of situations beginning with coaching within session, to applying between sessions and *in vivo*. In this example the therapist had begun with the belief that 'If I do not control my thoughts, then I will become unwell' and with the individual had transformed this to 'If I can ignore unwanted thoughts, I will feel better'.

As behavioural interventions were implemented and practised, these changes are consolidated through the review and examination of individuals' beliefs concerning the control, stigma, shame, and/or fear associated with illness. The therapist aims to assist the individual in accommodating new information gained during intervention into pre-existing assumptions concerning illness, in comparison with the beliefs tested during treatment.

Conclusions

There remains a major challenge to researchers and clinicians alike. The evidence for CBT in the prevention of relapse is limited unless CBT is dedicated to the prevention of relapse. We learned a lot about relapse prevention through our participants' stories. In particular they described significant problems in relation to the emotional adaptation to their experiences. For many, this was linked to feelings of fear of recurrence, shame about psychosis, feelings of defectiveness and undeservedness. In this context, relapse could be understood as a major source of threat and trauma. It was apparent when faced with the immediacy of a potential recurrence that many participants felt overwhelmed by the surge of emotion and sources of help (e.g. family, friends and services) became sources of threat (e.g. fear of rejection, disappointment or hospitalization). In this context, help seeking was a difficult challenge, therefore providing a timely, focussed and targeted formulation-based intervention was a significant improvement in their experience of services at that time.

However, many of the vulnerabilities to relapse reflected in problems regulating negative affect, problems in forming affiliating relationships with others (and with oneself), and problems in recognizing and responding productively to changes in mental states continued. These vulnerabilities could not be addressed within the therapy format described. Thus, more recently, we have developed Cognitive Interpersonal Therapy (CIT: Gumley and Schwannauer, 2006) that builds on our earlier experience described above (Gumley *et al.*, 2003). CIT explicitly aims to enhance service engagement and help seeking, reduce relapse vulnerability, and facilitate emotional recovery and personal re-organization in early psychosis. Therefore, this approach is explicitly concerned with a primary focus on affect, drawing upon an interpersonally based developmental understanding of affect regulation as a means of promoting emotional recovery and relapse prevention (Gumley *et al.*, 2010; Gumley, 2011). This approach has a specific focus on emotional adaptation with an emphasis on: (a) appraisals of shame, humiliation, loss and stigma; (b) coping strategies including avoidance, sealing over, self-criticism; and (c) their developmental and interpersonal context. Engagement emphasizes the development of a timeline, which constructs experiences of psychosis (or psychiatric admission), life events, coping and social support. The development of a timeline naturally reveals linkage between these domains and clarifies key areas of resilience and vulnerability. Diagrammatical portrayal of timelines enables reflection, narrative development and collaborative agreement of therapeutic priorities, which guide the use of cognitive behavioural and interpersonal change strategies. Our approach emphasizes emotional recovery and relapse prevention as co-primary outcomes, de-emphasizing the focus of traditional CBTp on distress associated with positive symptoms. While CBTp plays a crucial role in alleviating distress and promoting recovery from psychotic experiences, we hope that CIT will enhance emotional and interpersonal functioning as a means of protecting against further mental health crises linked to psychosis.

References

Alvarez-Jimenez, M., Parker, A.G., Hetrick, S.E. *et al.* (2011) Preventing the second episode: A systematic review and meta-analysis of psychosocial and pharmacological trials in first episode psychosis. *Schizophrenia Bulletin, 37,* 619–630.

Barrowclough, C., Haddock, G., Lobban, F. *et al.* (2006) Group cognitive-behavioural therapy for schizophrenia: randomised controlled trial. *British Journal of Psychiatry, 189,* 1–7.

Bechdolf, A., Knost, B., Kuntermann, C. *et al.* (2004) A randomized comparison of group cognitive-behavioural therapy and group psychoeducation in patients with schizophrenia. *Acta Psychiatrica Scandinavica, 110,* 21–28.

Birchwood, M., Mason, R., MacMillan, F. *et al.* (1993) Depression, demoralisation and control over illness: A comparison of depressed and non-depressed patients with a chronic psychosis. *Psychological Medicine, 23,* 387–395.

Dunn, G., Fowler, D., Rollinson, R. *et al.* (2012) Effective elements of cognitive behaviour therapy for psychosis: results of a novel type of subgroup analysis based on principal stratification. *Psychological Medicine, 42,* 1057–1068.

Garety, P.A., Fowler, D.G., Freeman, D. *et al.* (2008) Cognitive-behavioural therapy and family intervention for relapse prevention and symptom reduction in psychosis: randomised controlled trial. *British Journal of Psychiatry, 192,* 412–423.

Gleeson, J.F., Cotton, S.M., Alvarez-Jimenez, M. *et al.* (2009) A randomized controlled trial of relapse prevention therapy for first-episode psychosis patients. *Journal of Clinical Psychiatry, 70,* 477–486.

Gumley A.I. (2007) Staying well after psychosis: A cognitive interpersonal approach to emotional recovery and relapse prevention. *Tidsskrift for Norsk Psykologorening, 5,* 667–676.

Gumley, A.I., Braehler, C., Laithwaite, H. *et al.* (2010) A compassion focused model of recovery after psychosis. *International Journal of Cognitive Psychotherapy, 3,* 186–201.

Gumley, A.I., Karatzias, A., Power, K.G. *et al.* (2006) Early intervention for relapse in schizophrenia: Impact of cognitive behavioural therapy on negative beliefs about psychosis and self-esteem. *British Journal of Clinical Psychology, 45,* 247–260.

Gumley, A.I. and Macbeth, A. (2006) A trauma based model of relapse in psychosis. In W. Larkin and A.T. Morrison (eds) *Trauma and Psychosis.* Chichester: John Wiley and Sons.

Gumley, A.I., O'Grady, M., McNay, L. *et al.* (2003) Early intervention for relapse in Schizophrenia: Results of a 12-month randomised controlled trial of cognitive behavioural therapy. *Psychological Medicine, 33,* 419–431.

Gumley, A.I., O'Grady, M., Power, K.G. *et al.* (2004) Negative beliefs about illness and self-esteem: a comparison of socially anxious and non-socially anxious individuals with psychosis. *New Zealand and Australia Journal of Psychiatry, 38,* 960–964.

Gumley A.I. and Schwannauer M. (2006) *Staying Well After Psychosis: A Cognitive Interpersonal Approach to Recovery and Relapse Prevention.* Chichester: John Wiley and Sons.

Gumley, A.I., White, C.A. and Power, K. (1999) An interacting cognitive subsystems model of relapse and the course of psychosis. *Clinical Psychology and Psychotherapy, 6,* 261–279.

Herz, M. and Melville, C. (1980) Relapse in schizophrenia. *American Journal of Psychiatry, 137,* 801–812.

Jørgensen, P. (1998) Early signs of psychotic relapse in schizophrenia. *British Journal of Psychiatry, 172,* 327–330.

Karatzias, T., Gumley, A.I., Power, K.G. *et al.* (2007) Illness appraisals and self-esteem as correlates of anxiety and affective co-morbid disorders in schizophrenia. *Comprehensive Psychiatry, 48,* 371–375.

Kuipers, E., Garety, P., Fowler, D. *et al.* (1997) London-East Anglia randomised controlled trial of cognitive-behavioural therapy for psychosis. I: Effects of the treatment phase. *British Journal of Psychiatry, 171,* 319–327.

Lewis, S., Tarrier, N., Haddock, G. *et al.* (2002) Randomised controlled trial of cognitive-behavioural therapy in early schizophrenia: acute-phase outcomes. *British Journal of Psychiatry, 181,* 91–97.

Lynch, D., Laws, K.R., and McKenna, P.J. (2009) Cognitive behavioural therapy for major psychiatric disorder: does it really work? A meta-analytical review of well-controlled trials. *Psychological Medicine, 40,* 9–24.

Robinson, D., Woerner, M.G., Alvir, J. *et al.* (1999) Predictors of relapse following response from a first episode of schizophrenia or schizoaffective disorder. *Archives of General Psychiatry, 56,* 241–246.

Rooke, O. and Birchwood, M. (1998) Loss, humiliation and entrapment as appraisals of schizophrenic illness: a prospective study of depressed and non-depressed patients. *British Journal of Psychology, 37,* 259–268.

Startup, M., Jackson, M. and Bendix, S. (2004) North Wales randomized controlled trial of cognitive behaviour therapy for acute schizophrenia spectrum disorders: Outcomes at 6 and 12 months. *Psycholological Medicine, 34,* 413–422.

Tait, L., Birchwood, M. and Trower, P. (2002) A new scale (SES) to measure engagement with community mental health services. *Journal of Mental Health, 11,* 191–198.

Tarrier, N., Yusupoff, L., Kinney, C. *et al.* (1998) A randomised controlled trial of intensive cognitive behaviour therapy for chronic schizophrenia. *British Medical Journal, 317,* 303–307.

Valmaggia, L., van der Gaag, M., Tarrier, N. *et al.* (2005) A randomized controlled trial of cognitive behavior therapy with treatment refractory positive symptoms of schizophrenia. *British Journal of Psychiatry, 186,* 324–330.

Wykes, T., Steel, C., Everitt, B. *et al.* (2008) Cognitive behavior therapy for schizophrenia: Effect sizes, clinical models, and methodological rigor. *Schizophrenia Bulletin, 34,* 523–537.

8

CBT to Address and Prevent Social Disability in Early and Emerging Psychosis

David Fowler, Paul French, Jo Hodgekins,
Rebecca Lower, Ruth Turner, Simon Burton
and Jon Wilson

The Problem

Psychosis is the illness of working age adults most frequently associated with poor social outcome. Less than 50 percent of people with non-affective psychosis achieve a social recovery (Harrison *et al.*, 1996; Hafner and an der Heiden, 1999), and only 10–20 percent of people return to competitive employment despite the majority suggesting that they wish to work (Mueser *et al.*, 2001). The personal and economic costs of this social disability in schizophrenia are large. The lives of young people are disrupted at a crucial stage of development and, as a consequence, many continue to struggle over the long term to achieve key milestones in terms of personal achievement and social roles (Wiersma *et al.*, 2000; Lenior *et al.*, 2001). A recent estimate of the cost of lost productivity due to unemployment and absence from work associated with schizophrenia was 3.4 billion pounds (Mangalore and Knapp, 2007). Long-term follow-up studies indicate that poor social outcomes in psychosis tend to emerge early, often become stable, and are closely associated with long-term social course (see Fowler *et al.*, 2010 for a review). Early intervention services have shown considerable success in improving social outcomes in first episode psychosis by providing assertive case management and supported employment interventions.

CBT for Schizophrenia: Evidence-Based Interventions and Future Directions,
First Edition. Edited by Craig Steel.
© 2013 John Wiley & Sons, Ltd. Published 2013 by John Wiley & Sons, Ltd.

However, despite provision of such services a substantive proportion of cases remain to some degree socially disabled (Fowler *et al.*, 2009). More specific targeting of those cases showing early signs of delayed social recovery in first episode psychosis using cognitive behaviour therapy may be an important way to further improve the effectiveness of early intervention and is a central topic of ongoing research.

It is also now widely recognized that most socially disabling chronic and severe mental health problems begin in adolescence with much social disability developing before the onset of first episode psychosis. Of all severe and chronic mental illnesses 75 percent emerge between the ages of 15 and 25 (Kim-Cohen *et al.*, 2003; Kessler *et al.*, 2005). A series of retrospective studies have consistently shown that severe mental illness is often preceded by social decline, that this often becomes stable, and that such pre-morbid social disability is predictive of the long-term course of the disorder (Fowler *et al.*, 2010). Between 3 percent and 5 percent of adolescents present with complex mental health problems associated with social disability (Kim-Cohen *et al.*, 2003). The young people at highest risk of long-term social disability present with emerging signs of social decline, in association with low-level psychotic symptoms, emotional and behavioural disorder (often accompanied by substance misuse problems and risk to self and others). Despite poor outcomes and the cost of disorders leading to social decline, young people with complex needs frequently do not access treatment. More complex cases are found in areas of social disadvantage, and in youth justice, local authority care and learning disability services. It is now widely recognized that there is a major gap in identifying and managing the mental health problems of young people.

New approaches to detection and intervention are required to meet the needs of young people with social disability and psychosis. In this chapter we highlight the rationale for cognitive behaviour therapy to improve social disability among people with early and emerging psychotic disorder, and illustrate procedures with reference to a case which illustrates both the possibility of early detection and the use of techniques to address key features of typical presenting problems of people with early psychotic disorder.

Specific Characteristics of a Multisystemic Cognitive Behavioural Approach: The Need to Weave in Systemic and Assertive Case Management Practice in Delivering CBT to Promote Social Recovery

Young people with social disability problems are frequently hopeless and can be difficult to engage, they present with a range of complex mental health problems and are often stuck in a lifestyle of social withdrawal. This lifestyle may be both maintained and compounded by social disadvantage and negative attitudes of others. To effectively address these problems therapists need to be prepared to work in a flexible way that integrates cognitive behaviour therapy with an awareness of multisystemic formulation and interventions. This may involve addressing the attitudes of others such as family members or other professionals in the multidisciplinary context and assertive case management practice. The ability to use cognitive behaviour therapy skills is important. In particular in this approach therapists need to be thoroughly grounded in techniques to manage depression and social anxiety, as these are frequently the primary targets of intervention as much as psychotic symptoms. Techniques of promoting hope and motivation and behavioural activation and behavioural experiments are to the fore. However, our experience is that the traditional mode of working as a clinic based cognitive behavioural therapist is not sufficient to create change among young people with psychosis and severe social disability.

We have observed that real gains in terms of changing hope and promoting a sense of agency and positive beliefs about self and others in young people occur as a result of the person achieving meaningful changes in their lives or working toward them, including relationships with others, work, education, and valued social activities. To achieve this against a background of often years of social withdrawal and social advantage means that cognitive behaviour therapists have to be prepared to adopt practices more typically associated with case management, including: assertive community treatment, supported education and work and multisystemic working and integrate this with cognitive behavioural practice. The focus of this chapter is mainly to highlight techniques for cognitive behaviour therapists and it is beyond the scope of this chapter to discuss other approaches in depth. However it is worth noting that systemic and positioning approaches can effectively complement CBT, particularly when the client is part of a complex system. For instance, family members may sometimes encourage withdrawal as a result of their fears of relapse, in such cases some family meetings to address such attitudes may be important in creating a context for change. It is also the case that sometimes the attitudes of powerful professionals can create a barrier to the person's motivation to improve. In particular conservatism over the need to avoid stress, the fear of relapse, or over medication can be an issue. Here again, discussions with other professionals may be needed to ensure a consistent message of change and hope is provided. Similarly, the attitudes of education providers and work colleagues and employers can present real social barriers to the opportunities available to people. Here, meetings or phone calls to assist the creation of opportunity or to support the employer or education provider may be enough to keep a social opportunity open.

It is important that cognitive behaviour therapists who focus on social recovery are able to formulate these types of barriers and make steps to overcome them. Taking a systemic or positional approach can help the therapist/worker adopt strategies with regard to the client's wider systems that can facilitate the progress of the CBT or therapy of choice. Detailed knowledge of multisystemic working is not suggested but it is useful for the therapist to be a person who is confident to work in people's homes and liaise with families, other professionals and employers and education providers. A basic grounding in systemic ideas and also working in the context of a creative multidisciplinary team to provide back-up assists this work and provides the ground and context for CBT to promote social recovery. Adopting a case management or supported employment approach may mean visiting the person at home and liaising with employers or education providers to create a social opportunity. The behavioural experiments and cognitive behavioural symptom management techniques may then focus on assisting the person to maintain hope and motivation and achieve by overcoming symptoms. Done well this integration of different styles of working is seamless and automatic. Indeed, many cognitive behaviour therapists who work in the UK NHS (National Health Service) in the context of multidisciplinary early psychosis or assertive outreach teams will already implicitly work in this way.

Research Evidence

Research trials of CBT for psychosis have already shown promising indications of an impact on social disability where assessed as a secondary outcome. The systematic review of studies of CBT in psychosis carried out by Wykes *et al.* (2008) highlights an effect of CBT on social disability where assessed as a secondary outcome with a mean effect of 0.38 (15 studies), although social disability was not specifically targeted. Crucially, these interventions may be able to improve social outcomes in the face of limitations imposed by impairments such as residual psychotic symptoms, emotional disorder, and cognitive deficits. This is important as when targeting social recovery in psychosis, particular care must be taken to avoid over-stimulation. Past clinical trials of interventions to promote social activity without taking account of sensitivity to psychosis and anxiety, have shown increased risk of relapse, especially among people who still show psychotic symptoms (Hogarty *et al.*, 1974; Hogarty *et al.*, 1997). There is also clear support from systematic reviews of randomized controlled trials for a particular type of vocational intervention – Individual Placement and Support (IPS; Drake *et al.*, 1999; Mueser *et al.*, 2004). IPS is clearly effective in improving employment outcomes and retaining people in services. However, while IPS works well for those who are symptomatically recovered, the improvements for those who have a degree of residual symptoms, emotional dysfunction or drug abuse, are relatively modest and the effects on symptoms equivocal (Mueser *et al.*, 2004). Outcomes for IPS may be improved by using Cognitive Behaviour Therapy (CBT) to help people to identify and pursue more meaningful career goals, and to address cognitive impairments and symptoms. An intervention that combines techniques of CBT with those of vocational case management may be indicated for people with psychosis who wish to work but have some degree of residual problems. The form of the intervention presented here amalgamates CBT techniques with the supported employment and case management approaches and thus may overcome such problems.

The ISREP MRC trial platform study

We used an MRC (Medical Research Council) trial platform grant to develop our multisystemic approach to CBT addressing both social recovery and hopelessness, while managing psychotic symptoms and emotional disturbance and conducted a preliminary study to evaluate its efficacy (Fowler *et al.*, 2009). The intervention was focused on improving constructive social behaviour while managing sensitivity to stress, social anxiety, psychotic symptoms, and the potential consequences of cognitive deficits. Our MRC trial platform study involved 77 participants recruited from secondary mental health teams presenting with a history of unemployment and poor social outcome. The study was a single blind randomized controlled trial: 35 participants received CBT plus TAU (case management) and 42 participants received TAU alone. Participants were assessed at baseline and post-therapy (9 months after randomization), and stratified for non-affective and affective psychosis. The intervention was a cognitive behavioural intervention specifically targeting social recovery, with a median of 15 sessions delivered over a 9-month period. The primary outcome measures were hours in 'constructive economic' and 'structured' activity. Secondary outcomes comprised symptoms and hopelessness; and mediators included beliefs about self and others, schizotypal symptoms, and neuropsychological impairment. We found differential effects for people with affective and non-affective psychosis. In the non-affective psychosis group, Social Recovery Cognitive Behaviour Therapy (SRCBT) showed clear and significant superiority of outcome for weekly hours spent in constructive economic and structured activity. In addition, significant superiority was also seen for PANSS (Positive and Negative Syndrome Scale) scores and other secondary outcomes. In the health economic analysis of the pilot trial SRCBT was associated with large gains on the EQ-5D compared to treatment as usual (Barton *et al.*, 2009). This suggests that the intervention has the potential to be highly cost-effective. Results at 2-year follow up showed clear benefits in the proportion of people who had been involved in paid employment: 25 percent of the CBT group versus none of the controls had been employed. Results showed an effect of therapy on hopelessness with an effect size of 0.6 and an effect on positive beliefs about self and others. We found that changes in positive beliefs about self were a mediator of change in activity in the therapy group.

Current evidence for effective interventions to address social disability among young people who are in the early course of severe mental illness is very limited (Fowler *et al.*, 2010) but the type of intervention tested in the ISREP study may be highly applicable. In clinical cohort studies we have found it is feasible to apply this type of intervention with younger age participants who are at risk of social disability. In summary, CBT offers considerable promise in both improving social recovery in people with psychosis and in preventing the onset of social disability at an early stage of the disorder and we are currently undertaking further trials.

Future and Ongoing Trials

A series of trials are ongoing and planned. As part of the SuperEDEN NIHR programme grant on the evaluation of UK early intervention services we are carrying out a multicentre pilot trial of an intervention that specifically targets improving the social functioning of early psychosis patients who continue to show evidence of persistent poor social functioning after the initial year of treatment within an Early Intervention Service. The approach will draw extensively from the techniques used in the ISREP trial but will add in components of therapy to specifically address social anxiety problems, which we know to be highly prevalent in early psychosis and closely associated with social outcome. It will involve 150 participants in Norfolk, Birmingham and Manchester. We are also undertaking pre-liminary trials of the use of the approach at an early stage to prevent social disability in people presenting with At Risk Mental States (ARMS) and complex youth mental health syndromes.

Time Use as the Primary Outcome

A key feature of studies in this area is a focus on social recovery as the primary outcome, with this being operationally defined as time engaged in structured activity. The main aim of social recovery interventions is to assist the person in managing ongoing problems (which may include vulnerability to psychotic symptoms, emotional disorder and cognitive deficits) so that they can improve the amount of time they spend engaged in meaningful activity. This may include work and educational activity, but also household tasks and voluntary and social activity. Existing assessments of social disability in psychosis are often loosely defined and do not necessarily address the same dimensions as engagement in economic or social activity. We have found it useful simply to define social recovery as the amount of time a person spends in constructive economic and structured social activity. An adaptation of the Office for National Statistics (ONS) time-use survey (TUS; Short, 2006) is the optimal assessment for these purposes. As well as assessing time spent in employment and education, time use diaries and interviews capture the range of economic production and consumption activities that take place outside the paid economy (Gershuny, 2011). A recent study showed that the TUS is sensitive to change and has good reliability with other well-known scales of quality of life and social functioning, but is less confounded with psychotic symptoms (Fowler *et al.*, 2009). It is also a scale which users and other interested parties find readily and directly understandable.

A Cognitive Behavioural Model of Social Disability in Psychosis as Avoidance

Despite being regarded as a key outcome, social recovery from schizophrenia is poorly understood. It has long been known that time spent doing nothing may be a critical driver of poor mental health in schizophrenia (Wing and Brown, 1970). We also know that pushing vulnerable people with psychosis into activity can increase symptoms (Hogarty *et al.*, 1974; Hogarty *et al.*, 1997). Various factors play a role in impeding social recovery in psychosis. These include the presence of: continuing positive symptoms (delusions and hallucinations); negative symptoms (anhedonia, lack of motivation); cognitive deficits and disorganization; depression, hopelessness and social anxiety; and negative beliefs about self, others and the future. We know little about how these different factors interact to influence activity.

The patterns of low activity and social withdrawal, which characterize social disability among people with psychosis, may be usefully characterized as functional behavioural patterns of avoidance. Such avoidance may derive from self-regulation of the experience of psychosis, affect, confusion and information overload. As such, low motivation, avolition, and anhedonia may be characterized as arising at least in part as cognitive and emotional experiential avoidance. Avoidant behaviour and withdrawal can often be regarded as safety behaviours to manage anxiety and psychotic symptoms. A cognitive behavioural approach can provide a useful analysis of how avoidance may be central to understanding psychotic problems and especially for understanding and treating low levels of activity that characterize social disability.

Primary avoidance

Primary avoidance may occur as a direct result of the way vulnerability to psychosis may be manifested in the context of day-to-day stressors. Vulnerability to psychosis can be experienced as states of confusion, heightened arousal, and salience that can lead to aversive states of information overload, thus leading to withdrawal. In both the early stages of psychosis and among people recovering from psychosis these experiences can be subtle, occurring before the onset of frank psychotic symptoms. However, the continuing presence or vulnerability to psychotic states as a result of long duration of untreated psychosis or partial treatment, accompanied by the experience of information overload may naturally lead to a need to withdraw to cope with this toxic state. Current cognitive models also suggest that the experience of salience and cognitive confusion can also lead to anxiety being associated randomly with the environmental situations and also with internal states and images (Corr, 2011). This toxic emotional overload can lead to behavioural, cognitive and emotional avoidance. Recovery after psychosis may therefore require new adaptation to the environment and overcoming avoidance patterns. Where psychosis has been short term, this may occur naturally with encouragement. However in those cases with persistent psychosis, or where there is persistent low level vulnerability, the primary avoidance may need to be tackled and other approaches to manage information overload and anxiety assisted. The individual may need to be helped to gradually explore the world while learning to manage anomalous experiences and to cope with feelings of information overload. Strategies which help the person normalize and decatastrophize the experience of anomalies and confusion may also be important.

Secondary avoidance

It is also be important to recognize that there may be patterns of secondary avoidance arising from processes in depression and social anxiety, typical co-morbidities of psychosis. Hopelessness and extreme negative beliefs about self, others, and the world may lead to behavioural patterns of withdrawal typical of chronic depression. Furthermore social anxiety often occurs in psychosis and may need to be targeted directly. In many cases, both social anxiety and depression may have existed for long periods pre-morbid to psychotic problems. These problems need to be overcome and strategies learnt that can help individuals to adapt and deal with anomalies in a way that enables them to lead a meaningful and purposeful life. The types of procedures useful in overcoming avoidance in depression and social anxiety may then be relevant in psychosis.

The key is a cognitive behavioural formulation, which assesses presenting problems and in particular the problems an individual has in undertaking activity. The nature of the avoidance can then be identified and tackled in a systematic manner. Often the problems are complex and may involve a multilevel intervention.

Social Recovery Cognitive Behavioural Therapy (SRCBT)

Our intervention uses a focused subset of specific therapeutic procedures, many of which have already been described in our existing cognitive behaviour for psychosis treatment manuals (Fowler *et al.*, 1995; French and Morrison, 2004). Predominant among these are: assessment procedures to identify meaningful personal goals and key presenting problems, symptoms and impairments; and techniques to address negative evaluations of self and others, address self-regulation of psychotic symptoms (including training of coping strategies), and to improve social activity. The approach also draws on behavioural experiment approaches to manage social anxiety (Butler, 1999) and depression (Beck *et al.*, 1979). A novel aspect of this work involves a primary focus on social recovery (treating symptoms where they represent barriers to recovery but not as primary targets) and combining the therapist role with case management roles. For example, therapists are asked to adopt an assertive outreach worker style of contact, most frequently visiting people at home or in the workplace to carry out behavioural experiments. Therapists are also encouraged to adopt a pragmatic and problem-solving approach to assist people to overcome work-related problems, using techniques associated with IPS vocational interventions. This often involves setting up interviews with education and work placements and discussing problems in joint interviews with employment and education providers and the client. Participants will receive up to 24 sessions of SRCBT over a 12-month period. We have refined and tested tools to assess the adherence and competence of therapists' delivery of this intervention as part of our MRC trial platform pilot study.

Here we provide an illustration of the use of this type of approach in a case initially presenting with At Risk Mental State (ARMS) who developed a psychotic episode and became increasingly withdrawn. The case illustrates both the early detection and intervention points as well as techniques to address social disability once it has emerged.

> Lesley started to experience difficulties when she was at university. She was generally described as a quiet individual but had a number of close friends in whom she tended to confide and had a close family who she missed while away at university. There was nothing particularly of note in her background; she was frequently described as quiet by people who met her although this never appeared to be a problem for Lesley. The only area of slight concern was that she occasionally dieted at times of stress, which tended to be quite extreme, although things tended to resolve when the stress was removed.
>
> Things had been going reasonably well at university until a relationship ended with someone she had met at university. She worried that this individual may talk to his friends about their intimate moments so she contacted him asking for him not to say anything of this nature. During their conversation he apparently said that he was 'hardly going to post things on Facebook'. Lesley didn't feel reassured and in fact became increasingly worried to the point that she started to wonder if some of their intimate moments had been videoed and posted on the Internet – why did he mention Facebook? She could find no evidence for this but contacted him again to confront him. The boy vehemently denied even considering this but she became more and more worried that this had been done. Lesley found it increasingly difficult to focus on her studies and went home from university to spend time with her family. Her family were concerned and Lesley was taken to her GP. While the GP was concerned, she felt that it was a case of depression brought on by the stress of leaving home and the relationship breakup and prescribed a course of antidepressants. Lesley was encouraged to take a week off and then go back to university to continue with her studies.
>
> Lesley felt better at home and not as worried, although she spent most of her time inside with her family and not going out very much. She would also spend her time searching the Internet checking to see if there was anything about her, although she was able to dismiss these thoughts when she was with her family. After a couple of weeks at home she felt able to return to university to continue with her studies. Lesley was worried that she might become stressed once back at university, however, she kept this from her parents.

This would potentially have been an excellent intervention point and one where Lesley was still flexible and would have been able to reflect on and challenge her beliefs. She was starting to reduce her social contacts and social network but they were still intact. In general it is a great deal easier to maintain social networks than establish new ones. Also Lesley was still registered at university and had strong links with her parents and friends. These are important to maintain. Early detection strategies to offer interventions at this point may be very important, although Lesley would not meet criteria for a first episode psychosis service. Unfortunately, this opportunity was missed.

> When Lesley returned to university, her friends rallied round sharing their notes and asking how she had been. Lesley explained that she had been diagnosed with Glandular Fever and she may take a little while to get over things. Her friends accepted this explanation readily. However, while exiting a lecture she saw her ex-boyfriend laughing with some friends in a corridor and started to think that he was telling them about her and the video. This thought preoccupied her all day; she was unable to focus on her studies and spent all night searching the Internet again for signs of the video.
>
> Lesley found it harder to go out becoming increasingly concerned that someone may have seen the video and recognize her. She also spent hours at a time searching the Internet to see if she could find anything about her. Lesley found it difficult to see her friends and became more and more isolated, eventually returning home again. Her family was again concerned and contacted the GP who at this point referred her to the local mental health services. The response was to send an appointment at the local mental health unit. Lesley was finding it increasingly difficult to go out at this point and worried that someone would recognize her having seen this video. She had started to notice that people looked at her when she went out and many people seemed to smirk or laugh as she went past. She took this as further evidence for the existence of the video.
>
> Lesley was eventually seen at home by members of the mental health team after not attending a number of clinic appointments. It was decided that she had an emerging psychosis and she was prescribed antipsychotic medication, allocated a therapist and also a case manager. Lesley struggled to get to the therapy sessions as these were provided by a therapist who had limited time and had to offer sessions through a clinic in order to meet service standards of contacts. The case manager made repeated offers to help drive Lesley to the appointments but she would frequently not open the door when he turned up due to overwhelming feelings that she may be recognized while they were in the car driving to the appointment. In the meantime Lesley and her family decided she should defer her studies and agreed with her tutors that she should start again next year. Lesley was becoming increasingly isolated. She continued with the medication which certainly seemed to be helping with her sleep, but she was also putting on weight which she found very upsetting. She felt increasingly self-conscious and was really struggling to keep her weight down. This was further reason for Lesley to stay in because she felt so fat and, in her eyes, unsightly. This led to her overeating as there was little else in her life that gave her pleasure. Lesley became progressively more withdrawn and isolated.

In managing social recovery we know there is evidence that recovery focused assertive outreach case management has benefits. This particular style of outreach work is person focused, practical, and actively outreaching, typically into the persons home or wider environment. The focus is on social as opposed to symptomatic recovery and therefore needs to be delivered in the context of the wider environment that the individual inhabits, as opposed to the clinic setting. In the case of Lesley, we can see the importance of the therapist being willing to work in an assertive outreach manner. Clinic-based therapists are unlikely to either initially engage with clients or maintain therapeutic contact, leading to increased delays in delivering appropriate treatment and increasing levels of social disability before the onset of intervention.

The assertive outreach style of intervention is a good starting point for working with withdrawn non-engaging young people with psychosis. The platform of CBT is usually best to tie in with this. The therapist needs to be flexible to work in an assertive outreach manner and use case management techniques where relevant. A clinic-based typical therapy appointment style will not work with many severely withdrawn non-engaging clients who are likely to represent those most at need. It is also important to recognize that the social circumstances may often be adverse and there are medication regimes and other factors coming into play.

Also important are supported employment type interventions that give people hope to re-engage with work or education and career opportunities. Again there is strong evidence for this type of intervention. The key here is offering hope to gain placement in real community activity and work, which the person finds meaningful and is committed to. The largest changes occur where people gain real social achievements. Therefore, the direction of activity towards real social role gains and support in roles is important. However, CBT techniques may be useful and indeed essential where the person is too withdrawn, or too overwhelmed by symptoms to take up offers of supported employment. The case management and supported employment practices are important as these acknowledge the reality of working with a group for whom there are real social disadvantages and systemic blockages to progress. These include social position mental illness, stigma, weight gain, neuroleptics, problems in social position housing. Family members and professional staff may also sometimes present barriers relating to overprotection and concerns over the person's sensitivity. The key is assessing and acknowledging the presence of such systemic blockages to the person's recovery and working with the individual and the system to promote hope and negotiate pathways to overcome them.

In working with young people who have delayed social recovery after a first episode of psychosis, cognitive therapists will be targeting people who have not been able to make a natural recovery from psychosis. Furthermore these are likely to be cases for which case management and supported employment interventions have not been successful. The target group may sometimes be more complex than the case described above, with more prominent psychotic symptoms and persistent and engrained problems with social withdrawal. In addition, such cases may be very complex and may present with depression, social anxiety, low-level psychosis and sensitivity to psychosis, cognitive difficulties, drug abuse, and risk to self and others. The nature of the problems may differ widely from case to case. This complexity and heterogeneity implies the need for careful assessment and formulation in informing a structured approach to recovery.

The starting point is gaining an understanding of the complexity of problems. The initial steps to overcoming emotional avoidance involve assisting the individual to understand and accept their difficulties. This work is done alongside specific attempts to convey hope, while also accepting the problems people in very stuck social positions associated with psychosis face. Offering hope to the individual that they can live lives of purpose and meaning facilitates the engagement process and promotes feelings of personal agency and motivation to engage in activity. The next step is promoting activity and understanding the problems that arise as a result of engagement in specific social activity, for example, overcoming avoidance. Understanding problems of avolition, apathy and social withdrawal as functional patterns of avoidance is the first step to overcoming it. This is a primary difference between a cognitive behavioural approach and a purely case management approach. The process of therapy is a continual feedback loop between assessment, understanding and action.

Assessment and Formulation of an Individual's Problems

The starting point is carrying out an assessment of the person's problems in their current context, with particular reference to their existing pattern of activity, and problems undertaking activity. This is done in collaboration with the person. The assessment covers symptoms, current cognitions beliefs about self and others, and hopelessness. It also covers behavioural patterns with particular reference to patterns of avoidance and ideally also involves a behavioural test of the problems experienced when undertaking activity. The assessment also looks at the person's goals and motivation to carry out future roles as well as hopes and expectations. There is also a review of the history of the current problems with examination of the pathway to current behaviour, how this has evolved in reaction to circumstances, and how past goals and hopes may have been disrupted.

An important factor in formulating people's barriers to social recovery is to consider the meaning of psychosis to them. Each individual will have their own idiosyncratic beliefs about what it means to have experienced psychotic symptoms, to take antipsychotic medication, and to receive help from mental health services. These beliefs are important in understanding the 'stuckness', as they can contribute to a range of emotions. For example, an individual who believes that people who have experienced psychosis are more dangerous may become increasingly concerned about their angry, irritable or frustrated feelings, and may avoid social situations for fear that they hurt someone. These kinds of stigmatizing beliefs are common and have been identified by Birchwood *et al.* (2006) as being important in the development of social anxiety following a psychotic episode. In this model the internalized cultural values of mental illness stigma lead to a sense of external shame, anger and anxiety.

> Lesley's therapist spent time understanding her problems from a formulation-based perspective and identifying her problems and goals. Lesley explained that she was almost constantly preoccupied worrying about the video on the Internet and that she also wanted to get back to university to finish her studies and become a teacher. The therapist worked with her to shape the problems and goals:
>
> Problems
>
> 1 I spend hours worrying about the video
> 2 I have let my studies slip and want to get back to university
> 3 Putting on lots of weight
> 4 I don't think I will ever become a teacher now all this happened
>
> Goals
>
> 1 Reduce the amount of time I spend worrying about the video by 50 percent
> 2 To start doing 2–3 hours of university work on a weekly basis while at home
> 3 Stop putting on weight
>
> They both felt that having some hope in relation to problem number 4 was important but could not agree what a short-term goal would look like but if they could achieve goals 1 and 2 then this would start to help with problem number four.

The next step is a collaborative attempt to share the formulation and problem list, which help to agree a collaborative way forward. The aim of this is more than simply summarizing and clarifying the problems. This is a critical aspect of the intervention and the first step in overcoming emotional avoidance via acceptance. The aim is to assist in the management of emotions by empathy and validation, and to promote a 'good enough' positive view of self to serve as basis to move forward. The therapist summarizes and conveys understanding of the problems and provides a narrative that promotes hope and positive self-concept and allows the person to face up to and accept their current problems without feeling overwhelmed. This is important as the problems are often complex, multiple and longstanding and can feel overwhelming. The predicaments of people can often be sad and difficult and may have involved considerable suffering and struggle. The most frequent useful metaphor we have found to use is that of self as a hero. This metaphor does not avoid the painful reality of what people have been through. However, it empathizes with the individual's struggle to manage day-to-day life as a young person with the burden of emotional difficulties and psychotic disorder. It highlights the person's resilience and strengths and acknowledges that they have done their best to get through these difficult experiences. It connotes the struggle to adapt to life positively and empathizes with the difficulties faced. It highlights that at times there has been no choice but to withdraw during periods of time when emotions and strange experiences have felt overwhelming. However, because the individual has been working so hard to get rid of these difficult experiences, they have had to put their life on hold while they engage with this struggle. The message to get across to the person is one of hope in which the therapist emphasizes that there may be a different way to respond to these difficulties. The start is accepting where the person is now. It needs a new way of examining how to achieve the place in life the person wants, and new ways of managing experiences, the environment and others while accepting the obstacles and challenges.

Following this, the therapist moves on to a more detailed discussion of what the individual wants to achieve in their life. Depending on the stage of intervention this will require different amounts of time and input. Individuals in the early stages of illness, for example ARMS cases, are likely to have more access to their hopes and dreams and may even still be in pursuit of them, albeit temporarily disrupted. As the individual experiences increasing social exclusion it will require increasing effort on the part of the therapist, involving exploring the past history of what they once wanted to do and examining how this has been blocked. The aim is to help the individual regain a sense of life direction and awareness of what is important and of value in their life. From these values, concrete behaviours, goals and activities can then be defined, which are consistent with the valued direction they want in their life.

The aim is to clarify more specific, realistic longer term objectives. To clarify hope and expectations to work toward these objectives while accepting and recognizing the barriers. The key here is to foster goals with meaning and purpose for the individual. Often these can be around specific and diverse roles that should be explored with the individual with diverse desires, for example, wanting to become a childminder, a musician, a computer engineer. In order for the individual to face up to and overcome their psychological barriers, there needs to be a purpose for them doing so, rather than encouraging engagement in activities simply for the sake of filling a person's time. Often you will see more progress if goals are meaningful to the person, as individuals are more likely to be able to tolerate difficult feelings or increases in symptoms if they see this as being in line with working towards what is important in their lives.

> Lesley wanted to be a teacher but was losing sight of ever achieving this; she was not at university, was becoming increasingly isolated, and was preoccupied with the potential video on the Internet. In addition Lesley believed that taking antipsychotic medication meant that she was 'not normal'. She felt sure that these two factors would prevent her from ever entering the teaching profession. The aim was to identify with Lesley the realistic optimism that her goal could be achieved. That there was work to be done in terms of managing problems and that leaving university represented a challenge but there was a way back. An important aspect of this was working with Lesley, her family, and the admissions staff at university to examine the potential pathways back to education. Shorter term goals of voluntary work or university study from home were important in helping Lesley maintain hope that she was moving towards her valued direction of becoming a teacher. This added motivation to the more day-to-day work on managing her preoccupation with checking the Internet and her experience of paranoia when going out in social situations. In addition, normalizing interventions to challenge Lesley's stigmatizing beliefs about taking medication helped her to build up a more positive view of herself.

The focus is to build around the notion of personhood and identity the key values of the person an individual wants to be. Goals are often linked to living independently, having a relationship, achieving educational goals, living the life of young people, playing sport, having friends, going to clubs, as well as contributing to society by voluntary work and living a worthwhile life. The person is encouraged to see such goals as possibilities even if given their current situation this may seem some way off, or even a dream fantasy. Experienced therapists can use stories of the recovery of similar individuals to encourage the possibility of change. It is important this is realistic, but also encourages a sense of hope for the individual and opens them up to the possibility of responding differently to their experiences and struggle.

Akin to Dialectical Behaviour Therapy (DBT) and Acceptance and Commitment Therapy (ACT), the use of metaphors can be important to convey hope promoting the possibility of change while accepting problems. A good example is like the ship at sea when a storm arrives; the captain of the ship may have to concentrate on battling the storm for a period of time and forget about the course it had plotted but when the storm abates then it resets its course once again.

This metaphor was shared with Lesley to reinforce that she should not lose sight of her goal to achieve a job as a teacher but that what was needed at the present time was to get through the storm. This required different short-term goals, but goals that were still consistent with her valued life direction. These goals included managing her fear of being stared at and her preoccupation with checking the Internet before she could once again set off on her chosen course of becoming a teacher.

Behavioural Strategies

The work outlined above sets the stage for the use of specific behavioural strategies, which involve encouraging activity leading to mastery and pleasure. Here the classic approaches to behavioural activation, as outlined in Beck *et al.* (1979) are appropriate and well rehearsed. The key is persistence in promoting day-to-day activities that lead to a sense of agency and feelings of mastery and pleasure. The person is encouraged to link these patterns of activity to their feeling of valued role, as most people experience an increased sense of hope and vitality when their actions line up with their chosen values. Individuals are also often more willing to tolerate difficult experiences and overcome barriers to activity if they feel this activity is in pursuit of their values. Often the person in the early stages may be asked to 'act as if' they were in the part of the role or to 'fake it' if they don't feel it in the beginning. The key is getting the person to experiment with new activity and to explore and notice feelings of agency, pleasure and mastery as they emerge.

The aim is to promote and test the experience of agency, pleasure, and mastery by at first undertaking very simple and small day-to-day tasks. The person is set tasks to see and experience small joys and pleasures of the day-to-day. These may include making and preparing cups of tea, walks in the sun, small steps to undertaking exercise (swimming, running, gym), preparing and eating food, meeting up with someone, shopping, getting a haircut, bathing, smelling nice, having a makeover, playing football, going to the cinema, to the pub or to a party.

The need for persistence is vital. The problems of avoidance to be overcome are not likely to be simple. If they were obvious, the person would most probably have made a natural recovery or responded to past case managers or family advice to move on. Occasionally it can be surprising, if the activity is meaningful to the individual the movement and progress can be rapid as the person quickly discovers the benefits of actions and their sense of agency is restored. More often, the therapist will be presented with problems of various natures and will need perseverance to continue encouraging the individual to undertake activities.

The issue here is to use the problems in undertaking activity as an opportunity to understand the problems leading to lack of activity. The need is for the therapist to return to careful assessment of the way symptoms arise in context and then to address these problems. These problems can be associated with depression such as anhedonia, avolition and extreme affect associated with the triggering of negative self-regard. Other issues may include problems associated with social anxiety and problems associated with psychosis, including experience of anomalous experience, cognitive confusion, voices and paranoia.

> Lesley was becoming increasingly overweight but was doing very little exercise. Due to her enforced isolation she had very little to think about and was preoccupied with the Internet and thoughts of the video. She had been encouraged to go for a run or swimming by the mental health team and her parents but she had not taken this up. Her new therapist worked with Lesley on her problem list and they also used their formulation to see how they could move forward. It was clear that Lesley did very little with her time apart from spending time on the Internet. It was agreed that one of the things they could do together was go for a walk. Lesley lived quite close to some land that ramblers sometimes used but Lesley felt that she could either stay out of their way as she could see them coming from some way off and would be able to get off the main path. She also felt that ramblers were less likely to use the Internet. They agreed a time that suited them both and went for a walk. Lesley wore what could almost be described as a disguise with hat and dark glasses but she made it out and managed to go out for 45 minutes with her therapist who purposefully diverted the conversation towards things that were around them such as the birds singing, the weather and the scenery. This enabled Lesley to take her mind off her worries, something she had not done for quite some time. On return the therapist encouraged Lesley to reflect on how she had felt while she was out and if this had been any better than spending time on the Internet searching for clues about the video. The therapist helped Lesley recognize that she had spent a long time searching for the video but had turned up nothing, perhaps she needed to consider alternative approaches to managing her problems as her old strategies, while understandable, did not appear to have helped or worked. In addition, while she spent time doing this, her pursuit of what was important to her had stopped, therefore increasing her sense of hopelessness and negative feelings towards herself. The achievement of a first walk outside the house after many months led to a graded plan to go out every day and gradually to start going out without the safety net of the disguise.

Problems Associated with Depression

Many of the problems associated with avolition, anhedonia and severe behavioural apathy in psychosis are akin to those found in chronic depression. Indeed depression among people with psychosis is a common problem. Among those with persistent recovery problems the depression may be chronic and often may have existed pre-morbidly. A programme of work by Beck and others in Philadelphia and Yale has successfully used such techniques with people with severe negative symptoms.

Akin to chronic depression, very severe emotional avoidance may lead to states where the therapist may find it difficult to assess emotions. An individual may say they are fine when the evaluation of life circumstances would suggest severe anxiety or depression. Another common response is that they may report no feelings.

Encouraging the person to act is vital but be prepared that the person is likely to express there is no point and find many reasons not to do anything. These problems may need careful management, pushing the person can result in extreme emotions and anger ('you don't understand!'). Extreme emotion can also occur if an activity has previously provoked extreme negative beliefs about self (e.g. 'you are useless, worthless hopeless, bad'). Another common problem is that going out can feel worse. Here the issue is to return to formulations of avoidance and link any proposed activity to the individual's formulation and values. It may well be true in the short term that the person feels worse when they engage in activities. The key is to manage this so that it is not catastrophic and can be worked through to achieve a long-term gain. It can be useful to come back to the 'self as hero' metaphor to emphasize how positive it is that they are attempting to pursue their goals despite these difficult experiences. Another option is to reframe success, placing more emphasis on the process of pursuing valued goals rather than the actual attainment of them. For example, an agoraphobic may not be able to reach his designated goal of walking to the end of his street, but any movement towards this goal, no matter how small (i.e. even making it outside the front door) can be framed as movement towards his valued direction, as values unlike goals are not evaluative and cannot ever be completed but instead are an ongoing process. Returning again and again to models of avoidance and safety behaviours, the key here is not to give up but to feedback in to the loop, start smaller goals, and return to fostering positive self-image as described above. The person is encouraged to act in role while allowing the negativity to pass like a storm such as in the metaphor described earlier.

Similar types of techniques can be applied to anhedonia, the lack of experience of pleasure. The person may describe there is no point as they feel nothing. The issue is to test this out. The person may well feel nothing sitting indoors with all windows blacked out, and sleeping and ruminating most of the day. The key is first steps, to taste a strong cup of coffee (or juice if that is the person's preference) to sit for a while in the sun and feel it on their skin, the person may need to be encouraged to experience at this basic tactile level in the early stages. This is also the case with small steps to achievements in preparing food, sorting out their bedroom, buying a CD, and so forth. With Lesley, testing out the experience of being outside versus being in the house started a process of becoming gradually more active. This led to short runs, and eventually going to the gym and swimming pool at quiet times.

The key is repeated formulation of avoidance and persistence continually coming back to small gains that are meaningfully linked to living a valued life. Often gains occur slowly with big breakthroughs when the therapist and patient chance on something that is meaningful. For example the chance to sit in with a child group for an hour a week made significant changes for someone who wanted to become a childminder. It gave motivation to change appearance, look tidy, and make other changes in her daily routines to prepare for this. With Lesley, a lot of the work was around motivating her to prepare to return to meeting old friends and returning to university.

Managing Emotions, Intrusions, and Psychotic Experiences while Undertaking Activity

Many people who have social withdrawal and social activity problems in recovering from psychosis will experience anxiety, strange experiences, and sometimes psychotic symptoms including voices and paranoia when they undertake new experiences. Fear that this may induce relapse may lead to them to stop engaging in these new activities and returning to a pattern of avoidance. Others in their system, including both family members and health professionals, may regard withdrawal as functional as it reduces stress and may therefore encourage avoidance. Some liaison with others may be necessary to overcome such fears, otherwise changes may be blocked. Fear of relapse and the toxic experience of emotion and confusion may also be a strong reason for the person to justify not taking action. The approach then needs care but we have found that these problems can be overcome. Indeed, with most patients the demands of daily life mean that they have to undertake some form of activity despite how they are feeling, although many clients will employ safety behaviours, for example, shopping at night. In general, safety behaviours are seen as a bad thing, preventing disconfirmation of the feared catastrophe. However, in this stage of intervention, activity would be prioritized above removal of safety behaviours, especially if this was to lead to further reductions in activity. The general approach is one of graded exposure, with acceptance type strategies for allowing emotions and odd experiences to occur but continuing regardless. The person is gradually encouraged to consider a rationale for overcoming safety behaviours and for expecting and managing emotions and strange experiences, not fighting them, or making them worse. The key is assisting the person to work persistently to achieve their goals, despite moment to moment experiences which may be aversive. The aim is to continually assist the person into routines of meaningful activity that work for the individual (e.g. childminder, playing music, sport, teacher) and helping them manage their experiences in these contexts. The approaches are individualized to different types of problems, for example, social anxiety, anomalous experiences, cognitive confusion, voices, paranoia. This is described below.

Assessment and Management of Social Anxiety

Many patients with psychosis experience thoughts and images typical of those experienced in classic anxiety states, for example, 'I am fat and everyone is looking at me'. Also common are social anxiety images associated with stigma such as 'I have a mental illness and everyone can see that I act oddly'.

> Lesley had made some headway, she was now going out alone for walks without her therapist and this had enabled her to achieve one of her goals – she was not putting on any more weight, but she was not losing it. She was concerned that she was still fat and that people would stare at her and she was now worried that people may know she was mentally ill. Lesley had made great gains in being able to go out alone but this was only to the local park and for up to an hour a day. The next step was to extend this activity. Specific behavioural experiments were set up around helping her to manage her thoughts that others were staring at her and her shame and stigma about feeling that other people knew about her mental illness. These involved attentional training and perspective taking exercises.
>
> Lesley's therapist worked with her to identify a new problem and goal but also formulated any barriers that would stop her achieving the new goal. This collaborative approach suited Lesley and the ability to formulate new goals was something she valued. She was also becoming used to this process and was starting to engage with it and do it more herself. Her therapist had encouraged Lesley to become active in therapy not just a recipient.

We have found that exposure-based approaches based on detailed under-standing of the problem can be vital. This is not a new form of intervention; in fact classic approaches following Butler (1999) can be extremely useful.

This has a focus on education, simple attentional training, and self- and observer-rated tests. This can be beneficial, particularly where the problem is solely social anxiety, and very large gains can occur relatively quickly, even in cases who have been withdrawn for some time. Again, the key is persistence in focusing on activity while allowing for the complexity of problems. Sometimes therapists and patients become overwhelmed by the complexity of problems faced and neglect to move towards activity. The focus is a balance on moving onto the activity work that leads to purpose and meaning for the patient. It is the changes in activity that lead to purpose and meaning for the patient, which then lead to change.

Problems with Paranoia, Voices and Anomalous Experiences

Basic cognitive models of psychotic states provide an understanding of how the experience of emotion and features of the environment feeling abnormally salient can lead to paranoia, anomalous experiences and in some cases overwhelming information overload (Garety *et al.*, 2001). This can result in generalized anxiety for no apparent reason. People may describe odd visual sensations in the world (e.g. cars looking like tigers, colours being strange), odd auditory and tactile experiences. Disorganization and problems with the processing and misunderstanding of emotion can make social situations awkward, complex and aversive. People may describe interactions with others as awkward and confused, and not being able to speak properly. Others may have forms of referential ideas, feelings of thoughts being read and so forth. The key here is decatastrophizing and normalizing rationales, promoting the acceptance of unusual experiences. In these examples, existing cognitive strategies for managing psychotic experiences should be encouraged but always with the goal of moving beyond this to achieving an activity on the problem list.

> In Lesley's case this involved specific behavioural experiments around managing her paranoid thoughts about others. This was done in a graded way, moving from being active in quiet situations to gradually gaining experience in more complex social situations in town, public social situations, meeting friends and then returning to her university. These experiments involved first rehearsing expected and imagined scenarios, before specific practice in managing the paranoia. This work involved some degree of normalizing the experience of paranoia, by talking about how sensitivity around intimate moments can often lead to fears and images, and that as Lesley had experienced these before it was likely they would return as she practiced again. Decatastrophizing such experiences helped her to manage them and

overcome her social withdrawal. Also important was work around managing her use of checking on the Internet. This was formulated in a way that explained that by engaging with checking she was essentially putting her life on hold. The key was assisting her to live with the uncertainty of what was on the Internet, while moving forward with her life.

Conclusion

In summary, the principles of this approach are not novel. The principles and skills should be familiar to any trained CBT therapist. It focuses on the behavioural aspects of CBT for psychosis previously described (Fowler *et al.*, 1995; French and Morrison, 2004) and draws heavily from behavioural activation, but adds in specific strategies to manage depression, social anxiety and psychosis. However, here the focus is on social recovery and increasing the time the person spends in constructive and social activities. The major emphasis is on hope, agency and the promotion of a positive active sense of self and this we have found to be a mediator of therapy. It requires the expertise of a skilled CBT therapist, as although the principles are simple, effective practice may require the integration of CBT skills in creative and flexible ways with the experience of working and engaging with the complex presentations of people with psychosis. The integration of CBT with the style of approaches recommended in assertive outreach case management, supported employment, and multi-systemic interventions are necessary.

References

Barton, G.R., Hodgekins, J., Mugford, M. *et al.* (2009) Cognitive behaviour therapy for improving social recovery in psychosis: Cost-effectiveness analysis. *Schizophrenia Research, 112,* 158–163.

Beck, A.T., Rush, A.J., Shaw, B.F. *et al.* (1979) *Cognitive Therapy for Depression.* New York: Guilford Press.

Birchwood, M., Trower, P., Brunet, K. *et al.* (2006) Social anxiety and the shame of psychosis: A study in first episode psychosis. *Behaviour Research and Therapy, 45(5),* 1025–1037.

Butler, G. (1999) *Overcoming Social Anxiety: A Self-Help Guide using Cognitive-Behavioural Techniques.* London: Constable and Robinson.

Corr, P. (2011) Anxiety: Splitting the phenonmeonological atom. *Personality and Individual Differences, 50,* 889–897.

Drake, R.E., Becker, D.R., Clark, R.E. *et al.* (1999) Research on the individual placement and support model of supported employment. *Psychiatric Quarterly, 70(4),* 289–301.

Fowler, D., Garety, P.A., and Kuipers, E. (1995) *Cognitive Behaviour Therapy for Psychosis: Theory and Practice*. Chichester: John Wiley and Sons.

Fowler, D., Hodgekins, J., Arena, K. *et al.* (2010) Early detection and psychosocial intervention for young people who are at risk of developing long term socially disabling severe mental illness: should we give equal priority to functional recovery and complex emotional dysfunction as to psychotic symptoms? *Clinical Neuropsychiatry, 7*, 63–71.

Fowler, D., Hodgekins, J., Painter, M. *et al.* (2009) Cognitive behaviour therapy for improving social recovery in psychosis: a report from the ISREP MRC Trial Platform study (Improving Social Recovery in Early Psychosis) *Psychological Medicine*, 1–10.

French, P. and Morrison, A.P. (2004) *Early Detection and Cognitive Therapy for People at High Risk of Developing Psychosis: A Treatment Approach*. New York: John Wiley and Sons.

Garety, P.A., Kuipers, E., Fowler, D. *et al.* (2001) A cognitive model of the positive symptoms of psychosis. *Psychological Medicine, 31*, 189–195.

Gershuny, J. (2011) *Time-Use Surveys and the Measurement of National Well-Being*. Swansea, UK: Office for National Statistics.

Hafner, H. and an der Heiden, W. (1999) The course of schizophrenia in the light of modern follow-up studies: the ABC and WHO studies. *European Archives of Psychiatry and Clinical Neuroscience, 249*, 14–26.

Harrison, G., Croudace, T., Mason, P. *et al.* (1996) Predicting the long-term outcome of schizophrenia. *Psychological Medicine, 26*, 697–705.

Hogarty, G.E., Goldberg, S.C., Schooler, N.R. *et al.* (1974) Drug and sociotherapy in the aftercare of schizophrenic patients, II: Two-year relapse rates. *Archives of General Psychiatry, 31*, 603–608.

Hogarty, G.E., Kornblith, S.J., Greenwald, P. *et al.* (1997) Three-year trials of personal therapy with schizophrenics living with or independent of family, I: Description of study and effects on relapse rates. *American Journal of Psychiatry, 154*, 1504–1513.

Kessler, R.C., Berglund, P., Demler, O. *et al.* (2005) Lifetime prevalence and age of onset distributions of DSM-IV disorders in the National Comorbidity Survey Replication. *Archives of General Psychiatry, 62*, 593–602.

Kim-Cohen, J., Caspi, A., Moffitt, T.E. *et al.* (2003) Prior juvenile diagnoses in adults with mental disorder: developmental follow-back of a prospective-longitudinal cohort. *Archives of General Psychiatry, 60*, 709–717.

Lenior, M.E., Dingemans, P.M., Linszen, D.H. *et al.* (2001) Social functioning and the course of early-onset schizophrenia: Five-year follow-up of a psychosocial intervention. *British Journal of Psychiatry, 179*, 53–58.

Mangalore, R. and Knapp, M. (2007) Cost of schizophrenia in England. *Journal of Mental Health Policy and Economics, 10*, 23–41.

Mueser, K.T., Clark, R.E., Haines, M. *et al.* (2004) The Hartford study of supported employment for persons with severe mental illness. *Journal of Consulting and Clinical Psychology, 72(3)*, 479–490.

Mueser, K.T., Salyers, M.P. and Mueser, P.R. (2001) A prospective analysis of work in schizophrenia. *Schizophrenia Bulletin, 27*, 281–296.

Short, S. (2006) *Review of the UK 2000 Time Use Survey.* London: Office for National Statistics.

Wiersma, D., Wanderling, J., Dragomirecka, E. *et al.* (2000) Social disability in schizophrenia: its development and prediction over 15 years in incidence cohorts in six European centres. *Psychological Medicine, 30,* 1155–1167.

Wing, J.K., and Brown, G. (1970) *Institutionalism and schizophrenia: a comparative study of three mental health hospitals 1960–1968.* London: Cambridge University Press.

Wykes, T., Steel, C., Everitt, B. *et al.* (2008) Cognitive behaviour therapy for schizophrenia: Effect sizes, clinical models and methodological rigor. *Schizophrenia Bulletin, 34,* 523–537.

9

Group Cognitive Behavioural Social Skills Training for Schizophrenia

Jason Holden and Eric Granholm

Schizophrenia typically leads to profound functional disability (Knapp and Kavanagh, 1997; Department of Veterans Affairs, 2002). Poor functional outcome in schizophrenia shows a stronger relationship with cognitive impairments, negative symptoms and social skills deficits than with positive symptom severity (Green *et al.*, 2000). Although positive symptom reduction remains an important treatment goal, intervention targets for severe mental illness have expanded in the past two decades to include functioning in social and instrumental role domains, such as independent living, socialization, education and employment. Antipsychotic medications can reduce psychotic symptoms, but have little impact on negative symptoms and daily functioning (McEvoy *et al.*, 2007; Kahn *et al.*, 2008; Guo *et al.*, 2010). Treatment strategies that integrate pharmacotherapy to protect against biological vulnerabilities with psychotherapy, focused on setting valued goals, teaching social skills (e.g. enhancing coping, training communication skills, and reducing social isolation), and challenging defeatist performance beliefs have been found to improve outcomes in patients with schizophrenia in many studies (Kurtz and Mueser, 2008; Pratt *et al.*, 2008; Wykes *et al.*, 2008; Kurzban *et al.*, 2010).

CBT for Schizophrenia: Evidence-Based Interventions and Future Directions,
First Edition. Edited by Craig Steel.
© 2013 John Wiley & Sons, Ltd. Published 2013 by John Wiley & Sons, Ltd.

Model of Functional Outcome in Schizophrenia

It is well established that neurocognitive deficits are associated with poor functional outcome in schizophrenia (Green, 1996; Green *et al.*, 2004; Kurtz *et al.*, 2005; Milev *et al.*, 2005), but this relationship is at least partially mediated by several factors (Figure 9.1). Neurocognitive abilities and learning opportunities determine functional skill capacity (e.g. as measured on performance-based measures), but several personal factors determine whether skills are actually performed (e.g. attitudes, expectations, motivation, anhedonia, moods, insight) (Wiersma *et al.*, 2000; Friedman *et al.*, 2001; Twamley *et al.*, 2002; Robinson *et al.*, 2004; Bowie *et al.*, 2006; Grant and Beck, 2009; Horan *et al.*, 2010). In particular, the premise that cognitions, like expectations and performance beliefs, can influence symptoms and functional outcome is a key component of the generic cognitive model that guides cognitive behavioural therapy (CBT) interventions for schizophrenia. Several researchers (Rector *et al.*, 2005; Avery *et al.*, 2009; Grant and Beck, 2009; Horan *et al.*, 2010) have found that defeatist beliefs (e.g. 'Why bother, I always fail', 'It's not worth the effort') may contribute to negative symptoms and poor functioning in schizophrenia. Rector *et al.* (2005) proposed that dysfunctional attitudes about the personal costs of applying energy can lead to passivity and avoidance of activities that require effort, as a defence against anticipated failure and negative evaluations by others. This avoidance and lack of effort manifests as: diminished motivation (avolition-apathy), loss of pleasure (anhedonia-asociality) and lack of engagement in goal-directed functioning activities.

Defeatist beliefs and low expectations for success have been found to be associated with neurocognitive impairment (Grant and Beck, 2009) and this may be because neurocognitive impairment can lead to discouraging everyday failure experiences that lead to low success expectancies. Barch and Dowd (2010) also concluded that pathophysiological processes associated with cognitive impairment in schizophrenia can lead to impairment in a reward prediction mechanism mediated by the striatum that may disrupt the process of generating accurate expectations of success. In social learning theory (Bandura, 1986, 1997), self-competency beliefs are also central to motivation for achievement and engagement in goal-directed activities. People who expect to succeed are more willing to try new tasks, choose harder tasks and expend more effort because they think they will succeed (Bandura, 1997; Wigfield and Eccles, 2000). Social learning theory and the generic cognitive model applied to schizophrenia, therefore, suggest that low self-competency and defeatist beliefs may lead to disengagement from effortful social and community functioning activities as a defence against anticipated failure and negative evaluations by others, which manifests as negative symptoms and poor functioning.

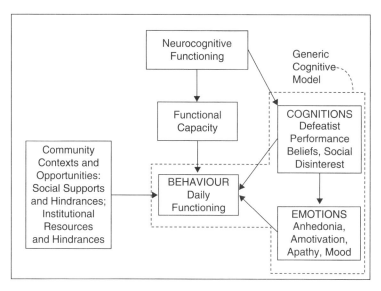

Figure 9.1 Model of functional outcome in schizophrenia

Group Cognitive Behavioural Social Skills Training (CBSST)

We developed and manualized a group psychotherapy intervention called Cognitive Behavioural Social Skills Training (CBSST) that targets several factors in this functional outcome model. CBSST targets dysfunctional attitudes, social skills (capacity) deficits and cognitive impairments (especially problem-solving) that interfere with psychosocial functioning in people with schizophrenia. CBSST draws upon the strengths of CBT and social skills training (SST) approaches and takes advantage of a group therapy setting to facilitate change in functioning. One of the primary goals in combining CBT and SST interventions is to use CBT interventions to address symptoms and dysfunctional thoughts that interfere with successful skills performance in the real world.

Most prior CBT for psychosis studies used an individual format, but recent promising results have been reported using group CBT (Wykes, Parr, and Landau, 1999; Gumley *et al.*, 2003; Kingsep *et al.*, 2003). The vast majority of SST studies have used group therapy (Kurtz and Mueser, 2008). Our prior CBSST trials have used group therapy or combined group and individual therapy. In a recent meta-analysis by Wykes *et al.* (2008), studies that used group versus individual formats of CBT for psychosis did not differ significantly on any outcome. In our recent review (Granholm *et al.*, 2009), we found that four of the six studies reviewed (66 percent) that used a group format found significant improvement in functioning on at least one measure, and eight of the twelve studies reviewed (66 percent) that used an individual format found significant improvement in functioning. Functioning outcomes, therefore, appear comparable between group and individual formats.

It is important to try to understand how groups can promote change in functioning. Groups can promote socialization and connections with peers struggling with common concerns. Groups can also impact social support systems and allow practice of communication and other social skills, which may be important for interventions that target social functioning. In fact, we found that regular supportive interactions with peers and therapists in group interventions lead to improvement in important social attitudes and interest in interacting with others, regardless of whether or not therapists used cognitive therapy interventions to target dysfunctional social attitudes (Granholm *et al.*, 2009). Group therapy may have greater potential than individual therapy for impacting attitude components of social anhedonia, like social disinterest, which in turn, could impact change in social functioning. In groups, there is greater opportunity for supportive interactions with peers that can provide behavioural experiments that demonstrate the value of interacting with others to solve problems and achieve functioning goals.

CBSST Clinical Trials

While most CBT studies have focused on positive symptom outcomes, effect sizes for functional outcome negative symptom reduction have been found to be at least as large as for positive symptom reduction in CBT (Rector and Beck, 2001; Wykes *et al.*, 2008). In a meta-analysis of 23 clinical trials of CBT for schizophrenia (Wykes *et al.*, 2008), 15 studies included functioning measures and the average effect size for functional improvement (.378) was comparable to that for positive symptoms (.372). A respectable average effect size was also found for improvement in negative symptoms (.437). We (Granholm *et al.*, 2009) reviewed 18 CBT trials that included at least one functioning measure and found that approximately two-thirds of studies showed significant gains in functioning, even when functioning was not the primary target. In a meta-analysis of 22 clinical trials of SST for schizophrenia, Kurtz and Mueser (2008) found a large effect size for proximal content-mastery outcomes (d=1.20), moderate effect sizes for intermediate outcomes, such as performance-based measures of social and daily living skills (d=0.52), community functioning (d=0.52), and negative symptoms (d=0.40) and small effect sizes for more distal outcomes, such as other symptoms (d=0.15) and relapse (d=0.23).

We examined the efficacy of CBSST intervention that combines these effective CBT and SST interventions. In an initial pilot study (Granholm *et al.*, 2002), we found that CBSST improved functioning and resulted in medium to large effect sizes for symptom reductions. This pilot study justified a larger clinical trial (Granholm *et al.*, 2005), in which 76 outpatients with chronic schizophrenia or schizoaffective disorder (M age=54) were randomized to treatment-as-usual (TAU) or CBSST+TAU. Groups did not differ significantly on any demographic or outcome variable at baseline. The majority of patients were high school educated, single, unemployed and living in assisted housing. Blind assessments of multiple outcomes were made at baseline and end of treatment (6 months), including psychosocial functioning, cognitive insight, positive and negative symptoms and CBSST skills mastery. Only 4 patients failed to engage in CBSST (i.e. dropped out before attending 4 sessions), 100 percent of patients who engaged in treatment completed at least half the 24 CBSST sessions, and 97 percent attended at least 75 percent of sessions. Intention-to-treat analyses showed significant treatment group effects for psychosocial functioning, cognitive insight and CBSST skills mastery (Granholm *et al.*, 2005; Granholm *et al.*, 2007). Patients in CBSST+TAU were able to learn cognitive-behavioural coping skills, showed improved psychosocial functioning and became more flexible and objective in their thinking about symptoms (improved cognitive insight). In an ongoing trial, we are comparing CBSST with an active goal-focused supportive contact control condition in people with schizophrenia aged 18 and over.

Clinical Assessment

Measuring clinical and functional improvement in group members is a useful way to monitor progress over the course of participation in CBSST groups. With limited resources in clinical settings, it can be challenging to measure outcomes without staff trained to reliably administer clinical interviews and performance-based assessments. However, several useful, conveniently-administered self-report inventories are available. The primary treatment target in CBSST is functioning. The validity of self-reports of functioning has been questioned in this population, but the major concerns are with scales that ask consumers to rate the quality of their performance of functioning tasks. Scales that simply ask whether or not a specific functioning behaviour was performed do not rely on judgments about how well the behaviour was performed. The Independent Living Skills Survey (ILSS: Wallace *et al.*, 2000) is a self-report scale that queries only whether specific functioning behaviours were performed during the past month for ten domains of functioning, ranging from activities of daily living to socialization and work/education. There is also an informant version of the ILSS, if a provider or family member is available who has frequent contact with the consumer. The Psychosocial Rehabilitation Toolkit (PSR Toolkit, Arns *et al.*, 2001) is a scale completed by a provider or other staff person with little consumer burden, based primarily on documentation (e.g. pay stubs, school transcripts) about the consumer's functioning. Symptom distress improvements can be measured using the Beck Depression Inventory-II (BDI-II; Beck *et al.*, 1996) and the Beck Anxiety Inventory (BAI; Beck and Steer, 1990) self-report instruments. The Psychotic Symptom Rating Scales (PSYRATS; Haddock *et al.*, 1999) is an interview measure that can be used for multiple dimensions of hallucinations and delusions, including severity, distress and dysfunction related to symptoms, as well as delusional conviction and beliefs about voices (e.g. external agency, control). The Life Satisfaction Index (LSI; Wallace and Wheeler, 2002) is a self-report measure to assess subjective well-being on several dimensions (e.g. zest vs. apathy, self-concept, optimism). We have found changes on all of these instruments in our previous research.

Group Member Inclusion

Referring clinicians often ask how to determine which potential group members are eligible or appropriate for CBSST. In our previous CBSST trials, the inclusion and exclusion criteria utilized were purposefully general to ensure a representative sample of individuals with severe mental illness. Participants were not excluded, for example, for substance abuse, or disorganization or cognitive impairments. If consumers did not require more intensive inpatient treatment for substance abuse, psychosis, suicidality/homicidality or medical illness, they were offered outpatient CBSST group therapy. We also assessed neuropsychological impairment in a previous trial (Granholm *et al.*, 2008) and found that severity of neurocognitive impairment did not moderate outcome in CBSST. Comparable benefits were found relative to treatment as usual for consumers with good and poor neurocognitive functioning. While negative symptoms and disorganization can present challenges in any goal-focused group, these problems can be addressed in the group session through various accommodations or interventions. We address negative symptoms by targeting the defeatist attitudes discussed above, which can underlie amotivation, apathy and withdrawal. By working with a group member to develop a meaningful, attainable, functioning goal, and challenging defeatist attitudes (e.g. 'Why try? I'm just going to fail'), they can overcome avolition and enjoy successful accomplishment of smaller steps along the way to achieving larger goals. Disorganization and cognitive impairment can be addressed through the brief and structured format of the CBSST skills training. Acronyms, simplified and focused skills, and written worksheets can all be useful strategies for helping a group member who is disorganized to focus their efforts and successfully work towards their goals. The material in all of the modules is well suited to asking group members to read out loud as well as asking a group member to complete an in-session activity on a whiteboard to more fully engage and focus a group member in that session. In the Social Skills module, simple three-step methods for expressing positive and negative feelings are included and we have found it helpful to frame disorganized and tangential speech as a communication problem that interferes with a consumer's goals. This can then be addressed in communication training role-plays and coaching (e.g. 'keep it short and sweet'). We believe the best way to determine whether a consumer will benefit from CBSST is to offer the intervention and give it a try.

CBSST Protocol

CBSST is delivered in three modules with approximately six sessions per module. While it is possible to complete the program in 18 sessions, group members are strongly encouraged to go through the modules a second time for a total of 36 sessions. We have found that doing so greatly increases the effectiveness of the program and reinforces the skills learned during each module. Improvements in real-world functioning take time. The improvements we see in group members after their second exposure to the content and skills is often quite impressive. The modules described below are delivered using a modular rolling admissions procedure, whereby consumers can enter groups at the start of any module, rather than starting the same group of patients at the same time and completing the entire intervention before enrolling a new group. The rolling admissions approach is more practical in most clinic settings. In addition, existing group members can gain a sense of mastery and self-competence when they help new members joining the group gain the skills they have previously practised.

Setting personalized treatment goals chosen by consumers is a key component of effective psychosocial rehabilitation treatment planning (Bellack and Mueser, 1993; Cook *et al.*, 1994). The initial sessions of each CBSST module include goal-setting and goal-progress discussions and exercises that encourage group members to focus on setting personalized, functioning goals. These goals then become the focus of the thought challenging, communication skills training and problem-solving interventions in later CBSST sessions. If a group member identifies a symptom-oriented goal, such as 'I want to get rid of my voices', a discussion follows during which the group member is encouraged to consider how their life would be different if they if they weren't experiencing symptoms ('What would you do differently each day if you woke up and your voices were gone?'). Individualized goal setting can effectively be done in a group setting by encouraging the group member to draw upon the experiences of other group members, brainstorm alternative goals, identify specific steps toward a particular goal and ways of overcoming obstacles. Members are encouraged to set SMART goals that are Specific (behavioural), Manageable, Attainable, Realistic goals and identify the Resources needed to achieve goals that Transfer to meaningful, valued change in quality of life.

Cognitive Skills Module

Cognitive therapy is the focus of this module, although these techniques are also used throughout the other two modules. Group members are introduced to the general concepts of CBT, including the relationship between thoughts, feelings and behaviours (generic cognitive model), automatic thoughts, thought challenging by examining evidence for beliefs and mistakes in thinking (e.g. jumping to conclusions, mind reading, all-or-none thinking). Specific dysfunctional thoughts, like expectancies ('It won't be fun'), self-efficacy beliefs ('I always fail'), and anomalous beliefs ('I will be harmed by spirits if I go out') can interfere with the performance of adaptive behaviours, despite intact skill capacity. Reducing the negative impact of these beliefs on social functioning is a goal of CBSST. By challenging defeatist performance beliefs, consumers are more likely to engage in effortful goal-directed behaviours and use the skills they have. Through group discussion and exercises, thought records, and homework assignments, patients are taught to identify thoughts, identify relationships between thoughts, feelings and behaviours, and identify mistakes in thinking. Behavioural experiments are conducted inside and outside the group (in session activities and homework) in order to gather evidence to evaluate beliefs. Alternatives therapy, Socratic questioning and thought chaining (Beck and Rector, 2000) are used to help patients examine the logic of beliefs and generate more adaptive alternatives to mistakes in thinking or thoughts without sufficient evidence. The primary thoughts targeted are beliefs about social functioning activities (e.g. expecting failure, pleasure predicting, expecting harm), hallucinations (e.g. external agency, omnipotence/control, and omniscience of voices) and beliefs about daily events (e.g. coincidences) that group members use as evidence to confirm delusions. To simplify learning and help group members remember and use cognitive techniques in everyday life, mnemonic aids are provided (e.g. laminated wallet cards containing

> **Catch It**: Identify the thought
>
> **Check It**: Identify evidence that supports and disputes the thought and mistakes in thinking
>
> **Change It**: Modify the thought so it is more accurate and helpful

Figure 9.2   The 3Cs acronym

information about skills). For example, to foster thought challenging, we use an acronym, 'The **3Cs**: **C**atch it, **C**heck it, **C**hange it'; the 'it' is the thought (see Figure 9.2).

Social Skills Module

The primary goal of this module is to improve communication skills and psychosocial interactions in everyday life experiences. The predominant therapeutic technique in this module is the behavioural role-play, and practice and reinforcement are key interventions. Important role-plays focus on socialization and leisure activities with friends and family, assertive communication and getting needs met through case managers and other service providers. Short, three-step techniques are taught to facilitate expression of positive and negative feelings and making positive requests (Bellack *et al.*, 2004), to improve assertive, clear and comfortable sharing of feelings in social interactions. Improving everyday activities and psychosocial functioning are common role-play topics for these skills (e.g. asking a roommate to change their behaviour; asking someone to go to the movies; assertive interactions with co-workers/employers). Group members critique the strengths and weaknesses of their own performance and each other's performance, according to a list of key verbal and non-verbal skill components displayed on a poster board (e.g. eye contact, speech volume). This feedback is then used in subsequent role-plays until the group member feels confident in their ability to execute the skill in the community.

Thoughts and beliefs also play an important role in the Social Skills module. Assisting the group member in identifying defeatist performance attitudes prior to the role-play (i.e. not believing that they will be able to express their frustration, expectancies about negative reactions from the other person etc.) is often helpful. Self-efficacy and performance beliefs are elicited and scaling is used before and after role-plays (0–10 ratings of how successful you think you will be/were) to challenge defeatist beliefs about communication abilities. Following the role-play, the group discusses these thoughts and possible changes in beliefs (i.e. 'I didn't think I could do it', 'That wasn't so bad', etc.) to promote real-world performance of the skills developed.

Problem-Solving Module

The focus of this module is on increasing problem-solving skills to address everyday challenges, overcome obstacles to goal achievement, and develop plans for collaborating with case managers or other support persons to solve real-world problems. Problems related to illness and disability are also addressed, such as coping with symptoms and stress, remembering to take medications, increase leisure activities, relationships and hygiene/health. Basic problem-solving skills are taught using the acronym, **SCALE**, to scale a mountain of problems one step at a time (see Figure 9.3).

When specifying the problem, it is vitally important to break down problems and define very specific, manageable steps (e.g. 'I need to wash the dishes on Tuesday by 5:00 PM' is a more specific problem than 'I need to keep my apartment cleaner'). Considering possible solutions is a very important, and often challenging, step. Possible solutions are generated and written down on worksheets and/or a white board, without censoring any solutions or assessing the best solution, yet. Consumers often perseverate on one solution or begin to doubt the potential success of solutions, so therapists must work to help group members brainstorm as many solutions as possible. Then, the group begins to assess solutions and selects two or three solutions to evaluate in detail, but weighing the good and not-so-good aspects of each (e.g. listing these on the worksheet and/or white board). Once the group decides the best solution, a plan to execute the solution is defined in detail, including potential obstacles that might come up and ways to address them. The group member with the problem is then assigned the plan to execute for homework, and the success of the plan is evaluated in the next session.

The role of thoughts and beliefs and the impact they have on behaviour is also addressed in this module. Often, not effectively executing a problem-solving plan is due to failure expectancies (e.g. 'This plan will never work') or a lack of self-efficacy beliefs (e.g. 'I'll never be able to remember my doctor's appointments'). Thoughts about the expected success or failure of plans are elicited before executing a plan and evidence about extent of success is reviewed after trying a plan to challenge defeatist beliefs. Group facilitators assist group

Specify the problem
Consider all possible solutions
Assess the best solution
Lay out a plan
Execute and **E**valuate the outcome

Figure 9.3   SCALE: Basic problem-solving

members in identifying any dysfunctional thoughts and encourage the group member to address the thoughts, such as through a 3Cs exercise.

Clinical Application of CBSST

Mary, a 54-year-old, married, African-American female presented with a DSM-IV diagnosis of schizoaffective disorder and a history of narcotic dependence, mood symptoms and chronic pain. Mary reported that she experienced auditory hallucinations and occasional visual hallucinations of seeing people that no one else could see. She said the voices were 'very derogatory' and occasionally talked to each other about her. They would often make her the subject of a joke or would blame her for her son's death. Mary believed that she was responsible for her infant son's death because she did not put her children's needs before her own. She said she 'allowed' her son to die by not doing everything she could do to cure his illness. Mary also believed that her psychiatrist 'conspired' with her therapist to have her committed to a hospital, that she received coded messages from the TV about other people's lives, and that she was a 'chosen one of God'.

While serving in the military in her early twenties, Mary's symptoms increased in frequency and severity following the death of one of her children. She started drinking alcohol on a regular basis at that time and she described feeling very depressed. Her voices began frequently instructing her to do things, such as harm herself. Mary's first suicide attempt was at the age of 23 and according to her medical records has attempted suicide ten times since then. In addition to periods of heavy alcohol use, Mary has frequently smoked marijuana and has been addicted to narcotic pain medications. At the time of the interview, Mary denied substance use and reported at least 1 year of abstinence.

Mary has numerous documented periods of medication non-adherence. This often led to symptom exacerbation and, as a result, she has had at least 20 psychiatric hospitalizations. Two of the hospitalizations occurred in the 12 months prior to the interview with the most recent occurring 10 months prior. Mary completed high school and a 2-year associate's degree and later served in the military for 3 years. She had not worked in 25 years. Mary was separated from her second husband of 9 years citing a strained relationship due to her husband being in jail for domestic violence and alcohol abuse. Mary has two sons and a daughter. She had been living with her daughter and four grandchildren for 7 months prior to the interview. Mary was not able to identify much social support outside her immediate family and often isolated herself from others. She said she is very religious and often uses prayer as a way to cope with her symptoms. Mary used a wheelchair, despite being ambulatory, stating it is due to her chronic pain.

During the first two sessions, several potential areas of focus were identified. Mary frequently expressed frustration and anger with others who she believed were taking advantage of her. She expressed uncertainty about how to handle these situations and was not assertive. Her inability to place limits on others' behaviour often created feelings of dysphoria and displaced anger. Mary had a history of putting others' needs before her own. She would 'put on a different face' to meet the needs of others while not being honest about her own feelings and needs. She often gave too much of her time, money and material goods to others, which often negatively affected her. 'I give them money so they won't suffer, but sometimes they take advantage of that and I can't do anything about it'. This defeatist, hopeless attitude prevented her from taking action to get her own needs met. Mary also thought she was unable to 'deal' with her problems and would often 'run away' (withdraw) when she felt overwhelmed, expecting to fail if she tried to change things. This defeatist belief led her to avoid confrontation and she even moved to different cities to avoid resolving problems. In CBSST, problem-solving training was used to brainstorm solutions to these interpersonal problems, SST was used to increase assertive communication and thought challenging was used to address these defeatist beliefs.

In CBSST, the initial sessions of each module include a discussion on goals and the homework asks group members to set goals. This provides an opportunity for a discussion of goal setting for new members, progress toward goals, and problems/obstacles that are inferring with the goals. Goals are related to recovery and functioning. For example, symptom reduction (e.g. 'I want to get rid of my voices') is not a useful functioning goal in itself. Rather, focusing on what the group member would be doing if his or her voices were not so bad (e.g. socializing more with friends, get a job) are much more useful goals. In Mary's case, she initially stated she would like to work on 'impulsivity, chronic pain, getting rid of voices, and feeling guilty' as goals. While important to Mary, these were not functional goals. Mary was asked what she would be doing differently in her life if she was less impulsive, experiencing less pain, was not troubled by voices and felt less guilt. After some consideration, Mary responded by saying she would be able to improve her relationships by maintaining better boundaries. More specifically, she would not loan people money to people and would prioritize her own needs before others, when appropriate. She set a goal of making one new friend outside of her family. Mary added that she would like to live independently in an apartment, rather than living with and supporting her extended family, and would work towards this goal by initially locating three possible apartments she could visit.

In the Cognitive Skills Module, Mary began to learn how to use the 3Cs. She started to apply the skills to some of her thoughts and in one of her early sessions, Mary did a 3Cs exercise on the thought 'I'm not useful'. This

---

3Cs Exercise

<u>Catch It:</u>

　'I'm not useful.'　　　　　　　　　　Feelings: Sad, hurt

<u>Check It:</u>

　　　　Evidence for:　　　　　　　　　　　**Evidence against:**

1. My voices tell me I'm not useful　　　1. I do a lot to take care of my grandchildren
2. I'm getting old　　　　　　　　　　2. The voices aren't always right
3. I'm in a wheelchair　　　　　　　　3. I give money and other
4. My kids criticize me for not　　　　　　things to my children
　 helping them enough financially　　　4. My kids tell me I'm a good mother

　　<u>Mistakes in Thinking:</u>

　　　　1. All-or-nothing (the thought suggests she isn't useful AT ALL)
　　　　2. Personalization (it's HER fault that her kids aren't doing well financially and need
　　　　　 help)

<u>Change It:</u>

'I may not be a perfect mother or grandmother, but I do a lot to help them and can still be
useful to them.'

Figure 9.4　　3Cs exercise

was the thought Mary identified as driving her feelings of worthlessness. It was also negatively impacting her behaviour in her relationships with others, because the thought would lead her to be unassertive and give too much of her time and money to others in order to feel like she was being useful. She ultimately expected to fail in relationships, because others would discover she was useless. Mary also acknowledged that this belief was maintained by the derogatory voices that she regularly experiences (e.g. 'You are a waste', 'You should just kill yourself'). An example of a 3Cs form she completed is shown in Figure 9.4.

During one session, Mary complained about her family not celebrating 'Grandparents Day' with her. 'No one even called me', she said. With some guidance, Mary identified the thought that, if she was useful and important, they would have called and that, 'I didn't get a call, so I'm a bad grandmother'. Mary's perceived value as a grandmother seemed dependent upon the behaviour of her daughter and grandchildren, which was interpreted as evidence for her own self-value. The group facilitator guided Mary through a 3Cs exercise to challenge the thought (as in the 3Cs figure above).

Mary expressed frustration with the miscommunication that occurred with her transportation to a particular group session. After discussing the situation with the group, she was able to identify the thoughts she had during and shortly after the situation. From there, the group facilitator guided Mary and the other group members through an exercise during which Mary labelled her thoughts with mistakes in thinking and discussed why each thought can be classified as a 'mistake in thinking'. Mary identified the thoughts 'The driver doesn't like me' (mind reading: making assumptions about how the driver feels about her), 'This group is never going to work for me' (all-or-nothing thinking and fortune telling: Mary used an absolute word 'never' and is predicting the future), and 'The driver forgot me on purpose' (jumping-to-conclusions: came to a decision based on very little evidence). Once Mary recognized the above patterns in her thinking, she was able to modify her thinking and acknowledged that she felt less frustrated after discussing it.

When Mary arrived for her 12th session, she reported to the group that she had moved out of her daughter's house the previous weekend. Mary described a situation in which she became frustrated with her daughter's boyfriend and decided she had 'enough of it all'. Mary made the decision to move into her own apartment and identified feeling 'very relieved' the moment she had the keys to her new apartment in her hands. This was a significant event for Mary and the group positively reinforced Mary for her decision to move out of the house. It also indicated a shift in Mary's beliefs about herself and the potential consequences setting limits may have on her relationships within her family. Mary also expressed some concerns about being able to live on her own again. Shortly after moving in, she identified the thought, 'I can't live by myself'. For homework that week, Mary completed a 3Cs exercise on that thought. While discussing her homework in the group session, the downward arrow technique was used to identify the core belief 'I'm a failure'. Mary acknowledged that this belief often impacts her feelings and behaviour, making her reluctant to try new activities or pursue her goals. When asked about evidence that supports and disputes this thought, Mary said she often felt like a failure because of the difficulties she had due to her schizophrenia symptoms. The symptoms made it an overwhelming challenge to maintain a job and led to the poor behaviour she demonstrated as a mother by not being as attentive and supportive of her children while they were younger. Mary's vocational and familial struggles reinforced the belief that she is a failure. They also led to defeatist performance beliefs that served as obstacles in the way of her setting and working towards goals.

In the Social Skills module, Mary focused on increasing her direct, assertive communication with others. Mary described a situation in which she was attempting to effectively communicate her desire for her son to wash her car, but did not have success. In the session, Mary participated in a role-play to practice communication skills and making a positive request. First, the two group therapists performed the role-play with each other to model the skill, while group members followed along with a handout. Then, Mary was asked what thoughts she has about doing the role-play. She said she was 'nervous' about doing it since it is something she finds difficult to do, but she made a first attempt:

You do a really good job of washing my van. Can you wash my van?

Mary was then given constructive feedback by the group members. She demonstrated poor eye contact and she was having difficulty making a direct request of the person because it felt 'uncomfortable'. Instead, the message she was attempting to communicate was implied. Mary said it feels more comfortable being indirect and acknowledged that she prefers to communicate by 'hinting' at what she is trying to communicate to the person. After some discussion and suggestions from the other group members on how to improve the wording, Mary tried the role-play again:

> I would really appreciate it if you would wash my van. It would make me very happy.

Mary received positive feedback from the other group members for improving her eye contact, adding the statement about how she would feel, and being more direct. Mary said making the request in this way still feels a little uncomfortable, but she said she recognized how it can be more helpful. Further discussion about feeling uncomfortable with being direct helped Mary identify thoughts related to these types of situations. These thoughts included, 'I will be rejected' and 'I will be disappointed'. This illustrates the importance of addressing cognitions when doing experiential exercises, as is done in CBSST. The thoughts and feelings Mary was having about being assertive and making requests of others, as well as those in the session about participating in role-plays, would have greatly decreased the likelihood of Mary completing the exercise, if only the skill was addressed. Identifying thoughts before and after the role-play can be very informative for both the group member and the group facilitators and can assist in addressing any potential obstacles that may impede trying a new behaviour.

Although the focus of the module is on communication skills, this is a very good example of how exercises in other modules can help identify thoughts that can be challenged using a 3 C's exercise. Improving her communication skills helped Mary to be more assertive and it quickly had an impact on her relationships. A couple of weeks later, Mary reported that she had 'survived' seeing her estranged husband at a family gathering. She said in the past she would have 'run away' and not faced the situation with the same courage that she did. By being courageous and utilizing the communication skills she had been learning, Mary said she felt more confident confronting the situation directly, rather than avoiding it. She acknowledged that her tendency to 'want to run away' often gets in the way of her goals.

The Problem-Solving module provides an opportunity for group members to specify problems, such as obstacles that get in the way of their goals, and then identify potential solutions to the problem. Mary previously identified feeling lonely as a persisting problem. While feeling lonely is not

Specify: How can I meet more people?

Consider all possible solutions:
1. Go to church
2. Network through other friends
3. Join a club
4. Go to the shopping centre
5. Go to a coffee shop

Assess the best possible solution: Go to the shopping centre.

Pros	Cons
1. If I don't meet anyone, it is still a fun thing to do	1. It might be harder to introduce myself to someone there
2. I've met people there before	2. Sometimes my voices are worse in large crowds
3. It's near my house	3. People may not feel like socializing there
4. I can go there with the purpose of buying something	

Lay out a plan (After some group discussion/planning):
1. Review the communication skill section of my manual before I leave.
2. Go to the shops at 11:00 a.m. on Saturday
3. Go to the food court area.
4. Sit at a table near someone else.
5. Say something to the other person, such as a comment about the weather.
6. Think of three questions to ask the person and three interesting facts about myself I can share.
7. Have paper and a pen in case I exchange phone numbers with the person.

Execute and Evaluation:
Execute the plan to talk to someone at the shops and then evaluate what I could do differently to make the plan more effective next time. For example, should I try a different time or location? Should I approach someone in a different way?

The following session, Mary reported that she attempted to execute the plan, but discovered that her voices were exacerbated by the large number of people there on a Saturday morning and her anxiety about the task. Mary said she would modify the plan by making progressively longer trips to the mall to reduce her anxiety, and attempting to meet someone at 11:00 a.m. on a monday when there are fewer people and to have an objective while there.

Figure 9.5   SCALE in practice

a functioning goal in itself, further discussion led to a more functioning-related goal of increasing socialization. Mary completed a SCALE exercise by starting with the problem, 'How can I meet more people?' Phrasing the problem as a question can make it easier for group members to identify potential solutions to the problem since it allows them to 'answer' a question (see Figure 9.5).

Mary selected a solution and developed a plan to go to a shopping centre, since she knows based on prior experience that people will talk to her there. She can also go with the purpose of buying something she needs so it will encourage her to get out of her apartment. Group members are encouraged to select two possible solutions to assess. In the example above, just one of the two solutions Mary selected is presented. At the end of the session, Mary agreed to execute the plan during the coming week. Thoughts about expected success or failure were elicited before the end of the session. Mary stated that the plan was reasonable and she believed she could successfully execute the plan. It can also be helpful to ask the group member to rate their expectations on a scale of 1 to 10 (1=complete failure; 10=complete success) and then check again following an attempt to execute.

When Mary returned for the subsequent session, she reported that she had attempted to execute the plan, but was unsuccessful. This was a good opportunity for the group facilitators to discuss with Mary what got in the way of her not executing the plan. The discussion uncovered some thoughts and beliefs that were getting in the way of her completing this task along with an exacerbation of her voices. Mary said she had thoughts that included 'I won't be able to do this on my own' and 'I won't be able to help myself if something bad happens'. A 3Cs exercise could be used to challenge these thoughts, or an additional SCALE exercise could be completed by specifying a more specific problem (e.g. 'How can I go to the shopping centre on my own?') or modifying the plan the group member created in the original SCALE exercise. In Mary's case, she chose to modify the plan. Mary decided to take incrementally longer trips to the shops to feel more comfortable being away from her apartment for a longer period of time and would work towards attempting to meet someone at 11:00 a.m. on a Monday when there were fewer people about. She also devised a strategy to identify an objective for each trip to the mall, such as purchasing a needed item of clothing. Mary had reported feeling anxious at the start of this SCALE session (rated an 8 out of 10). Afterwards, the group facilitators asked Mary to rate her anxiety again and she said doing the exercise helped her feel more confident and, as a result, her anxiety decreased to a 4 out of 10.

Mary's beliefs about an inability to care for herself affected several areas of her life. The beliefs impacted her confidence to move out of her daughter's house and live independently. They also contributed to her use of a wheelchair. Mary identified thoughts about her use of the wheelchair such as 'I always need it with me because my pain will get worse' and 'I can't get through the day without it'. Mary brought her wheelchair to each session until her 24th session. Mary arrived without the wheelchair and this was quickly noted by the other group members. Mary received positive feedback from the other group members and she commented that she has been feeling good lately and wanted to try to make it through the day without it. When asked what was contributing to her improved mood, Mary informed the group that she met someone and started a romantic relationship and was very much enjoying spending time with this person.

As is recommend for all group members completing CBSST, Mary went through each module twice. The second time Mary completed each module, her understanding and application of the techniques had improved greatly. For example, while Mary was working through the Cognitive Skills Module a second time she stated that she had noticed changes in her thoughts, particularly beliefs about how she views herself and how it related to her goal of setting boundaries and being more assertive in relationships. 'I'm more important now. I have an opinion and it's going to be heard'. Mary acknowledged this was a significant change from her thinking earlier in the group, since she used to believe that she had to literally pay for the mistakes she made with others. She noted that she understood the mistakes in thinking she was making and was able to successfully change her thinking and ultimately her behaviour.

Mary also completed the Social Skills and Problem-Solving modules a second time, for a total of 36 sessions. In one of her final sessions, Mary became noticeably upset when another group member made a comment about her being overweight, yet she remained quiet and did not respond. The group facilitators used this as an opportunity to practice the communication skills 'Expressing Negative Feelings, and Making Positive Requests'. Mary attempted to communicate her feelings to the group member by saying, 'You shouldn't talk about someone's weight. I don't need a reminder'. With prompting and a reminder of the steps for Expressing Negative Feelings, Mary then said, 'I would like to make this request of you. Please do not talk about my being overweight in the group, because it makes me feel very uncomfortable'. Mary was able to directly and clearly express how she felt when the group member made the comment and then assertively request that the group member not bring up that topic again in the sessions. Mary's improved eye contact was noted by one group member and she also received positive feedback for her increased courage to express negative feelings.

Working toward her goals of being more assertive or 'giving a voice to [her] thoughts' (her words) and 'setting clear boundaries with others' remained a focus throughout her participation in the group. When introducing herself to new group members, Mary stated that attending the group sessions helped her set boundaries with people: 'I'm not letting people walk on me as much anymore. It feels good'.

During Mary's final session, she was given an opportunity to reflect upon the progress she had made since she started the CBSST group. Mary had written a lengthy journal entry about her experiences in the group that she shared with the other group members. Mary stated that some of her significant changes included not 'personalizing things' and blaming herself for certain events, setting better boundaries with her family and feeling more confident about putting her needs before others when necessary. Mary admitted these changes were 'scary at first', but she learned 'taking time out for [herself] is not a selfish act'.

References

Arns, P., Rogers, E.S., Cook, J. *et al.* (2001) The IAPSRS Toolkit: Development, utility, and relation to other performance measurement systems. *Psychiatric Rehabilitation Journal, 25(1)*, 43–52.

Avery, R., Startup, M. and Calabria, K. (2009) The role of effort, cognitive expectancy appraisals and coping style in the maintenance of the negative symptoms of schizophrenia. *Psychiatry Research, 167*, 36–46.

Bandura, A. (1986) *Social Foundations of Thoughts and Action: A Social Cognitive Theory.* New Jersey: Prentice Hall.

Bandura, A. (1997) *Self-Efficacy: The Exercise of Control.* New York: W.H. Freeman.

Barch, D.M. and Dowd, E. C. (2010) Goal representations and motivational drive in schizophrenia: The role of prefrontal-striatal interactions. *Schizophrenia Bulletin, 36*, 919–934.

Beck, A.T. and Rector, N.A. (2000) Cognitive therapy of schizophrenia: A new therapy for the new millennium. *American Journal of Psychotherapy, 54*, 291–300.

Beck, A.T. and Steer, R.A. (1990) *Manual for the Beck Anxiety Inventory.* San Antonio, TX: Psychological Corporation.

Beck, A.T., Steer, R.A. and Brown, G.K. (1996) *BDI–II, Beck Depression Inventory: Manual*, 2nd edn. Boston: Harcourt Brace.

Bellack, A.S. and Mueser, K.T. (1993) Psychosocial treatment for schizophrenia. *Schizophrenia Bulletin, 19*, 317–336.

Bellack A.S., Mueser, K., Gingerich, S. *et al.* (2004) *Social Skills Training for Schizophrenia: A Step-by-step Guide*, 2nd edn. New York: Guilford Press.

Bowie, C.R., Reichenberg, A., Patterson, T.L. *et al.* (2006) Determinants of real-world functional performance in schizophrenia subjects: Correlations with cognition, functional capacity, and symptoms. *American Journal of Psychiatry, 163*, 418–425.

Cook, J.A., Lefley, H.P., Pickett, S.A. *et al.* (1994) Age and family burden among parents of offspring with severe mental illness. *American Journal of Orthopsychiatry, 64*, 435–447.

Department of Veterans Affairs (2002) *Practice Matters: Effective Treatment for Schizophrenia.* Washington, DC: Department of Veterans Affairs, Health Services Research and Development Service.

Friedman, J.I., Harvey, P.D., Coleman, T. *et al.* (2001) Six-year follow-up study of cognitive and functional status across the lifespan in schizophrenia: A comparison with Alzheimer's disease and normal aging. *American Journal of Psychiatry, 158*, 1441–1448.

Granholm, E., Ben-Zeev, D. and Link, P.C. (2009) Social disinterest attitudes and group cognitive-behavioral social skills training for functional disability in schizophrenia. *Schizophenia Bulletin, 35*, 874–883.

Granholm, E., McQuaid, J.R., Link, P.C. *et al.* (2008) Neuropsychological predictors of functional outcome in Cognitive Behavioral Social Skills Training for older people with schizophrenia. *Schizophrenia Research, 100*, 133–143.

Granholm, E., McQuaid, J.R., McClure, F.S. *et al.* (2002) A randomized controlled pilot study of cognitive behavioral social skills training for older patients with schizophrenia. *Schizophrenia Research, 53*, 167–169.

Granholm, E., McQuaid, J.R., McClure, F.S. *et al.* (2005) A randomized controlled trial of cognitive behavioral social skills training for middle-aged and older outpatients with chronic schizophrenia. *American Journal of Psychiatry, 162*, 520–529.

Granholm, E., McQuaid, J.R., McClure, F.S. *et al.* (2007) Randomized controlled trial of cognitive behavioral social skills training for older people with schizophrenia: 12-month follow-up. *Journal of Clinical Psychiatry, 68*, 730–737.

Grant, P.M. and Beck, A.T. (2009) Defeatist beliefs as a mediator of cognitive impairment, negative symptoms, and functioning in schizophrenia. *Schizophrenia Bulletin, 35*, 798–806.

Green, M.F. (1996) What are the functional consequences of neurocognitive deficits in schizophrenia? *American Journal of Psychiatry, 153*, 321–330.

Green, M.F., Kern, R.S., Braff, D.L. *et al.* (2000) Neurocognitive deficits and functional outcome in schizophrenia: Are we measuring the 'right stuff'? *Schizophrenia Bulletin, 26*, 119–136.

Green, M.F., Kern, R.S. and Heaton, R.K. (2004) Longitudinal studies of cognition and functional outcome in schizophrenia: Implications for MATRICS. *Schizophrenia Research, 72*, 41–51.

Gumley, A., O'Grady, M., McNay, L. *et al.* (2003) Early intervention for relapse in schizophrenia: Results of a 12-month randomized controlled trial of cognitive behavioural therapy. *Psychological Medicine, 33*, 419–431.

Guo, X., Zhai, J., Liu, Z. *et al.* (2010) Effect of antipsychotic medication alone vs combined with psychosocial intervention on outcomes of early-stage schizophrenia: A randomized, 1-year study. *Archives of General Psychiatry, 67*, 895–904.

Haddock, G., McCarron, J., Tarrier, N. *et al.* (1999) Scales to measure dimensions of hallucinations and delusions: the psychotic rating scales (PSYRATS). *Psychological Medicine, 29*, 879–889.

Horan, W.P., Rassovsky, Y., Kern, R.S. *et al.* (2010) Further support for the role of dysfunctional attitudes in models of real-world functioning in schizophrenia. *Journal of Psychiatric Research, 44*, 499–505.

Kahn, R.S., Fleischhacker, W.W., Boter, H. *et al.* (2008) Effectiveness of antipsychotic drugs in first-episode schizophrenia and schizophreniform disorder: An open randomised clinical trial. *Lancet, 371*, 1085–1097.

Kingsep, P., Nathan, P. and Castle, D. (2003) Cognitive behavioural group treatment for social anxiety in schizophrenia. *Schizophrenia Research, 63*, 121–129.

Knapp, M. and Kavanagh, S. (1997) Economic outcomes and costs in the treatment of schizophrenia. *Clinical Therapeutics, 19*, 128–138.

Kurtz, M.M., Moberg, P.J., Ragland, J.D. *et al.* (2005) Symptoms versus neurocognitive test performance as predictors of psychosocial status in schizophrenia: A 1- and 4-year prospective study. *Schizophrenia Bulletin, 31*, 167–174.

Kurtz, M.M. and Mueser, K.T. (2008) A meta-analysis of controlled research on social skills training for schizophrenia. *Journal of Consulting and Clinical Psychology, 76*, 491–504.

Kurzban, S., Davis, L. and Brekke, J.S. (2010) Vocational, social, and cognitive rehabilitation for individuals diagnosed with schizophrenia: A review of recent research and trends. *Current Psychiatry Reports, 12*, 345–355.

McEvoy, J.P., Lieberman, J.A., Perkins, D.O. *et al.* (2007) Efficacy and tolerability of olanzapine, quetiapine, and risperidone in the treatment of early psychosis: A randomized, double-blind 52-week comparison. *American Journal of Psychiatry, 164*, 1050–1060.

Milev, P., Ho, B.C., Arndt, S. *et al.* (2005) Predictive values of neurocognition and negative symptoms on functional outcome in schizophrenia: A longitudinal first-episode study with 7-year follow-up. *American Journal of Psychiatry, 162*, 495–506.

Pratt, S.I., Van Citters, A.D., Mueser, K.T. *et al.* (2008) Psychosocial rehabilitation on older adults with serious mental illness: A review of the research literature and recommendations for development of rehabilitative approaches. *American Journal of Psychiatric Rehabilitation, 11*, 7–40.

Rector, N.A. and Beck, A.T. (2001) Cognitive behavioral therapy for schizophrenia: An empirical review. *Journal of Nervous Mental Disorders, 189*, 278–287.

Rector, N.A., Beck, A.T. and Stolar, N. (2005) The negative symptoms of schizophrenia: A cognitive perspective. *Canadian Journal of Psychiatry, 50*, 247–257.

Robinson, D.G., Woerner, M.G., McMeniman, M. *et al.* (2004) Symptomatic and functional recovery from a first episode of schizophrenia or schizoaffective disorder. *American Journal of Psychiatry, 161*, 473–479.

Twamley, E.W., Doshi, R.R., Nayak, G.V. *et al.* (2002) Generalized cognitive impairments, ability to perform everyday tasks, and level of independence in community living situations of older patients with psychosis. *American Journal of Psychiatry, 159*, 2013–2020.

Wallace, C.J., Liberman, R.P., Tauber, R. *et al.* (2000) The independent living skills survey: A comprehensive measure of the community functioning of severely and persistently mentally 111 individuals. *Schizophrenia Research, 26*, 631–658.

Wallace, K. and Wheeler, J. (2002) Reliability generalization of the life satisfaction index. *Educational and Psychological Measurement, 62*, 674–684.

Wiersma, D., Wanderling, J., Dragomirecka, E. *et al.* (2000) Social disability in schizophrenia: its development and prediction over 15 years in incidence cohorts in six European centres. *Psychological Medicine, 30*, 1155–1167.

Wigfield, A. and Eccles, J. S. (2000) Expectancy-value theory of achievement motivation. *Contemporary Educational Psychology, 25*, 68–81.

Wykes, T., Parr, A.M. and Landau, S. (1999) Group treatment of auditory hallucinations. Exploratory study of effectiveness. *British Journal of Psychiatry, 175*, 180–185.

Wykes, T., Steel, C., Everitt, B. *et al.* (2008) Cognitive behavior therapy for schizophrenia: Effect sizes, clinical models, and methodological rigor. *Schizophrenia Bulletin, 34*, 523–537.

10

Brief Acceptance and Commitment Therapy for the Acute Treatment of Hospitalized Patients with Psychosis

Brandon A. Gaudiano

Overview of ACT for Psychosis

Over the past two decades, numerous clinical trials have demonstrated the efficacy and effectiveness of cognitive-behavioural therapies for psychosis (CBTp) when combined with traditional medication treatment (Gaudiano, 2006; Rathod *et al.* 2010). Today, 'CBT' has come to denote a loose family of related interventions that share certain principles and procedures (Gaudiano, 2008). In *traditional* CBTp, cognitive strategies (e.g. Socratic questioning, cognitive restructuring) are introduced to target delusions and dysfunctional beliefs related to hallucinations, whereas behavioural interventions (e.g. problem solving, goal setting, pleasant events scheduling) are used as 'experiments' to provide information that will correct dysfunctional beliefs about psychotic experiences and to counteract negative symptoms such as anhedonia (Kingdon and Turkington, 2005). However, Tai and Turkington (2009) recently described how traditional CBTp has evolved over the years. They note that although earlier approaches emphasized identifying and reappraising distorted thinking patterns related to psychosis, newer CBT approaches are increasingly exploring ways to utilize acceptance versus change strategies to help patients cope with symptoms. Acceptance and Commitment Therapy (ACT; pronounced as the word not the individual letters) is one example of a newer CBT

CBT for Schizophrenia: Evidence-Based Interventions and Future Directions,
First Edition. Edited by Craig Steel.
© 2013 John Wiley & Sons, Ltd. Published 2013 by John Wiley & Sons, Ltd.

approach that uses mindfulness and acceptance in place of direct cognitive changes strategies (Hayes *et al.*, 1999). ACT has been applied successfully to a number of clinical and non-clinical problems (Hayes *et al.*, 2006). Recent meta-analyses of clinical trials demonstrate that ACT is efficacious for a wide range of disorders and effect size improvements are at least on par with more traditional CBT (Hayes *et al.*, 2006; Öst, 2008; Levin and Hayes, 2009; Powers *et al.*, 2009). First, a brief overview of ACT is presented, followed by a discussion of research applying it to psychosis.

What is ACT?

A detailed description of ACT theory and technique is beyond the scope of the current chapter, and thus it will only be summarized briefly here. Readers are referred to other books that provide a more comprehensive description of the approach (Hayes *et al.*, 1999; Hayes and Strosahl, 2004). ACT is rooted in a philosophy of radical behaviourism and proposes a newer behaviour analytic account of language and cognition (Hayes *et al.*, 2001). In essence, ACT combines acceptance and mindfulness strategies with overt behaviour change efforts to improve psychological flexibility. *Psychological flexibility* is defined as 'the ability to contact the present moment more fully as a conscious human being, and to either change or persist when doing so serves valued ends' (Hayes *et al.*, 2004). It is theorized that healthy psychological functioning is related to a person's ability to adaptively respond to an ever-changing environment. The opposite of this is psychological *in*flexibility or rigidity, which is proposed to underlie most, if not all psychopathology. In ACT, psychological rigidity is understood to be the result of the processes of cognitive fusion and experiential avoidance. *Cognitive fusion* is defined as 'the tendency of human beings to live in a world excessively structured by literal language' (Strosahl *et al.*, 2004). When a person is fused with cognitions, he/she is treating thoughts as literal descriptions of reality. For example, when a person is fused with a thought ('I am crazy'), he/she is experiencing that thought literally ('I'='crazy'). This cognitive fusion permits the content of thinking to dominate a person's behavioural responses and choices ('I can't have a successful relationship because I'm crazy'). Cognitive fusion also encourages *experiential avoidance*, which is defined as 'the attempt to escape or avoid the form, frequency, or situational sensitivity of private events, even when the attempt to do so causes psychological harm (Hayes *et al.*, 2004). When engaged in experiential avoidance, the person attempts to avoid or suppress undesirable private material such as thoughts, memories, emotions and bodily sensations as if they were inherently harmful, even though doing so can paradoxically worsen these problems

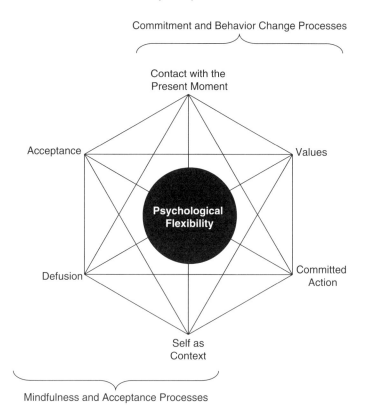

Figure 10.1   The six core ACT processes and their relationship to psychological flexibility (adapted from Hayes *et al.*, 2006)

in the long-run. ACT targets six processes which promote psychological flexibility: 1) acceptance or *willingness* to experience distressing internal experiences; 2) cognitive *de*-fusion so that the literal content of unhelpful thinking is delinked from behavioural choices; 3) awareness of ongoing mental events as they occur in the present moment; 4) a stable sense of self that is separable from its evaluative or descriptive content; 5) personally-defined values that serve as guides for meaningful behaviours and goals; and 6) committed actions that are consistent with those chosen values (see Figure 10.1).

ACT utilizes a variety of techniques and strategies to achieve these goals, many of which are inspired by or borrowed from other approaches to psychotherapy (e.g. humanistic, gestalt) (Hayes *et al.*, 1999). In particular, ACT makes liberal use of metaphors, stories, paradoxes and experiential exercises in addition to behavioural techniques such as behavioural activation and exposure. Experiential components of intervention strategies are stressed so that patients can experience the various ACT processes *in vivo*. ACT can be thought of as more eclectic at the level of technique than traditional CBT; although ACT is theoretically rooted in a particular form of behaviourism. The goal of these ACT strategies is to improve psychological flexibility by fostering acceptance of internal states of distress and cognitive defusion from problematic language-based processes.

How Does ACT Differ from Traditional CBT?

ACT and traditional CBT have similarities and differences. In terms of their similarities, Forman and Herbert (2009) note that both approaches emphasize the current and future more than the past; help people cope with distress; understand cognitions as observable and distinguishable from the self; foster increased awareness of internal experiences; incorporate behavioural strategies such as behavioural activation and exposure; employ 'homework' assignments between sessions; and emphasize the importance of a collaborative therapist–client relationship.

In terms of differences noted by Forman and Herbert (2009), traditional CBT proposes that psychiatric disorders have distinctive patterns of cognitive biases (Beck, 2008). In contrast, ACT posits that psychopathology is the result of the broader problem of psychological inflexibility which stems from ineffective attempts to control or avoid internal experiences (Hayes *et al.*, 2006). In terms of techniques, a CBT approach stresses the importance of identifying, evaluating and modifying specific distorted cognitions to correct information processing biases using strategies such as Socratic questioning, rational deliberation and behavioural experiments. ACT employs a broader array of techniques and strategies (e.g., metaphors, meditation exercises, paradoxical interventions) that are used to foster the six core processes of defusion, acceptance, present moment awareness, self-as-context, values clarification and committed action. ACT views the traditional CBT emphasis on directly targeting putatively distorted or dysfunctional cognitions as limited in utility and largely unnecessary. In contrast, ACT teaches meta-cognitive skills characterized by broader defusion strategies and promotes increased willingness to experience internal sources of distress (e.g. negative cognitions) in the service of valued goal attainment. CBT proposes that the treatment works by directly altering information processing biases using cognitive techniques, leading to symptomatic improvement. In contrast, ACT proposes that targeting excessive cognitive fusion and avoidance of internal distress improve psychological flexibility and lead to therapeutic improvement. ACT focuses more of the *process* of thinking, whereas traditional CBT focuses more on the *content*. Although CBT considers a variety of positive treatment outcomes, health has traditionally been defined as the alleviation of psychiatric symptoms. In contrast, the primary goal of ACT is living a self-defined valued life regardless of symptoms.

Research Related to ACT for Psychosis

Studies on the coping strategies of patients with psychosis support taking a more acceptance-based stance toward psychotic symptoms. Romme and Escher (1989) observed that individuals experiencing voices appeared to benefit from naturally increasing their acceptance of these experiences and using adaptive coping strategies to minimize the negative effects of these symptoms. Falloon and Talbot (1981) reported that attempts to suppress auditory hallucinations were ineffective in a sample of 40 patients with chronic schizophrenia. Farhall and Gehrke (1997) interviewed 81 patients with hallucinations and reported that 'resistance' coping efforts predicted poor distress reduction. Escher and colleagues (2003) reported that higher levels of 'coping defenses' at baseline were predictive of negative outcomes in a sample of adolescents who heard voices. Tait and colleagues (2003, 2004) followed patients after an acute psychotic episode for 6 months and found that a 'sealing-over' recovery style (i.e. characterized by avoidance of the psychotic experience) was associated with a history of negative childhood experiences, current negative self-evaluative beliefs and poor treatment engagement. More recently, Shawyer *et al.* (2007) investigated coping strategies that are more specifically targeted by ACT (i.e. experiential avoidance vs. acceptance). These researchers piloted a questionnaire called the Voices Acceptance and Action Scale (VAAS) in a sample of 43 patients with psychosis. Results showed that greater acceptance of voices was associated with lower depression, greater quality of life and greater confidence in resistant command hallucinations.

Several research groups are currently exploring the benefits from explicitly teaching patients to adopt more mindful and acceptance-based coping strategies for dealing with their psychotic symptoms. Mindfulness refers to bringing a non-judgmental awareness to a person's moment-to-moment experiences (Kabat-Zinn, 1994), with meditation practices being the most common method for fostering mindfulness. Chadwick and colleagues (2005, 2009) have shown the acceptability and potential benefits of a group-based meditation intervention for patients with psychosis in two preliminary studies. In addition, Chadwick (2006) has developed a more traditional cognitive-behavioural approach that includes mindfulness and acceptance components called Person-Based Cognitive Therapy for Distressing Psychosis, with preliminary support reported in an open trial (Dannahy *et al.*, 2011). Furthermore, Johnson and colleagues (2009) have presented case studies showing promising results for the use of a specific type of practice called loving-kindness meditation for improving negative symptoms associated with schizophrenia. However, to date only ACT has been studied in clinical trials with hospitalized patients with acute psychotic illnesses.

Most of the research on traditional CBTp has been conducted in psychiatric outpatient samples. Considerably less research has focused on CBTp for hospitalized patients with acute psychosis (Gaudiano, 2005); although what evidence is available supports interventions adapted for this population (Drury *et al.*, 1996; Hall and Tarrier, 2003; Startup *et al.*, 2004). Research also has shown that ACT provides a potentially usefully intervention for hospitalized patients with psychosis.

Bach and Hayes (2002) conducted the first study of ACT in the treatment of schizophrenia and related psychotic-spectrum disorders. Eighty patients with psychotic symptoms were randomly assigned to treatment as usual (TAU) or TAU plus four individual sessions of ACT beginning during a psychiatric hospitalization. Patients were encouraged to accept unavoidable events, to simply notice their psychotic symptoms without treating them as either true or false, and to identify and work toward valued goals despite whatever symptoms they might be experiencing. Self-ratings of the frequency, distress, and believability of psychotic symptoms were collected at pre-treatment and 4-month follow-up, along with rehospitalization data from medical records. The ACT group showed a significantly higher reporting of psychotic symptoms but lower believability in those symptoms compared with the TAU only group. This was interpreted as signifying that ACT patients were more accepting of their psychotic symptoms and thus more willing to report them. Rehospitalization rates in the ACT group (20 percent) were significantly lower than in the TAU only group (40 percent) at follow up. A 1-year follow up study continued to demonstrate lower rehospitalization rates in the ACT condition (Bach *et al.*, 2012).

Gaudiano and Herbert (2006) conducted a similar study on ACT for psychiatric inpatients with active psychotic symptoms. Patients (n=40) were randomly assigned to an enhanced treatment as usual (ETAU) condition or ETAU plus ACT. The number of ACT sessions varied based on length of hospital stay (an average of 3 over approximately 1 week) and were delivered in place of other milieu therapy provided to patients in the ETAU condition. Hospital care was enhanced by providing assessment information to the treatment team and informal support and brief check-ins to patients. This design helped to control for the potential confound of additional treatment in the Bach and Hayes (2002) study. Results showed that patients receiving ACT showed greater improvements in clinician-rated mood symptoms, self-reported impairment in social functioning and clinically significant changes (greater than 2 standard deviations improvement) in overall psychiatric severity relative to the ETAU group at hospital discharge. Both groups showed similar reductions in the self-reported and clinician-rated frequency and severity of psychotic symptoms by discharge. However, the ACT condition improved significantly more on hallucination-related distress. Only the ACT group showed significant decreases in believability of hallucinations over time. At 4-month follow up, the ACT group (28 percent) showed similar reductions in rehospitalization rates compared to the ETAU group (45 percent). A survival analysis controlling for baseline severity indicated that the time to rehospitalization was significantly lower in the ACT compared with ETAU condition (Bach *et al.*, in press).

Results from these studies also provide initial support for the theorized mechanisms of action of ACT for psychosis. Follow-up analyses showed that the effect of treatment condition on hallucination distress was statistically mediated by hallucination believability (Gaudiano *et al.*, 2010). This finding is consistent with the model that ACT produced greater changes in hallucination distress by decreasing hallucination believability compared with the TAU alone group. Hallucination believability was conceptualized as a measure of psychological flexibility and cognitive defusion in the study. Furthermore, an analysis conducted on the combined data from the Gaudiano and Herbert (2006) and Bach and Hayes (2002) studies showed that reductions in psychotic symptom believability also statistically mediated the effect of treatment on rehospitalization rates (Bach *et al.*, in press). However, further research with larger samples is needed. Currently, a study is underway comparing ACT versus supportive counselling for outpatients with medication-resistant psychosis (Thomas *et al.*, 2010).

Clinical Implications

There are a number of clinical implications that can be drawn from the two clinical trials of ACT for psychosis (Bach and Hayes, 2002; Gaudiano and Herbert, 2006). First, they show that hospitalization may represent a unique opportunity to engage patients in novel coping strategies for psychosis. Patients typically arrive at the hospital due to a crisis and there is an opportunity to bring awareness to the ways in which they are coping with psychotic experiences that may be counterproductive or unhelpful (e.g. excessive attempts at control or suppression). Furthermore, ACT offers unique strategies for engaging patients suffering from acute psychosis. Traditional CBTp approaches emphasize the need for a more extensive period of rapport building prior to instating strategies specifically targeting psychotic symptoms (Kingdon and Turkington, 2005). The studies of ACT for psychosis demonstrate that work can begin on active psychotic symptoms during the first session by emphasizing acceptance and mindfulness versus change of these experiences. Particularly in the US, the typical psychiatric hospital length of stay is relatively short, often less than a week in duration (Mechanic *et al.*, 1998). The ACT studies demonstrate that this approach can be adapted for very short hospital stays. Furthermore, the Gaudiano and Herbert study implemented ACT so that it could be used for varying lengths of stay. Each session was designed as a self-contained intervention that included all the major components of ACT. Different themes were rotated across sessions but patients could complete as many sessions as their stay would permit, making treatment delivery practical and responsive to the realities of routine practice settings. Also relevant to routine practice, ACT for psychosis research shows that the approach can be applied to patients with various diagnoses without the need to change major aspects of the treatment. The ACT studies contained patients diagnosed with both primary psychotic disorders such as schizophrenia as well as primary affective disorders such as psychotic depression. The primary study inclusion criterion was the presence of active psychotic symptoms. Finally, results of these studied showed that patients could benefit from interventions that focus on treatment targets other than symptom reduction as the primary goal. Psychosocial interventions can target outcomes that are not typically addressed by pharmacologic treatments, such as quality of life, social and occupational functioning, self-esteem, and personal goal attainment. For example, brief ACT treatment reduced rehospitalization rates and Gaudiano and Herbert (2006) showed that it decreased impairment related to illness. In summary, ACT for psychosis research shows that relatively low-intensity interventions provided to patients during an acute phase of illness in the hospital can produce better short and longer-term outcomes compared with routine care.

ACT for Psychosis Treatment Protocol

As mentioned, the treatment protocol used in the Gaudiano and Herbert (2006) study permitted patients to participate in treatment according to their length of stay on the hospital unit. In these 'stand alone' ACT sessions, all essential elements of the treatment were presented briefly during each session, including the basic ACT model, interventions to promote an acceptance and mindful stance toward private events in general and hallucinations and delusions in particular, as well as values and goals clarification work. Each 1-hour session contained a core set of components, and various themes were rotated over subsequent sessions. For example, regarding the presentation of the ACT rationale, the first session focused on examining unsuccessful past attempts to cope with symptoms, and

Box 10.1 Outline of ACT for hospitalized patients with psychosis

I. Session A
  a. Provide a normalizing rationale for psychotic symptoms (5 min)
  b. ACT Model (10 min)
     i. Explore avoidance-based coping and acceptance as an alternative
     ii. Describe the *Polygraph Metaphor* (pp. 123–124)*
  c. Acceptance/Mindfulness Exercise (15 min)
     i. Introduce mindfulness as the nonjudgmental awareness of present moment experience
     ii. Practice the *Leaves on the Stream Meditation* (pp. 159–161)
  d. Values/Goals Clarification (15 min)
     i. Elicit valued areas (e.g. family, relationships, work, health, recreation, etc.) and discuss specific behavioural goals consistent with values
     ii. Describe the *Skiing Metaphor* (pp. 220–221)
  e. Review 'take home' messages of the session
  f. Assign Homework (5–10 min)
     i. Practice brief (10 min twice daily) meditation exercises
     ii. Complete one values-consistent goal that can be accomplished immediately

II. Session B
  a. Review homework
  b. Discuss the continuum of normal and psychotic experiences
  c. ACT Model
     i. Introduce the concept of workability as a guide to choosing coping strategies
     ii. Describe the *Tug of War with a Monster Metaphor* (p. 109)
  d. Acceptance/Mindfulness Exercise
     i. Introduce wiliness of unwanted private events as an alternative to avoidance
     ii. Conduct *Contents on Cards Exercise* (p. 162)
  e. Values/Goals Clarification
     i. Promote commitment toward valued goals
     ii. Describe the *Gardening Metaphor* (p. 220)
  f. Review 'take home' messages from session
  g. Assign Homework

(continued)

Box 10.1   (cont'd)

    i. Choose to carry an index card with a distressing thought/
      voice written on it throughout the day
    ii. Complete one values-consistent goal

III. Session C
  a. Review homework
  b. Describe how life events affect symptoms
  c. ACT Model
    i. Discuss how the patient responds to unwanted experiences
      and their consequences
    ii. Introduce the *'Dirty' versus 'Clean' Discomfort Exercise* (p. 147)
  d. Acceptance/Mindfulness Exercise
    i. Explore how one can choose to remain consistent with
      goals despite what the mind 'says'
    ii. Conduct *'I Can't Do This' Exercise* (p. 162)
  e. Values/Goals Clarification
    i. Describe how setbacks and challenges are a natural part of
      moving along the valued life path
    ii. Describe the *Path Up the Mountain Metaphor* (p. 222)
  f. Review 'take home' messages from session
  g. Assign Homework
    i. Complete one values-consistent goal
    ii. Notice what the mind 'says' while completing valued goals

IV. Session D
  a. Review homework
  b. Discuss medication adherence and how it relates to valued goals
  c. ACT Model
    i. Help the person to contact a stable sense of self that is
      separate from his/her transient mental events
    ii. Describe the *Chessboard Metaphor* (pp. 190–192)
  d. Acceptance/Mindfulness Exercise
    i. Discuss how to identify avoidance and choose acceptance
      instead
    ii. Practice using the *FEAR/ACT algorithms* (pp. 245–246)
  e. Values/Goals Clarification
    i. Discuss willingness in the service of valued goal attainment
    ii. Describe the *Swamp Metaphor* (p. 248)
  f. Review 'take home' messages from session
  g. Assign Homework
    i. Use FEAR/ACT algorithm cards
    ii. Complete one values-consistent goal

Note: Page numbers refer to the text by Hayes *et al.*, 1999

introduced the concepts of acceptance and willingness as alternatives to control-oriented strategies. Future sessions expanded upon the work completed in the previous sessions, and introduced new concepts consistent with the ACT rationale, such as workability as a guide to coping, and the concept of an observer-self that is distinct from one's transient private experiences. Each session was designed to be self-contained, so that patients could participate in treatment as their length of stay dictated. An expanded session-by-session outline is presented in Box 10.1.

Session Summaries

Each session begins with a brief psychoeducational discussion. This serves the purpose of helping the therapist to begin the process of establishing rapport in a non-threatening way. In the initial session, the therapist discusses with the patient his/her hallucinatory or delusional experiences and provides a normalizing rationale. The therapist presents psychotic experiences as largely understandable reactions to various life situations and stressors. The therapist also might note other situations in which unusual beliefs or confusing sensory experiences can be produced (e.g. sleep deprivation).

Next the ACT model is introduced. As discussed, each session focuses on a different ACT-consistent theme. In the initial session, the therapist turns to a discussion of the ways in which the patient has attempted to cope with psychotic symptoms in the past. Unhelpful attempts to avoid or struggle with these symptoms are explored. The therapist highlights attempts by the patient to avoid or struggle with symptoms that paradoxically seem to cause increased distress, intensity or impairment. Stories such as the *Polygraph Metaphor* can be presented to explore the unworkability of controlling internal experiences. In this metaphor, the therapist describes a hypothetical 'anxiety' detector, similar to a lie detector, which happens to be 100 percent accurate. The patient is told that if he/she can remain completely free from any anxiety or nervousness for 30 minutes while hooked up to this machine, the person will win a reward (e.g. $1 million). However, if the machine detects any anxiety at all, the person will experience some bad outcome (e.g. being sentenced to life in prison). The story illustrates that sometimes no matter how much a person may be motivated to suppress unwanted internal experiences, it may be impossible to succeed in this goal. The therapist can then relate this story back to the previous discussion of the patient's experiences attempting to cope with psychotic symptoms and the paradoxical results that this produces.

Various experiential exercises can be conducted to help the patient work on ACT concepts in the present moment with the help of the therapist. For example, the experience of mindfulness can be introduced using various meditation practices. With mindfulness, the patient is asked to simply notice what the mind is doing in the present moment without treating it as true or false. This also is applied to any psychotic symptoms that may arise during the session. The therapist makes no attempt to challenge the validity of these experiences directly, but also refrains from colluding with the patient and reinforcing these symptoms. Instead, a stance of non-judgmental awareness is encouraged and modelled by the therapist. In the *Leaves on the Stream Meditation*, patients are asked to visualize leaves falling into a stream and to place any thoughts or feelings that arise on these leaves and watch them flow down the stream without trying to control them. The stated goal of this exercise is not to produce relaxation per se, but to teach non-judgmental awareness of the person's transient mental events. At first, patients often struggle and have difficulty letting go of their internal experiences when attempting to place them on their mental leaves. The therapist then parallels this experience with the previous discussion of how the person has attempted to cope with other symptoms in daily life. The therapist emphasizes that the aim of the meditation exercise is not to produce any particular outcome (e.g. to have less 'leaves') and that simply doing the exercise itself is considered a success.

Some reports suggest that intensive meditation practices are contraindicated in acutely psychotic individuals because they may pro-mote an unhelpful internal focus in those who already have reality testing problems (Sethi and Bhargava, 2003). Although as other research suggests that patients with active psychosis can benefit from relatively intensive meditation (Chadwick *et al.*, 2005), the use of these practices should be based on a careful clinical assessment of the particular patient. In cases in which the patient may be too actively psychotic, meditation exercises should be adapted to be less intensive or internally focused, such as practicing the mindful eating of a raison (Kabat-Zinn, 1990). The *Leaves on the Stream Meditation* is practiced only briefly (approximately 10 minutes) for this reason, or this activity is substituted for another ACT experiential exercise. ACT provides other ways of promoting mindfulness that do not involve intensive meditation practice, such as the *Take Your Mind for a Walk Exercise* (Hayes *et al.*, 1999, p. 163). In this exercise, the therapist follows behind the patient and acts as his/her 'mind,' making observations and commenting out loud while the person walks or does certain activities.

The concept of values is also introduced in the initial session. The therapist explores possible values that may be relevant to the patient (e.g. family, romantic relationships, work, health). Values are described as the things that give a person's life meaning and purpose. One relevant value is picked and discussed in more detail to produce an expanded narrative so that it can be individualized for the patient. Discrepancies between the person's valued area and his/her daily actions are highlighted. Often these discrepancies are associated with distress on the part of the patient. The therapist suggests that being more consistent with values can lead to a more fulfilling and healthy life. Specific behavioural goals are then discussed and a plan for implementing them after the session is developed. The therapist can present values as the person's life 'compass' that helps him/her to determine in which direction to move when he/she is uncertain. In contrast, goals are likened to a specific set of directions that tells the person how to get from point A to point B. The *Skiing Metaphor* is a story that highlights how the ongoing process of working toward values is important and meaningful in and of itself regardless of the specific outcome obtained (Hayes *et al.*, 1999).

Many hospitalized patients have cognitive limitations for a number of reasons, such as medication side effects, organic impairments or severe emotional distress. Therefore, the therapist reviews the take home messages of the session before concluding. The patient is then asked to complete homework assignments between sessions. In the initial session, he/she may be encouraged to practice the brief meditation exercise introduced twice daily for 10 minutes each. A recording with the meditation instructions can be provided to facilitate this. In addition, the patient is encouraged to complete one value-consistent behaviour discussed during session. The action should be a relatively small one that can be accomplished in between sessions, and the therapist always emphasizes the consistency between the action and the stated value as important. Mindfulness and acceptance can be applied to perceived barriers around goal completion.

Although delivering all the content of such a session in 1 hour may sound ambitious, the goal is for the therapist to simply begin to introduce these concepts to the patient. The conversation should flow naturally and move from topic to topic easily. The therapist does not overly focus on any one ACT process and attempt to train the person to expertise in it. Instead, the therapist remains flexible and adapts the content as needed to ensure direct relevance to the patient and his/her current experiences. Metaphors and exercises are chosen that are most relevant to the patient, and can be substituted for others that map onto the ACT processes. The therapist takes the lead from the patient and encourages the person to develop his/her own relevant stories and metaphors based on personal experience. Ultimately, the focus of each session is on helping the person to engage in more flexible coping strategies related to their psychotic symptoms and to use this as a vehicle for behaviour change.

The other sessions follow the same format but focus on related themes to further deepen and expand upon the ACT processes covered. In the second session, the choice of acceptance or willingness to experience an unwanted feeling is highlighted as an alternative to avoiding or struggling with it. The *Tug of War with a Monster* can be used to illustrate this alternative approach. The therapist asks the patient to imagine being in a life-or-death struggle with a horrible monster and he/she is sliding toward an abyss that is in between them. The option of simply 'dropping the rope' is explored and then applied to troublesome symptoms that the patient may be experiencing. In the *Contents on Cards Exercise*, distressing thoughts and feelings can be written down on index cards and the patient can then practice choosing to hold on to them versus trying to avoid them. The physicalizing of these experiences on the cards is theorized to promote distancing so that patients can explore alternative ways of coping with them. Homework can involve patients taking one of these cards (e.g. with the content of a distressing voice written down on it) with them between sessions to keep in their pockets. Values work is continued, and the *Gardening Metaphor* can be used to stress the importance of maintaining consistency with values even when there is no immediate reward. The therapist also continues to help the patient to formulate additional values-consistent goals to work on between sessions.

Additional sessions emphasize other relevant ACT processes. For example, the concept of 'dirty' versus 'clean' discomfort can be introduced in the third session. Clean discomfort is described as the uncontrollable life stress and negative events that happen to the person that are largely out of his/her control and provoke negative feelings. This is differentiated from the 'dirty' discomfort, or the negative feelings one has about being upset in the first place. Avoidance and struggle with the clean discomfort is highlighted as producing the additional distress. The therapist helps the person to accept or make more room for the clean discomfort. Sometimes this dirty discomfort is produced by the mind when the patient 'buys into' it in unhelpful ways. The therapist may attempt the *'I Can't Do This' Exercise* with the patient. In this experiential exercise, patients are instructed to complete a simple task (e.g. picking up a pen and holding it) while simultaneously repeating out loud that they cannot do the task that they are presently performing ('I can't hold this pen. I can't hold this pen…'). This represents a defusion exercise that helps patients to differentiate between what the mind tells them to do and what they can choose to do instead. This can be related to coping with command hallucinations that may instruct the patient to do things that they do not want to do. Patients learn that they can choose to behave in ways consistent with their valued goals despite what the voices command. Values work also continues in each session, and the *Path Up the Mountain Metaphor* is used to illustrate how setbacks and challenges are an inherent part of the journey and can be worked through to remain committed to their valued direction.

The final session format emphasizes the concept of the self-as-context in ACT. The therapist helps the patient to contact a more stable and consistent part of their self (self-as-context) that can be the observer of the evaluative content of their mind (self-as-content). This concept is not explained in an abstract or technical way. Instead, the *Chessboard Metaphor* is used to illustrate this idea. An actual chess set is helpful for this purpose. The chess pieces are used as examples of the content of the mind (e.g. depression, voices, low self-esteem, persecutory thoughts). The patient is encouraged to name each piece in relation to a distressing symptom. 'Good' pieces are also named by the patient. These pieces are contrasted with the chessboard, which represents the self-as-context, or the stable part of the self that holds the pieces. The therapist explains that whereas the chess pieces are engaged in a constant battle with each other that is endless (i.e. once one side wins the game starts over again), the board simply holds the pieces and is not directly affected by the game, regardless of which side wins and loses. The therapist may encourage patients to try 'being the chessboard' when they feel that they are struggling and getting caught up with their mental 'pieces' so that they can observe their mental content without reacting to it. In addition, the FEAR and ACT algorithms can be introduced at this point. This is a mnemonic device to help the patient remember and apply these strategies outside sessions. Patients are taught to identify when they are in the state of F.E.A.R.: F = 'Fused' with their thoughts; E = Evaluating themselves; A = Avoiding their experiences; and R = Reason giving for their problems. They are encouraged to A.C.T instead: A = Accept and stay present; C = Choose a valued direction; and T = Take action. The FEAR/ACT exercise can be presented in the form of worksheet that patients can complete between sessions. Psychotic symptom frequency, believability and associated distress can be assessed before each session to identify changes related to the treatment (See Box 10.2).

Case Illustration

Dawn, a 41-year-old African-American woman, was diagnosed with schizoaffective disorder, depressive type. She also was HIV positive and had a history of cocaine dependence in full sustained remission. She was on permanent disability due to her mental illness and lived in a group home. Dawn was admitted to the hospital after she was contacted out of the blue by her biological father. She described her father as sexually and physically abusive to her as a child, and this recent contact with him triggered increased symptoms of depression and psychosis. Dawn experienced disparaging voices that sometimes suggested suicide. She also developed paranoid delusions and started to believe that her housemates

Box 10.2   Self-ratings of psychotic symptoms

Specific hallucination assessed:_____

_____

Specific delusion assessed:_____

_____

Frequency

1. On average, how often have you heard voices [*or seen (hallucination); or thought about (delusion), as appropriate*] in the past week?
   (1) never, (2) less than once a week, (3) about once a week, (4) several times a week, (5) daily, (6) more than once a day, (7) almost constant

   1a. Hallucinations _____   1b. Delusions _____

Distress

2. On a scale from 0 to 10, how bothered are you when you hear the voices [*or see (hallucination); or think about (delusion), as appropriate*]? Zero means not bothered at all and 10 means the most bothered you've ever been.

   ```
         0    1    2    3    4    5    6    7    8    9    10
         L    /    /    /    /    /    /    /    /    /    L
   Not bothered                                    Most bothered
      at all                                    you've ever been
   ```

   2a. Hallucinations _____   2b. Delusions _____

Believability

3. On a scale from 0 to 10, how much do you believe that when you hear voices [*or when you see (hallucination); or when your think about (delusion) as appropriate*] that they are real [*or that it is true (for delusion)*]? Zero means that you are certain it is not real or true, and 10 means you are absolutely certain that it is real or true.

   ```
         0    1    2    3    4    5    6    7    8    9    10
         L    /    /    /    /    /    /    /    /    /    L
   Certain not                                        Certain
   real or true                             it is real or true
   ```

   3a. Hallucinations _____   3b. Delusions _____

Adapted from Bach and Hayes (2002) and Gaudiano and Herbert (2006) were conspiring to get her removed from the group home. This led her to become increasingly isolative and she stopped going to the vocational training job that she had previously found enjoyable.

Dawn was polite and cooperative on the inpatient unit but often isolated and failed to attend therapy groups. For the initial part of the session, Dawn was slow to warm up and exhibited poor eye contact. During the psychoeducational discussion, Dawn responded minimally, although she appeared to be interested in hearing what the therapist was saying. The therapist explained to Dawn that he had read her medical chart and encouraged Dawn to talk about her experience with voices and concerns about her housemates. At first she was reluctant to discuss these experiences with the therapist, but the therapist asked her to help him understand what problems might have led up to her recent hospitalization.

Dawn described how she would try to stop the voices by isolating in her room and sleeping because the voices seemed to be triggered by social interactions or trips outside the house. However, she acknowledged that the voices would only stop for a while and then return. She also described arguing with the voices ('Sometimes I stand up to them') and trying to contradict what they were saying about her (e.g. that she is a terrible person, a sinner, and that she didn't deserve to live). However, she noted that they would often increase in intensity when she attempted to argue with them. The voices also filled her head with thoughts about how her housemates were conspiring against her. Given her inability to escape these voices, even after becoming increasingly isolative, Dawn reported that she began feeling very hopeless and contemplating suicide by stepping in front of a moving car. The therapist used this opportunity to describe the *Polygraph Metaphor*. He first explained that sometimes he would relate stories to help her to make sense out of her experiences. Dawn's affect changed as the therapist related the story and she began to smile at times. At first, Dawn was confused by the discussion, but then after the therapist was finished with the story she started to relate it to her experiences. She described to the therapist how she had been shy as a child and would get anxious around groups of people and so predicted she would not be able to remain anxiety free. The therapist acknowledged that he would probably not fair any better in this situation, and that perhaps it is normal reaction. The therapist also encouraged Dawn to relate this story to her experience with her voices. She noted that she had never thought of her voices in this way before but that it made sense to her based on her experience that the more she tried to control them the more it seemed to make the voices worse.

Next, the therapist asked Dawn if she would be willing to try a meditation exercise to practice a different way of coping with these distressing thoughts and feelings. She reported that she had tried relaxation techniques before in therapy but the therapist clarified how meditation was different. Dawn was willing to try the exercise and the therapist played a recording of the meditation instructions, practicing the exercise with her. During the debriefing by the therapist Dawn reported experiencing frustration over not being able to keep her mind focused on the visualization. The therapist used this as an opportunity to stress that the goal of the exercise was simply the process of doing it and the fact that her mind wandered was not a problem but simply part of the experience. He suggested that she might be able to apply this practice to some of the things that were causing her distress, like her feelings of hopelessness and her disparaging voices.

Next the therapist introduced the values clarification work. Dawn described the importance of her vocational training job and her goal of eventually working full time and moving into an independent living situation. However, she noted that in the weeks preceding the hospitalization she had stopped going to vocational training in an attempt to control her increasing symptoms. Dawn felt guilty about this and embarrassed about the prospect of returning to the job following discharge. The therapist explored Dawn's value of 'work' in more detail. Working gave Dawn a sense of purpose and hope about the future, and she felt good after learning a new skill and applying it successfully. The therapist suggested that it might be helpful for Dawn to start moving in her valued direction, but that this would require her to learn to make more room for the negative feelings that could arise during this process. He suggested that she make a small goal for herself that was consistent with her value of work. Dawn agreed to call her employer between sessions to let her know that she was in the hospital, give her an update as to her progress, and discuss the possibility of returning to work after she recovered.

Future sessions with Dawn built upon the themes of the first session. Willingness as an alternative to avoidance was explored in more detail. The therapist encouraged Dawn to increase her willingness to experience negative thoughts and feelings while remaining consistent with her valued goals. He related the *Tug of War with a Monster Metaphor* to Dawn and helped her to practice 'letting go of the rope' when she found herself struggling with negative feelings that distracted her from her goals. At times, Dawn reported that she heard the voices during the session. The therapist used this as an opportunity to help Dawn practice taking a more mindful and accepting stance toward this experience while choosing to remain engaged in the session despite what the voices might be saying. Dawn expressed concerns at times about taking medications for her symptoms because she perceived it as a weakness and related it to her previous addiction with cocaine. The therapist helped Dawn to conceptualize medication treatment in the context of her values. Taking medications was presented to Dawn as something she chooses to do in service of her values of work and health as she acknowledged that they have been useful for these purposes in the past.

Dawn began to attend more therapy groups on the unit between sessions and no longer avoided them simply because she may be experiencing voice. However, Dawn's increasing social interaction on the unit would sometimes provoke paranoid thoughts about other patients and staff. Instead of trying to directly undermine the validity of these fears, the therapist asked Dawn to try to simply make more room for these thoughts and choose to carry them along with her while she continued working toward her goals. The *Chessboard Metaphor* appeared to be a helpful concept that Dawn could use to remind herself to defuse from these thoughts when they got in the way of what she wanted to do. Dawn completed four sessions over a period of 8 days. Upon discharge, Dawn reported less distress and believability about her voices, even though they were still occurring at times. She also expressed a desire to return to her vocational job following discharge.

Conclusion

Given the need for and benefit derived from psychosocial approaches to psychosis as part of a patient's overall treatment program, ACT offers one approach that appears to be particularly useful and potentially efficacious for acutely hospitalized patients suffering from psychotic symptoms. Inpatients require a brief psychosocial approach that can be integrated into the hospital environment. The focus of ACT on acceptance and mindfulness provides patients with alternative coping strategies that may not be available as part of the other treatments they are receiving. It is hoped that through this type of therapy, patients will become more psychologically flexible in managing their symptoms, instead of over relying on control-oriented strategies that ultimately may prove counterproductive. Although preliminary research from two controlled studies suggests that ACT is safe and effective for psychotic inpatients, further research will be necessary to clarify better the similarities and differences between ACT and traditional CBT for psychosis, as well as ACT's efficacy compared with alternative approaches. Nevertheless, given the recognition of the current limitations of pharmacotherapy for psychosis, particularly as it relates to long-term improvement and functioning, ACT offers an approach that offers an opportunity to capitalize on the strengths of patients.

References

Bach, P., Gaudiano, B.A., Hayes, S.C. *et al.* (in press) Reduced believability of positive symptoms mediates improved hospitalization outcomes of acceptance and commitment therapy for psychosis. *Psychosis: Psychological, Social, and Integrative Aspects.*

Bach, P. and Hayes, S.C. (2002) The use of acceptance and commitment therapy to prevent the rehospitalization of psychotic patients: A randomized controlled trial. *Journal of Consulting and Clinical Psychology, 70*, 1129–1139.

Bach, P., Hayes, S.C. and Gallop, R. (2012) Long term effects of brief Acceptance and Commitment Therapy for Psychosis. *Behavior Modification, 36(2)*, 165–181.

Beck, A.T. (2008) The evolution of the cognitive model of depression and its neuro-biological correlates. *American Journal of Psychiatry, 165*, 969–977.

Chadwick, P. (2006) *Person-based Cognitive Therapy for Distressing Psychosis.* New York: John Wiley and Sons.

Chadwick, P., Hughes, S., Russell, D. *et al.* (2009) Mindfulness groups for distressing voices and paranoia: A replication and randomized feasibility trial. *Behavioural and Cognitive Psychotherapy, 37*, 403–412.

Chadwick, P., Taylor, K.N. and Abba, N. (2005) Mindfulness groups for people with psychosis. *Behavioural and Cognitive Psychotherapy, 33*, 351–359.

Dannahy, L., Hayward, M., Strauss, C. *et al.* (2011) Group person-based cognitive therapy for distressing voices: Pilot data from nine groups. *Journal of Behavior Therapy and Experimental Psychiatry, 42*, 111–116.

Drury, V., Birchwood, M., Cochrane, R. *et al.* (1996) Cognitive therapy and recovery from acute psychosis: A controlled trial. I. Impact on psychotic symptoms. *British Journal of Psychiatry, 169*, 593–601.

Escher, S., Delespaul, P., Romme, M. *et al.* (2003) Coping defence and depression in adolescents hearing voices. *Journal of Mental Health, 12*, 91–99.

Falloon, I.R.H. and Talbot, R.E. (1981) Persistent auditory hallucinations: Coping mechanisms and implications for management. *11*, 329–339.

Farhall, J. and Gehrke, M. (1997) Coping with hallucinations: Exploring stress and coping framework. *British Journal of Clinical Psychology, 36 (Pt 2)*, 259–261.

Forman, E.M. and Herbert, J.D. (2009) New directions in cognitive behavior therapy: Acceptance-based therapies. In W. O'Donohue and J. E. Fisher (eds) *General Principles and Empirically Supported Techniques of Cognitive Behavior Therapy* (pp. 102–114). Hoboken, NJ: John Wiley and Sons.

Gaudiano, B.A. (2005) Cognitive behavior therapies for psychotic disorders: Current empirical status and future directions. *Clinical Psychology: Science and Practice, 12*, 33–50.

Gaudiano, B.A. (2006) Is symptomatic improvement in clinical trials of cognitive-behavioral therapy for psychosis clinically significant? *Journal of Psychiatric Practice, 12*, 11–23.

Gaudiano, B.A. (2008) Cognitive-behavioural therapies: achievements and challenges. *Evidence Based Mental Health, 11*, 5–7.

Gaudiano, B.A. and Herbert, J.D. (2006) Acute treatment of inpatients with psychotic symptoms using acceptance and commitment therapy: Pilot results. *Behaviour Research and Therapy, 44*, 415–437.

Gaudiano, B.A., Herbert, J.D. and Hayes, S.C. (2010) Is it the symptom or the relation to it? Investigating potential mediators of change in acceptance and commitment therapy for psychosis. *Behavior Therapy, 41*, 543–554.

Hall, P.L. and Tarrier, N. (2003) The cognitive-behavioural treatment of low self-esteem in psychotic patients: A pilot study. *Behaviour Research and Therapy, 41,* 317–332.

Hayes, S.C., Barnes-Holmes, D. and Roche, B. (2001) *Relational Frame Theory: A Post-Skinnerian Account of Human Language and Cognition.* New York: Kluwer Academic/Plenum Publishers.

Hayes, S.C., Luoma, J.B., Bond, F.W. *et al.* (2006) Acceptance and commitment therapy: Model, processes and outcomes. *Behaviour Research and Therapy, 44,* 1–25.

Hayes, S.C. and Strosahl, K.D. (2004) *A Practical Guide to Acceptance and Commitment Therapy.* New York: Springer-Verlag.

Hayes, S.C., Strosahl, K.D., Bunting, K. *et al.* (2004) What is acceptance and commitment therapy? In S.C. Hayes and K.D. Strosahl (eds) *A Practical Guide to Acceptance and Commitment Therapy* (pp. 3–29). New York: Springer-Verlag.

Hayes, S.C., Strosahl, K.D. and Wilson, K.G. (1999) *Acceptance and Commitment Therapy: An Experiential Approach to Behavior Change.* New York: Guilford.

Johnson, D.P., Penn, D.L., Fredrickson, B.L. *et al.* (2009) Loving-kindness meditation to enhance recovery from negative symptoms of schizophrenia. *Journal of Clinical Psychology, 65,* 499–509.

Kabat-Zinn, J. (1990) *Full Catastrophe Living: Using the Wisdom of your Body and Mind to Face Stress, Pain, and Illness.* New York: Delta.

Kabat-Zinn, J. (1994) *Wherever You Go, There You Are: Mindfulness Meditation in Everyday Life.* New York: Hyperion Books.

Kingdon, D. G. and Turkington, D. (2005) *Cognitive Therapy of Schizophrenia,* 2nd edn. New York: Guilford Press.

Levin, M. and Hayes, S.C. (2009) Is acceptance and commitment therapy superior to established treatment comparisons? *Psychotherapy and Psychosomatics, 78,* 380.

Mechanic, D., McAlpine, D.D. and Olfson, M. (1998) Changing patterns of psychiatric inpatient care in the United States, 1988–1994. *Archives of General Psychiatry, 55,* 785–791.

Öst, L.-G. (2008) Efficacy of the third wave of behavioral therapies: A systematic review and meta-analysis. *Behaviour Research and Therapy, 46,* 296–321.

Powers, M.B., Zum, M.B. and Emmelkamp, P.M.G. (2009) Acceptance and commitment therapy: A meta-analytic review. *Psychotherapy and Psychosomatics, 78,* 73–80.

Rathod, S., Phiri, P. and Kingdon, D.G. (2010) Cognitive behavioral therapy for schizophrenia. *Psychiatric Clinics of North America, 33,* 527–536.

Romme, M.A. and Escher, A.D. (1989) Hearing voices. *Schizophrenia Bulletin, 15,* 209–216.

Sethi, S. and Bhargava, S.C. (2003) Relationship of meditation and psychosis: Case studies. *Australian and New Zealand Journal of Psychiatry, 37,* 382.

Shawyer, F., Ratcliff, K., Mackinnon, A. *et al.* (2007) The voices acceptance and action scale (VAAS): Pilot data. *Journal of Clinical Psychology, 63,* 593–606.

Startup, M., Jackson, M. and Bendix, S. (2004) North Wales randomized controlled trial of cognitive behaviour therapy for acute schizophrenia spectrum disorders: outcomes at 6 and 12 months. *Psychological Medicine, 34,* 413–422.

Strosahl, K.D., Hayes, S.C., Wilson, K.G. *et al.* (2004) An ACT Primer: Core therapy processes, intervention, strategies, and therapist competencies. In S.C. Hayes and K.D. Strosahl (eds) *A Practical Guide to Acceptance and Commitment Therapy* (pp. 31–58). New York: Springer-Verlag.

Tai, S. and Turkington, D. (2009) The evolution of cognitive behavior therapy for schizophrenia: Current practice and recent developments. *Schizophrenia Bulletin, 35*, 865–873.

Tait, L., Birchwood, M. and Trower, P. (2003) Predicting engagement with services for psychosis: Insight, symptoms and recovery style. *182*, 123–128.

Tait, L., Birchwood, M. and Trower, P. (2004) Adapting to the challenge of psychosis: Personal resilience and the use of sealing-over (avoidant) coping strategies. *British Journal of Psychiatry, 185*, 410–415.

Thomas, N., Farhall, J., Shawyer, F. *et al.* (2010) *Randomized controlled trial of ACT for medication-resistant psychosis: Interim results.* Paper presented at the 6th World Congress of Behavioral and Cognitive Therapies, Boston, MA.

11

Improving Sleep, Improving Delusions: CBT for Insomnia in Individuals with Persecutory Delusions

Elissa Myers, Helen Startup and Daniel Freeman

Introduction

Over the past 10 years there has been substantial progress made in understanding the causes of persecutory delusions. Our current programme of research aims to improve significantly the efficacy of treatments for persecutory delusions by drawing upon this theoretical advance (see Freeman, 2011). Key causal factors are being targeted one at a time. The work described in this chapter is part of this programme, with disrupted sleep as the causal factor of interest. Our group's cognitive model identifies insomnia as a putative causal factor of persecutory delusions, consistent with a recent series of empirical studies. Therefore we have treated insomnia in individuals with delusions. A brief cognitive behavioural intervention for insomnia (CBT-I) was evaluated in a case-series of 15 patients with persistent persecutory delusions and insomnia. The results were extremely encouraging. Following the four-session intervention significant reductions were found both in levels of insomnia and persecutory delusions. In this chapter we provide an overview of this work, including a description of the intervention in practice.

*This work was supported by a Wellcome Trust Fellowship awarded to Daniel Freeman.

Developing CBT for Psychosis

There have been significant beneficial changes in the treatment of individuals with psychosis due to CBT, but the evidence indicates that the effect sizes on positive psychotic symptoms such as delusions and hallucinations are weak to moderate. Effect sizes from meta-analysis are estimated to be in the region of 0.3 to 0.5 (e.g. Pfammater *et al.*, 2006; Garety *et al.*, 2008; Wykes *et al.*, 2008). A limitation of the research considered in the meta-analyses is that trials tend to use a generic CBT, which aims to treat a wide range of symptoms and many potential key mechanisms. When measured, there has been no evidence that the mechanisms considered to underlie delusions have actually changed (e.g. Garety *et al.*, 2008). Therapy lags behind the advances in the understanding of psychotic symptoms. Our approach has been to: focus on one psychotic experience, delusions; demonstrate that a causal mechanism is changed by an intervention; and examine the subsequent effect on delusional experience (Foster *et al.*, 2010; Freeman, 2011; Hepworth *et al.*, 2011; Waller *et al.*, 2011).

According to one of the main cognitive models of delusions, sleep disturbance can act as both a trigger and a maintaining factor in the occurrence of persecutory delusions (Freeman *et al.*, 2002; Freeman, 2007). Four recent studies carried out by Freeman and colleagues (2009, 2010, 2011a, 2011b) have investigated for the first time the association between insomnia and paranoid thinking. In two large nationally-representative samples of the adult population strong associations were found between insomnia and paranoia (Freeman *et al.*, 2010; Freeman *et al.*, 2011a). This work was significantly extended by showing, in a longitudinal study, that insomnia predicts both the new occurrence of paranoid thinking and its persistence (Freeman *et al.*, 2011b). Further, in a clinical sample it was found that more than 50 percent of the individuals with persecutory delusions had moderate to severe insomnia (Freeman *et al.*, 2009). The causal link between insomnia and paranoia is very plausible. Insomnia is known to cause anxiety, depression and anomalies of experience (Chemerinski *et al.*, 2002; Smith *et al.*, 2005; Espie *et al.*, 2006; Necklemann *et al.*, 2007; Freeman, 2011), which are all risk factors associated with paranoia.

Of course insomnia in individuals with psychosis is also a clinical problem in its own right, irrespective of the effect on psychotic symptoms. Insomnia, in the general population, is associated with poorer quality of life, increased ill health, higher rates of mental health problems, impaired relationships, reduced daytime productivity, higher rates of drug and alcohol abuse, increased cardiac morbidity, greater levels of healthcare utilization, increased risk of accidents and higher rates of overall mortality (Morin *et al.*, 1999; Harvey, 2002; Espie *et al.*, 2006; NICE, 2004). At present, chronic insomnia is often poorly managed (NICE, 2004) and treatment of chronic insomnia with pharmacotherapy remains controversial because of issues of tolerance and dependency (Morin *et al.*, 1999; NICE, 2004; Espie *et al.*, 2006). Specifically in insomnia linked with schizophrenia, treatment often involves antipsychotics and sedative hypnotics, which are only partially effective in the long term and are often associated with a daytime 'hangover' effect, which can contribute to poor global functioning (Kantrowitz *et al.*, 2009).

A large body of research has found that non-pharmacological interventions based on cognitive behavioural theory and techniques are highly effective and without side-effects (e.g. Morin *et al.*, 1999; Smith *et al.*, 2005; Espie *et al.*, 2006), and there is some suggestion that they may be even more effective than pharmacotherapy (Jacobs *et al.*, 2004). There is a range of CBT-I strategies including: tackling unhelpful beliefs about sleep, cognitive restructuring, sleep hygiene, relaxation training, stimulus control therapy, and paradoxical intention (Harvey *et al.*, 2007). A review of 48 clinical trials and two meta-analyses of non-pharmacological treatments for insomnia revealed that such treatments produce reliable and durable change with moderate to mild effect sizes (Morin *et al.*, 1999). Around 70 to 80 percent of patients treated with non-pharmacological interventions benefit. Regarding the durability of non-pharmacological treatment effects, Morin *et al.* (1999) show that they are well-maintained in the short (3-month) and intermediate (6-month) terms.

Given the potentially important links between insomnia and persecutory delusions, and the demonstrated efficacy of CBT-I, we carried out a pilot study for patients with psychosis (Myers *et al.*, 2011). The aim of this trial was to evaluate for the first time the treatment of insomnia for individuals with persecutory delusions. It was predicted that a brief cognitive behavioural intervention for insomnia for individuals with persistent persecutory delusions and concurrent sleep difficulties would not only reduce the insomnia but that it would also reduce the paranoia. Our focus was on individuals with persecutory delusions, but these difficulties were within the context of a schizophrenia disorder, and hence many other symptoms, such as hallucinations, were present in those treated.

The CBT-I intervention was provided to 15 patients. The CBT-I was a standard-format, four-session intervention devised for the study, with our adaptations for this patient group. Psychoeducation about sleep was provided and factors maintaining sleep difficulties were discussed, leading to a simple formulation individualized for each patient. Targets for treatment varied according to the sleep profile of the individual but typically included: sleep hygiene, the establishment of appropriate night time routines, stimulus control (learning to associate bed with sleep), relaxation practice and exploration of beliefs about sleep. Finally all patients developed a relapse prevention plan. The four weekly sessions were provided to individual patients over 1-month. Assessments of insomnia, persecutory delusions, anomalies of experience, anxiety and depression were conducted at pre-treatment, post-treatment and 1-month follow-up. All participants completed the intervention and all of the assessments, indicating excellent engagement with CBT-I. Following the CBT-I intervention, significant large reductions were found in insomnia (effect size = 2.64) and the persecutory delusions (effect size = 1.07). The effect sizes were large and the changes were maintained at a 1-month post-treatment follow-up. At least two-thirds of participants made substantial improvements in insomnia and approximately half showed substantial reductions in the persecutory delusions. There were also reductions in levels of anomalies of experience, anxiety and depression.

The investigation was the first trial of a CBT-I intervention for persecutory delusions and co-morbid insomnia. Although it was an uncontrolled evaluation, without blind assessments, the results were highly promising, and certainly indicate no reason why CBT-I cannot be used for patients with psychosis experiencing sleep disruption. The research also highlights the importance of asking about sleep disturbance in the routine assessment of individuals experiencing persecutory delusions, and subsequently to discuss treatment options. Our clinical experience indicates – and indeed there was evidence within the pilot study – that CBT-I may also be helpful for people experiencing other psychotic symptoms such as hallucinations. A more rigorous evaluation of sleep interventions for individuals with psychosis is now required.

The Insomnia Intervention Protocol

The intervention used in the pilot trial of CBT-I for individuals with persecutory delusions was informed by a number of sources including: 'Overcoming Insomnia and Sleep Problems' by Colin Espie (2006); 'Know Your Mind' by Daniel Freeman and Jason Freeman (2009); research carried out by Espie *et al.*, (2006), Harvey, (2002), Morin (2004), Morgenthaler *et al.*, (2006), Smith *et al.*, (2005); and the investigators' theoretical and clinical knowledge. The sources cited above were used to create a newly-devised therapy book, which acted as a protocol for the sessions and for participants to use in-between sessions. A section of the booklet was given to participants at the end of each session. Sessions followed a standard CBT format including an agenda at the beginning of each session, frequent summaries, feedback, guided discovery and Socratic questioning (Beck, 1995). An outline of each section of the protocol is detailed below, followed with a clinical example from the pilot study to illustrate the intervention in practice.

Session 1: Psychoeducation, formulation and treatment goals

The first session of the protocol began with brief psychoeducation about sleep, including how common sleep problems are, accounts of how CBT-I can help, how much sleep people need, and what causes/maintains sleep problems (e.g. stress, anxiety, worry, depression, poor bedtime routine, lifestyle, surroundings, physical factors such as pain). Following psycho-education, questions were used to elicit the specifics of the individual's own difficulties, including when the sleep problems started, the number of nights he or she was affected, approximately how many hours sleep obtained each night, previous treatments or strategies and their effective-ness, and the impact of sleep problems on daytime activity. An important focus was identifying the factors disrupting sleep for the individual, draw-ing upon the list in the sleep intervention protocol (see Table 11.1).

Table 11.1 was used collaboratively with the individual to decide together what the main factors that maintained the sleep difficulties might be. A maintenance formulation was created, which included any unhelpful thoughts or thinking patterns, sleep related beliefs, arousal and distress, safety behaviours and other unhelpful behaviours (e.g. smoking when not able to sleep, staying in bed the next day, cancelling activities during the day), the physiological impact, and selective attention and monitoring. Information from the formulation and the identified maintenance factors were used to set sleep related goals.

Finally, sleep diaries were introduced and advice was given on how to fill them in, if the patient was willing. For example, individuals' were encour-aged to complete the diary each morning just after waking-up and to esti-mate sleep times. Sleep diaries included the following questions: How many hours were you asleep, approximately? What time did you go to bed? What time did you get up the next day? How long did it take you to fall asleep? How long were you awake during the night?

At the end of each session the patient, with the therapist, summarized the main points taken from the session and the aims of the between-session task. Feedback on therapy was always elicited at the end of each session.

Sessions 2 and 3: Targeting the sleep maintenance factors

The content of the subsequent sessions depended on the key sleep distur-bance factors identified for each patient. Typically the focus was on night time routines, sleep hygiene and learning to associate bed with sleep (stim-ulus control), but it could also include relaxation techniques and reviewing unhelpful beliefs about sleep.

Table 11.1 Screen to elicit sleep disturbance maintenance factors

What stops me sleeping?	1 Not at all	2 Some-what	3 Quite a lot	4 Very much
Thoughts go through my head and keep me awake.				
I have a lot of worries which keep me awake.				
I feel anxious when I am trying to sleep.				
I can't relax when I am trying to sleep.				
I worry about other people harming me.				
I hear voices.				
I have nightmares.				
I feel too upset to sleep.				
I don't do much during the day.				
I find it too noisy to sleep.				
My room it too light.				
My room is too hot/ cold.				
I snore heavily.				
I sleep during the day.				
I have a lot of caffeine (coffee, tea, coke, chocolate)				
I smoke before I go to bed.				
I drink alcohol before I go to bed.				
I don't have a regular bed time and waking time.				
I spend a lot of time lying in my bed not sleeping.				
I go to bed when I don't feel tired.				
Other (please specify):				
Other (please specify):				
Other (please specify):				

Sleep hygiene

Morin *et al.* (1999) state that sleep-hygiene education covers health practices (e.g. diet, exercise, substance use) and environmental factors (e.g. light, noise, temperature, comfortable bed, bedding and bedroom conditions) that may be beneficial or detrimental to sleep. These factors are rarely severe enough to be the primary cause of insomnia but they can hinder the treatment process or complicate the existing sleep problem (Manber *et al.*, 2008). The following sleep-hygiene recommendations were provided: (a) not to drink caffeine 4 to 6 hours before bedtime and to reduce excessive consumption; (b) cut down or reduce nicotine 4 to 6 hours before bedtime; (c) avoid alcohol as a sleep aid; (d) regular exercise, but not in the 3 hours prior to bedtime; (e) minimize excessive light (thicker curtains or cover window with a blanket), high temperatures and noises during the sleep period, and (f) avoid clock watching. Additional recommendations that may overlap with stimulus control included reducing daytime napping and time spent in bed not sleeping. Interestingly, poor sleepers have been found to be generally better informed about sleep hygiene, but still engage in more unhealthy practices than good sleepers (Lacks and Rotert, 1986). Sleep-hygiene education, therefore, aims to both inform and encourage these behaviours. Sleep hygiene was discussed and if any of these factors were relevant to the individual's sleep difficulties then a specific plan of action was agreed for the following week.

Stimulus control therapy

Stimulus control therapy is based on the idea that insomnia is a conditioned response to temporal (bedtime) and environmental (bed/bedroom) cues that are usually associated with sleep (Morin *et al.*, 1999). Someone without insomnia, therefore, has a conditioned response to sleep with bedtime and bedroom cues. Stimulus control therapy aims to train the individual to re-associate bedtime, bed and the bedroom with rapid sleep onset. This is done by changing sleep-incompatible activities, which serve as cues for staying awake, for example, watching TV, using the phone in bed or using the bed for other activities during the day. Morin *et al.* (2004) and Espie (2006) propose that stimulus control therapy consists of the following: (a) go to bed only when sleepy; (b) use the bed and the bedroom only for sleep and sex; (c) get out of bed and go into another room whenever unable to fall asleep or return to sleep within 15 to 20 minutes, and return to bed only when sleepy again; (d) maintain a regular rising time in the morning regardless of sleep duration the previous night; (e) having a wind-down routine 90 minutes before bedtime, and (f) avoid daytime napping. These were discussed with the individual and an appropriate wind-down routine and an agreed wake time were planned. Ideas were generated around how to maintain the wake time and avoid napping during the day. Any barriers to maintaining these sleep habits were discussed. This stimulus control work was a key component of therapy.

Relaxation
Insomnia is often associated with high levels of arousal (physiological and cognitive), both at night and during the day (Morin *et al.*, 1999). When required, individuals were given a CD and script for progressive muscle relaxation, body scan meditation and use of imagery for relaxation. They were asked to practice relaxation daily, sometimes as part of the wind-down routine, and, when possible, record daily practice in a relaxation diary.

Cognitive restructuring
This cognitive element of the intervention aimed to review unhelpful beliefs and attitudes about sleep. For example, beliefs that an individual must always get 8 hours sleep a night or catastrophic beliefs about the impact of lack of sleep on the body and/ or on performance. Unhelpful beliefs were identified to create a mini-formulation, illustrating how these beliefs often lead to increased arousal making it even more difficult to sleep. The aim was then to break this cycle using cognitive restructuring and attention shifting.

Session 4: Review and relapse prevention

The final session involved discussion of what had been learnt in the course of therapy, progress towards goals and a relapse prevention plan. Therefore the session covered: what factors maintained the sleep problems; a review of goals and progress towards goals; techniques that were helpful; strategies to continue working on; and the development of a relapse prevention plan. General feedback about the therapy was elicited.

A Clinical Example from the Pilot Study

Ms A, a 28-year-old woman, who had been diagnosed with paranoid schiz-ophrenia, had moved to the UK from Africa with her family when she was 3 years old. At secondary school she reported difficulties with her peers which she felt was because she didn't fit in. She was bullied and was bully-ing towards others. In her early teens she was involved in petty crime and when she was 14 years old she was charged with assault leading to a 9-month custodial sentence. During this time she developed depression, sleep difficulties including nightmares and started to self-harm after seeing other girls in prison doing it. She was badly beaten in a fight while in prison. After these events she started to use cannabis daily to try to forget about these experiences.

In her late teens she developed paranoid thoughts that included beliefs that people she knew and her family wanted her dead. She was also hearing voices, sounding like an echo saying bad things. These paranoid thoughts led to a significant break with her family. She moved out of the family home and was subsequently referred to a community mental health team from a hospital accident and emergency clinic after the police had taken her there after she had reported an intruder. At the time of referral to the insomnia study she was being treated with 3 mgs of Risperidone taken orally daily (which did not change during the course of therapy and follow-up), but had not had any previous psychological treatment.

At assessment she described feeling paranoid, uneasy on her own and hearing voices that she was unsure of whether they occurred inside or outside her head. Antipsychotic medication had helped her sleep longer but she still currently experienced not being able to get to sleep for 1–2 hours most nights and broken sleep. She tried to compensate for this sleep disturbance by staying in bed until late morning and napping during the day. At assessment she appeared anxious, with limited eye contact. She found it difficult to talk about her delusions and past experiences, explaining that it was too upsetting to talk about. However, she expressed a high level of interest in talking therapy and was keen to have help with overcoming sleep difficulties.

Assessment

Two baseline assessments were made, one that was a fortnight prior to treatment and the other just before the start of the therapy. Assessment involved standardized measures for insomnia, persecutory delusions, depression and anxiety. Sleep was assessed using the Insomnia Severity Index (ISI; Bastien *et al.*, 2001) and the Pittsburgh Sleep Quality Index (PSQI; Buysse *et al.*, 1988). These measures revealed Ms A was experiencing moderate clinical insomnia and significant sleep disturbance.

Delusions were assessed with an interview assessment, the Psychotic Symptoms Rating Scale: Delusions subscale (PSYRATS; Haddock *et al.*, 1999). This indicated that Ms A was experiencing her persecutory delusion with a 70 percent conviction rating and marked distress. Paranoid thoughts were also assessed with the Green *et al.* Paranoid Thought Scales (G-PTS; Green *et al.*, 2008) that captures ideas of persecution and reference and the Cardiff Anomalous Perception Scale (CAPS; Bell *et al.*, 2006) designed to assess perceptual anomalies such as changes in levels of sensory intensity, distortion of the external world, sensory flooding and hallucinations.

Depression and anxiety were assessed with the Depression Anxiety Stress Scales (DASS; Lovibond and Lovibond, 1995). Ms A's depression rating was 29 out of 42 and her anxiety rating was 26 out of 42.

The scores at the two baseline assessments were very similar suggesting stability in sleep and delusions prior to the intervention.

Intervention

Session 1

Following the setting of the agenda for the session, psychoeducation about insomnia was provided to normalize and adjust any unhelpful beliefs about sleep. Ms A had the belief that she needed 8 hours sleep per night, so she would always try to catch up the next day if she was not able to sleep at night. We explored this by looking at the variation in sleep needed in adults, that is, between 4 to 10 hours sleep each night. Ms A was surprised at this variation and was able to reflect on times when she had had less sleep and had managed to get on with her day.

What causes sleep difficulties was discussed and many factors that disrupted Ms A's sleep were identified (see Figure 11.1). These included: unhelpful beliefs about sleep (e. g. 'if I am not able to sleep, I will not be able do anything the next day'; 'I will not be able to sleep'; 'I must rest in bed if I cannot sleep'), feeling anxious and tense when trying to sleep, not having a regular waking time, spending a lot of time in bed not sleeping, smoking at night time and insufficient activity during the day. As a consequence, Ms A felt more anxious, depressed and engaged in less activity the next day. From this information a maintenance formulation was drawn up together (see Figure 11.1). On drawing this formulation out together, Ms A felt that this captured her sleep experience and helped her to make sense of how her sleep problems were maintained. We discussed breaking the negative cycle by tackling each aspect in turn, for example, learning new helpful sleep habits, practicing relaxation, challenging unhelpful sleep beliefs and becoming more active.

From the factors identified as disrupting sleep we discussed which Ms A wanted to prioritize and had confidence that she could work on. These became the following sleep related therapy goals:

1   A regular bedtime routine and regular getting up time
2   Reduce time spent in bed when not sleeping
3   Reduce smoking at night time
4   Learning relaxation
5   Being more active during the day

Finally sleep diaries were introduced and it was discussed with Ms A whether they could be kept for the duration of the intervention to provide

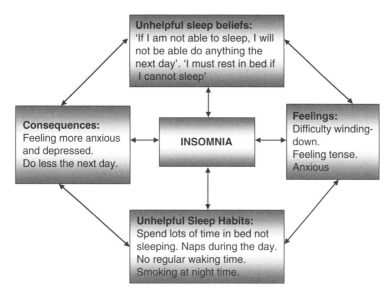

Figure 11.1 Maintenance formulation for Ms A's insomnia adapted from an integrated model of chronic insomnia
Source: Morin, 2002

more information on current sleep patterns and to monitor progress. Ms A and the therapist then summarized the session, key learning points and feedback was elicited. Ms A was given the first session booklet (which included sleep diaries) to read before the next session to reinforce what had been covered in the session. The session had lasted approximately 1 hour.

Session 2
In the second session we reviewed the sleep diary (see Table 11.2) and how it fitted with the formulation and goals from the last session. The sleep diary was used for guided discovery of factors that contributed to sleep difficulties. Ms A indicated that she had found it difficult to know exactly how long it took her to fall asleep or how long she was awake each night. She was reassured that it was only an approximation to gauge current sleep patterns and track progress over the course of therapy. From the sleep diary, Ms A observed that her sleep pattern was very irregular and felt frustrated that she would spend long periods in bed before going to sleep and would wake during the night. We reflected on reasons for her irregular sleep pattern by reviewing her maintenance formulation from Session 1 and how her goals aimed to tackle these.

We then discussed sleep hygiene and identified aspects that were relevant for Ms A. She recognized that her unhelpful sleep habits included: smoking before bed when she was trying to sleep, lack of regular exercise

Table 11.2 Sleep diary following session 1

Sleep Diary 1	Day 1	Day 2	Day 3	Day 4	Day 5	Day 6	Day 7
How many hours were you asleep (approximately)?	4 hrs	8.5 hrs	4 hrs	7 hrs	2.5 hrs	2 hrs	8 hrs
What time did you go to bed?	9 p.m.	3 a.m.	11 p.m.	12 a.m.	4.30 a.m.	3 a.m.	11 p.m.
How long did it take you to fall asleep?	4 hours	1.5 hrs	3–4 hrs	2 hrs	2 hrs	4 hrs	1 hr
How long were you awake during the night?	Felt like all night	Maybe 1 hour	3–4 hrs	3 hrs	1 hr	2 hrs	1 hr
What time did you get up in the morning?	12 p.m.	2 p.m.	11 a.m.	12 p.m.	9 a.m.	11 a.m.	9 a.m.

and activity during the day, and naps during the day. We set goals for the next week to tackle these. Ms A was currently smoking one or two cigarettes each evening. She aimed to cut down to just having half a cigarette before 9 p.m.. It was planned for her to go out for a 20/30 minute walk each day, stop napping during the day and not to talk or text on her mobile phone when in bed. We used an activity schedule to help her record her walk each day, whether or not she had had a nap and activities that replaced napping. She agreed to leave her mobile phone in another room to prevent temptation to talk on her phone or text when she was in bed. This also involved using her alarm clock instead of her mobile phone as an alarm in the morning.

Finally, we then started looking at stimulus control principles. Ms A recognized that a winding down routine and reducing time in bed would be useful. We drew up a detailed plan of an evening winding down routine to be used over the next week. As part of the winding down routine, we talked about the use of relaxation. Ms A was given a relaxation CD to use as part of this routine each day. Ms A selected a regular wake time of 8.30 a.m. with a bed-time of around midnight depending on when she felt tired. She also planned to try the 20 minute rule. Instead of lying in bed feeling frustrated and getting more anxious about sleeping, it was recommended that she get out of bed after approximately 20 minutes if she was unable to sleep to do something relaxing until she felt tired, and then going back to bed. Ms A only had one room where she lived so we agreed she would get out of bed to read a book or magazine in a comfy chair she had in her room and return to bed when she felt sleepy. We reviewed the session and she was given the next booklet, with the weeks goals outlined.

Session 3
The latest sleep diary and the techniques we had discussed in the previous session were reviewed. From the sleep diary there had been some improvements in Ms A's sleep which she thought could be attributed to using her new routine on most days, the relaxation CD, the winding down routine, not using her telephone in bed and smoking less at night time (half a cigarette before 9 p.m.). The therapist was very encouraging of these changes. We discussed what difficulties there were in this work. She had found it difficult not to nap during the day, to get up at her target time of 8.30 a.m. on the days she had not slept so well and to do the 20 minute rule. We problem-solved strategies to help her not to nap and to get out of bed at her target time of 8.30 a.m. This included: going for a walk, taking a shower, walking down to the shops or doing some housework, having a nice breakfast and having a regular morning routine. We recorded this plan in her activity schedule. She reflected that she had found the 20 minute rule difficult because she found it difficult to estimate 20 minutes and it was

sometimes cold in her room. We agreed that she would aim to get out of bed when she started worrying and felt frustrated about sleeping because this is when she felt more tense and then less likely to go back to sleep. When she got out of bed she would have a couple of blankets on her comfy chair in her room to keep warm.

Cognitive restructuring, Socratic questioning and guided discovery were then used to tackle some of her unhelpful sleep related beliefs. She believed that if she wasn't able to sleep then she could not do anything the next day and that time in bed resting was helpful if not able to sleep. We explored how tired she felt after a day in bed versus a day being active, the impact of activity on tiredness for her, and identified days she was able to carry out tasks following very little sleep and what this was like. She recognized that she generally felt more tired after spending a long time in bed or after napping but less tired after getting up and being a bit more active. This helped to reinforce her goals of getting up at her target time and not napping during the day. Finally, Ms A was asked to summarize the session and her plan for the next week and asked for her feedback on the session.

Session 4

In the final session we reviewed the latest sleep diary (see Table 11.3), discussed and problem solved implementing each of the strategies from the past two sessions, and outlined a relapse prevention plan. She had been more able to keep to the regular wake-time and not napping during the day after the problem-solving in the previous session. We reviewed and recorded in her relapse plan the strategies that she had found particularly helpful, for example, winding down routine including relaxation, having a regular wake time and bedtime. Strategies that she had found less helpful or not been able to implement were also discussed, this included the 20 minute rule. She planned to continue working on these strategies and if she had sleep disturbance in the future she could go back to them and review the booklets from the sessions. However, she was worried about whether she would continue making progress without a therapist to 'check in' with. We talked about possible solutions. She had already discussed the intervention with her care coordinator who she met regularly and thought it would be helpful to report progress to her and to continue to complete sleep diaries. These reflections and plans were recorded in a relapse prevention plan that we completed in session. At the end of therapy Ms A was asked for her feedback on her experience of the therapy. Ms A reflected that she had found the therapy really helpful, and that it had improved her sleep and her mood. Following the intervention, she reported that she felt better in herself and felt more control over her sleep.

Table 11.3 Sleep diary after session 3

Sleep Diary 3	Day 1	Day 2	Day 3	Day 4	Day 5	Day 6	Day 7
How many hours were you asleep (approximately)?	8 hrs	7.5 hrs	8 hrs	7 hrs	8.5 hrs	8 hrs	7.5 hrs
What time did you go to bed?	11.30 p.m.	12.30 a.m.	midnight	midnight	midnight	11.30 a.m.	midnight
How long did it take you to fall asleep?	.5 hrs	.5 hrs	0 hrs	1 hrs	.5 hrs	5.hrs	.5 hrs
How long were you awake during the night?	.5 hrs	.5 hrs	.5 hrs	.5 hrs	.5 hrs	.5 hrs	.5 hrs
What time did you get up in the morning?	8.30 a.m.	9 a.m.	8.30 a.m.	8.30 a.m.	9.30 a.m.	8.30 a.m.	8.30 a.m.

Outcome

At post-treatment and follow-up Ms A's insomnia had reduced to 'sub-threshold' as measured by the Insomnia Severity Index (ISI; Bastien *et al.*, 2001), and no significant sleep disturbance was indicated by the score on the Pittsburgh Sleep Quality Index (PSQI; Buysse *et al.*, 1988) (see Figure 11.2). There had been a substantial improvement in levels of insomnia.

Persecutory delusions were assessed with the PSYRATS (Haddock *et al.*, 1999), and the G-PTS (Green *et al.*, 2008). It can be seen in Figure 11.3 and Figure 11.4 that there were reductions in the persecutory delusions, as well as in anomalous experiences assessed by the CAPS, following the intervention.

Depression and anxiety scores as assessed with the Depression Anxiety Stress Scales (DASS; Lovibond and Lovibond, 1995) showed substantial reductions from pre-treatment to post-treatment (see Figure 11.5).

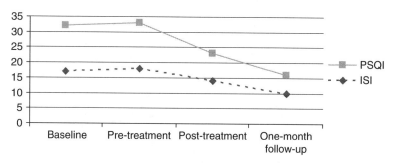

Figure 11.2 Insomnia Severity Index (ISI) and Pittsburgh Sleep Quality Index (PSQI) scores at baseline, pre-treatment, post-treatment and at follow-up

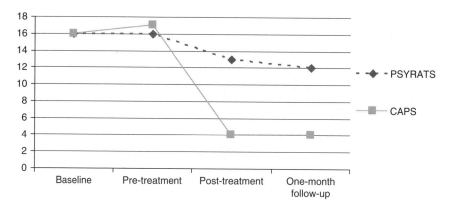

Figure 11.3 Psychotic Symptoms Rating Scale: Delusions subscale (PSYRATS) and Cardiff Anomalous Perception Scale (CAPS) scores at baseline, pre-treatment, post-treatment and follow-up

Case study discussion

This case study outlined a four-session CBT-I intervention for Ms A, a 28-year-old woman diagnosed with paranoid schizophrenia and concurrent insomnia. The intervention was based on standard evidence-based CBT-I techniques adapted for people with persecutory delusions. At assessment, Ms A reported worries about others intentions to harm her, heard voices and had a long history of insomnia. In the first session, psychoeducation about sleep difficulties was provided and discussed. Maintenance factors of Ms A's insomnia were identified and formulated, which led to sleep related therapy goals. The second and third sessions covered sleep hygiene, stimulus control, relaxation and cognitive re-structuring of unhelpful sleep related beliefs. The final session reviewed progress and difficulties implementing sleep strategies and a relapse prevention plan.

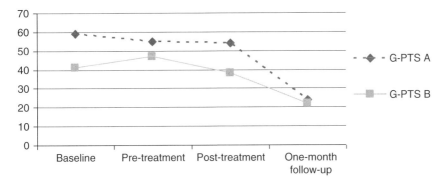

Figure 11.4 The Green *et al.* Paranoid Thought Scales (G-PTS) scores at baseline, pre-treatment, post-treatment and follow up.

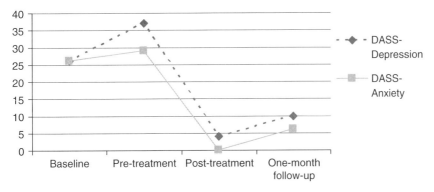

Figure 11.5 Depression and anxiety scores as assessed with the Depression Anxiety Stress Scales (DASS) scores at baseline, pre-treatment, post-treatment and follow up

Assessments were taken at baseline, pre-treatment, post-treatment and 1-month follow-up. Following the intervention, assessments revealed a significant improvement in symptoms of insomnia, paranoia, anxiety and depression.

In therapy, Ms A was initially anxious but motivated as she had had a long history of sleep difficulties and recognized that when she was not able to sleep it impacted negatively upon her mood and ability to carry out tasks during the day. She had some insight into her delusions but found it difficult and upsetting to discuss them in detail. However, since the focus of this intervention was insomnia, it did not require in-depth discussion of her delusions.

The intervention covered a number of sleep strategies, which required changes in behaviour and beliefs. Through guided discovery and formulation Ms A became aware that her previous routine was unhelpful in relation to her sleep patterns because she was spending long periods of time in bed not sleeping. This made her feel more tired and added to her low mood and anxiety. She also felt frustrated that it stopped her getting on with daily activities. This helped motivate her further to be able make changes. Since we covered a number of strategies in a short space of time it was important to use frequent summaries within sessions, check understanding and use the newly-devised book alongside therapy. The booklet had sections to complete to record what had been discussed in the session and plan for the next week, which Ms A found a really useful reminder between sessions. Ms A also found it difficult to remember when her sessions were which was overcome by the therapist calling her the morning of the appointment as a reminder. The selection of four sessions was in order for the intervention not to seem too burdensome for patients and to make sure the work was highly targeted upon sleep. However, it clearly is a limited amount of time to deliver the intervention and allow time for behavioural changes and cognitive re-structuring. Our view after the pilot work, and the encouraging comments of the patients, is that six sessions will be more beneficial, to allow more time for change, cover strategies at a slower pace, allow for additional problem-solving over obstacles and allow for further cognitive restructuring.

Overall, Ms A found the intervention extremely helpful as the strategies allowed her to feel in control of her sleep, which she found empowering. She reported a significant improvement in her sleep and overall mood and was really surprised at how having a more regular sleep routine impacted on how she felt during the day. She was concerned about how she would continue implementing what she had learnt in therapy when sessions had finished. This was helped with the relapse prevention plan but again emphasizes the benefits of incorporating additional sessions into the intervention.

Summary

This chapter has provided an overview of a potentially clinically important area of intervention for individuals with psychosis: disrupted sleep. Epidemiological research has identified close links between insomnia and paranoia, while patients frequently report sleep difficulties. Our work indicates that insomnia should routinely be assessed in individuals with delusions, and that appropriate strategies from CBT are likely to prove beneficial, both in reducing sleep problems and psychotic experiences. This forms part of a broader therapy development strategy of targeting key causal processes in the occurrence of distressing delusions (Freeman, 2011).

References

Bastien, C.H., Vallieres, A. and Morin, C.M. (2001) Validation of the insomnia severity index as an outcome measure for insomnia research. *Sleep Medicine, 2*, 297–307.

Beck, J.S. (1995) *Cognitive Therapy: Basics and Beyond*. New York: The Guilford Press.

Bell, V., Halligan, P.W. and Ellis, H.D. (2006) The Cardiff Anomalous Perceptions Scale (CAPS). *Schizophrenia Bulletin, 32*, 366–377.

Buysse, D.J., Reynolds, C. F., Monk, T.H. *et al.* (1988) The Pittsburgh Sleep Quality Index: A new instrument for psychiatric practice and research. Psychiatry Research, *28*, 193–213.

Chemerinski, E., Beng-Choon, H., Flaum, M. *et al.* (2002) Insomnia as a predictor for symptom worsening following antipsychotic withdrawal in schizophrenia. *Comprehensive Psychiatry, 43*, 393–396.

Espie, C. (2006) *Overcoming Insomnia and Sleep Problems: A Self-help Guide using Cognitive Behavioral Techniques*. London: Robinson.

Espie, C.A., MacMahoon, K.M.A., Kelly, H. *et al.* (2006) Randomized clinical effectiveness trial of nurse-administered small-group cognitive behaviour therapy for persistent insomnia in general practice. *Sleep, 30*, 574–584.

Foster, C., Startup, H., Potts, L. *et al.* (2010) A randomised controlled trial of a worry intervention for individuals with persistent persecutory delusions. *Journal of Behavior Therapy and Experimental Psychiatry, 41*, 45–51.

Freeman, D. (2007) Suspicious minds: The psychology of persecutory delusions. *Clinical Psychology Review, 27*, 425–457.

Freeman, D. (2011) Improving cognitive treatments for delusions. *Schizophrenia Research, 132*, 135–139.

Freeman, D., Brugha, T., Meltzer, H. *et al.* (2010) Persecutory ideation and insomnia: findings from the second British National Survey of Psychiatric Morbidity. *Journal of Psychiatric Research, 44*, 1021–1026.

Freeman, D. and Freeman, J. (2009) *Know Your Mind: Everyday Emotional and Psychological Problems and How to Overcome Them*. Basingstoke: Pan Macmillan.

Freeman, D., Garety, P.A., Kuipers, E. *et al.* (2002) A cognitive model of persecutory delusions. *British Journal of Clinical Psychology, 41*, 331–347.

Freeman, D., McManus, S., Brugha, T. *et al.* (2011a) Concomitants of paranoia in the general population. *Psychological Medicine, 41*, 923–936.

Freeman, D., Pugh, K., Vorontsova, N. *et al.* (2009) Insomnia and paranoia. *Schizophrenia Research, 108*, 280–284.

Freeman, D., Stahl, D., McManus, S. *et al.* (2011b) Insomnia, worry, anxiety and depression as predictors of the occurrence and the persistence of persecutory ideation. *Social Psychiatry and Psychiatric Epidemiology*, online publication.

Garety, P.A., Bentall, R. and Freeman, D. (2008) Research evidence of the effectiveness of cognitive behavioural therapy for persecutory delusions: more work is needed. In D. Freeman, R. Bentall and P. Garety (eds) *Persecutory Delusions* (pp. 329–351). Oxford: Oxford University Press.

Garety, P., Fowler, D., Freeman, D. *et al.* (2008) A randomised controlled trial of cognitive behavioural therapy and family intervention for the prevention of relapse and reduction of symptoms in psychosis. *British Journal of Psychiatry, 192*, 412–423.

Green, C., Freeman, D., Kuipers, E. *et al.* (2008) Measuring ideas of persecution and reference: The Green *et al.* Paranoid Thoughts Scale (G-PTS). *Psychological Medicine, 38*, 101–111.

Haddock, G., McCarron, J., Tarrier, N. *et al.* (1999) Scales to measure dimensions of hallucinations and delusions: the psychotic symptom rating scales (PSYRATS) *Psychological Medicine, 29*, 879–889.

Harvey, A.G. (2002) A cognitive model of insomnia. *Behaviour Research and Therapy, 40*, 869–893.

Harvey, A.G., Sharpley, A.L., Ree, M.J. *et al.* (2007) An open trial of cognitive therapy for chronic insomnia. *Behaviour Research and Therapy, 45*, 2491–2501.

Hepworth, C., Startup, H. and Freeman, D (2011) Developing treatments for persistent persecutory delusions: the impact of an emotional processing and metacognitive awareness (EPMA) intervention. *Journal of Nervous Mental Disorders, 199*, 653–658.

Jacobs, G.D., Pace-Schott, E.F., Stickgold, R. *et al.* (2004) Cognitive behavior therapy and pharmacotherapy for insomnia: a randomized controlled trial and direct comparison. *Archives of Internal Medicine, 164*, 1888–1896.

Kantrowitz, J., Citrome, L. and Javitt, D. (2009) $GABA_B$ receptors, schizophrenia and sleep dysfunction, *CNS Drugs, 23 (8)*, 681–691.

Lacks, P. and Rotert, M. (1986) Knowledge and practice of sleep hygiene techniques in insomniacs and poor sleepers. *Behaviour Research and Therapy, 24*, 365–368.

Lovibond, S.H. and Lovibond, P.F. (1995) *Manual for the Depression Anxiety Stress Scales*, 2nd edn. Sydney: Psychology Foundation.

Manber, R., Edinger, J.D., Gress, J.L. *et al.* (2008) Cognitive behavioural therapy for insomnia enhances depression outcome in patients with comorbid major depressive disorder and insomnia. *Sleep, 31*, 489–495.

Morgenthaler, T., Kramer, M., Alessi, C. *et al.* (2006) Practice parameters for the psychological and behavioral treatment of insomnia: An update: An American Academy of Sleep Medicine report. *Sleep, 29*, 1415–1419

Morin, C.M. (2002) Contributions of cognitive-behavioural approaches to the clinical management of insomnia. *Journal of Clinical Psychiatry, 4(1)*, 21–26.

Morin, C.M. (2004) Cognitive-behavioral approaches to the treatment of insomnia. *Journal of Clinical Psychiatry, 65(16)*, 33–40.

Morin, C.M., Hauri, P.J., Espie, C.A. *et al.* (1999) Nonpharmacologic treatment of chronic insomnia. *Sleep, 22*, 1134–1156.

Myers, E., Startup, H. and Freeman, D. (2011) Cognitive behavioural treatment of insomnia in patients with persecutory delusions. *Journal of Behavior Therapy Experimental Psychiatry, 42*, 330–336.

National Institute for Clinical Excellence (NICE) (2004) *Technology Appraisal 77. Guidance on the Use of Zaleplon, Zolpidem and Zopiclone for the Short-term Management of Insomnia*, April. London: NICE.

Necklemann, D., Mykletun, A. and Dahl, A. A. (2007) Chronic insomnia as a risk factor for developing anxiety and depression. *Sleep, 30*, 873–880.

Pfammater, M., Junghan, U.M. and Brenner, H.D. (2006) Efficacy of psychological therapy in schizophrenia: Conclusions from meta-analyses. *Schizophrenia Bulletin, 32*, 64–80.

Smith, M.T., Huang, M.I. and Manber, R. (2005) Cognitive behaviour therapy for chronic insomnia occurring within the context of medical and psychiatric disorders. *Clinical Psychology Review, 25*, 559–592.

Waller, W., Freeman, D., Jolley, S. *et al.* (2011) Targeting reasoning biases in delusions. *Journal of Behaviour Therapy and Experimental Psychiatry, 42*, 414–421.

Wykes, T., Steel, C., Everitt, B. *et al.* (2008) Cognitive behaviour therapy for schizophrenia: effect sizes, clinical models, and methodological rigor. *Schizophrenia Bulletin, 34*, 523–537.

12

Compassion Focused Group Therapy for Recovery after Psychosis

Christine Braehler, Janice Harper and Paul Gilbert

This chapter outlines the application of an evolutionary model of emotion regulation, Compassion Focused Therapy (CFT),[1] in a group therapy that aims to promote emotional recovery from psychosis. CFT was specifically developed for people with high shame and self-criticism (Gilbert, 2000, 2010a, 2010b). We will describe the theoretical principles of CFT and suggest that the regulation of threat processing through stimulation of soothing and affiliation is a valid and promising therapeutic focus in the treatment of psychosis.

Theoretical Background

Emotional recovery from psychosis

Emotional recovery is a key dimension of overall recovery from psychosis (Birchwood, 2003). Problematic emotional recovery is characterized by depression, hopelessness and suicidal thinking (Birchwood *et al.*, 2000a), social anxiety (Gumley *et al.*, 2004; Birchwood *et al.*, 2006) and trauma (Morrison *et al.*, 2003). In addition, shame and stigma (Iqbal *et al.*, 2000; Rooke and Birchwood, 1998), feeling trapped in one's illness (Karatzias *et al.*, 2007) and the fear of recurrence (White and Gumley, 2009) significantly

CBT for Schizophrenia: Evidence-Based Interventions and Future Directions,
First Edition. Edited by Craig Steel.
© 2013 John Wiley & Sons, Ltd. Published 2013 by John Wiley & Sons, Ltd.

undermine emotional recovery. Although CBT for psychosis has demonstrated effectiveness in alleviating distressing persisting positive psychotic symptoms, there is less evidence for its effectiveness on key aspects of emotional recovery (Wykes *et al.*, 2008). The roles of affect regulation, attachment, mentalizing and self-organization in the development and recovery from psychosis are increasingly recognized (Garfield, 1995; Gumley and Schwannauer, 2006).

Threat and psychosis

Many psychopathologies are linked to threat processing focusing on the external world (e.g. the action of others) or the internal world (e.g. one's own feelings, thoughts or intrusive memories) (Gilbert, 1993). Psychosis is also strongly linked to negative affect and threat appraisal (Freeman and Garety, 2003).

There are many reasons why people can become highly sensitized to threat. The high rates of psychosocial stressors in early life such as losing a parent before the age of 16 (Morgan *et al.*, 2007), childhood abuse and neglect (Read *et al.*, 2005), parenting marked by control in the absence of warmth (Read and Gumley, 2008), bullying, witnessing violence at home, homelessness, being in care, assault (Bebbington *et al.*, 2004), poverty (Harrison *et al.*, 2001) and racial discrimination (Bhugra *et al.*, 1997) might partly account for the pronounced threat sensitivity seen in people with psychosis (Myin-Germeys and van Os, 2007). High rates of insecure, especially dismissive, and disorganized attachment styles have been identified in this population (Dozier, 1990; Tyrrell and Dozier, 1997; Berry *et al.*, 2008). Central to these findings is that they seem to reflect a lack of individuals' experience of safeness in early relationships and in their ability to self-soothe (Liotti and Gumley, 2009).

Following a psychotic episode people experience major internal threats. Bullying voices, traumatic memories, low self-worth, shame and self-attacking (often related to delusional beliefs) maintain a high level of internal threat, conflict, distress and entrapment (Birchwood *et al.* 2000; Gilbert *et al.*, 2001; Longe *et al.*, 2010). The generation of voices is associated with voice hearers misidentifying critical internal signals/speech as critical external signals/speech (McGuire *et al.*, 1996). This external attribution in turn increases threat and entrapment by reducing the sense of control individuals perceive to have over their mental state (Birchwood *et al.*, 2000).

They way in which the individual experiences the external world relating to them and to their psychotic experience determine the level of social threat. The trauma of the psychosis itself and its often devastating impact may further dysregulate affect (Gumley and Schwannauer, 2006). Relapses and being (re)traumatized by coercive service responses (Frame and Morrison, 2001) pose actual threats, which can interfere with people's willingness to engage with services and to disclose distress. Fears of being victimized, physically harmed, stigmatized and excluded also foster submission, social withdrawal and isolation. Hypervigilance of social threats followed by active avoidance is thought to contribute to paranoia and social anxiety, which in turn increase the perception of social threat (Green and Phillips, 2004). Shame and stigma are common in psychosis and block affiliative connections to others, promote avoidance and increase social anxiety (Gilbert and Andrews, 1998; Birchwood *et al.*, 2006).

Avoidant coping strategies such as submitting to voices or to others by complying or appeasing (Birchwood *et al.*, 2000), thought suppression (Spinhoven and van der Does, 1999), or 'sealing over' (McGlashan, 1987) are common and understandable attempts to cope. Unfortunately, sealing over strategies such as down-regulating threats by minimizing the impact of the psychosis, being reluctant to talk about the psychosis or to explore its underlying emotional issues are linked to worse engagement (Tait *et al.*, 2003), impaired mentalizing (Braehler and Schwannauer, 2011) and worse outcome (Thompson *et al.*, 2003).

In summary, the data suggest that people with psychosis suffer from major difficulties in regulating threat.

The role of affiliation in the regulation of threat

The evolution of attachment as a protective and provisioning relationship for the infant has had profound effects on subsequent evolution and on affect regulation and social cognition in particular (Gilbert, 1989, 2005; Porges, 2007). Research over the past 20 years has shown just how powerful – especially early – attachment relationships are in shaping physiological and phenotypic development (Belsky *et al.*, 2007; Cozolino, 2007; Porges, 2007). Specialized neurophysiological systems underpinning our capacity to process affiliation (Depue and Morrone-Strupinsky, 2005) have been found to down-regulate fear (Kirsch *et al.*, 2005). Affiliation and affection play major roles in the maturation of the brain, in particular of areas involved in social cognition and empathy (Schore, 1996). Feelings of safeness and security as provided by experiences of affiliation and attachment have profound effects on abilities to process social information, mentalize and regulate affect (Fonagy *et al.*, 2002). Some people with psychosis might become fearful of others due to a heightened threat sensitivity and due to difficulties in affect recognition, mentalizing and theory of mind skills – rendering the 'minds of others' strange and unfathomable (Penn *et al.*, 1997; Russell *et al.*, 2000). Therefore, poor affiliation skills to self and to others may reduce mentalizing (MacBeth *et al.*, 2011) and may increase distress, avoidance, social withdrawal and risk of relapse (Gumley *et al.*, 2010).

Given that individuals with psychosis may have increased threat sensitivity and decreased affiliative capacity, it follows that one therapeutic target would be to increase the abilities for affiliation both with self and with others.

Definition of compassion

Compassion can be defined in different ways (Gilbert, 2010). In CFT compassion is related to a number of attributes that include – developing the *motivation* to be caring in order to address distress and suffering; capacities to be *attentive* to suffering within the self or others; to be emotionally engaged (in sympathy and in tune with) and moved by suffering of self and others; to be *tolerant* of emotions of distress that can be aroused; abilities to develop *empathic* insights into the causes and sources of suffering of self and others; capacities to take a non-condemning, open and mindful orientation to the process. Common misunderstandings about compassion are that it involves a striving to attain a state of serene bliss or 'niceness' free from negative emotions. In keeping with attachment theory, CFT helps build an internal secure base and trains us in capacities for soothing and courage, which allow us to descend into, turn towards and contain our emotional pain.

Evidence-base of compassion-based interventions in psychosis

Research on the application of CFT in psychosis is at an early stage. Questions about the understandability, relevance, effectiveness and common difficulties of using this approach with people with psychosis require further attention. In a first attempt to address these questions Mayhew and Gilbert (2008) used a single case design with three individuals who heard distressing malevolent voices, but who were not actively psychotic. Following 12 individual sessions of CFT, two did very well and one less so. The clients who significantly improved found the compassion focus a new way of relating to themselves and others. The individual who did less well felt he 'didn't deserve compassion' and was dominated by intrusive fantasies that he felt too ashamed to discuss. This is not an uncommon problem and speaks of the complex relationship between self-compassion and shame (Gilbert, 2010). Johnson and colleagues evaluated the effects of Loving Kindness Meditation in 18 outpatients with persistent negative symptoms (Johnson *et al.*, 2011). After six sessions participants reported a significant increase in positive emotions, self-acceptance, mastery, life satisfaction and a significant decrease in negative symptoms mainly in anhedonia. In a study of 20 sessions of group CFT for 19 clients with psychosis in a high security psychiatric setting, Laithwaite and colleagues (2009) found a large magnitude of change for levels of depression and self-esteem. In addition moderate effects were found for social comparison and general psychopathology, with a small magnitude of change for feelings of shame. These changes were maintained at 6-week follow-up. Braehler and colleagues (in press) assessed the feasibility of randomization and the acceptability of group CFT in a community setting. Twenty-two clients with psychosis received 16 sessions of group CFT and treatment as usual. Relative to TAU, CFT was associated with greater clinical improvement and an increase of compassion of large magnitude. In the CFT group increases in compassion were associated with reductions in depression and social marginalization. The evidence, albeit limited at this stage, suggests that CFT is safe and acceptable to use with this population.

Compassion focused group therapy for recovery after psychosis

The present protocol further developed a forensic group manual (Laithwaite *et al.*, 2009) by running groups in a community setting (Braehler *et al.*, in press). A compassion-focused formulation of recovery stresses the adverse emotional and interpersonal consequences that psychotic experiences typically have on a person's life (Gumley *et al.*, 2010). At the heart of group CFT for psychosis (CFTgp) is the development of compassionate relating to threats experienced in psychosis. Emotional resilience is developed through the gradual desensitization to self-compassion using psychoeducation, mindfulness and compassion practices, reframing, interpersonal learning, building of peer attachments and narrative tasks. Recommendations for interpersonal group therapy in psychosis (Kanas, 1996; Yalom, 1983) and aspects of mindfulness training (Nairn, 1999; Segal *et al.*, 2002) were also taken into account.

Practical Considerations

Selecting group participants

Case studies and feasibility data suggest that the majority of people recovering from psychosis may be able to engage with and benefit from CFT (Mayhew and Gilbert, 2008; Laithwaite *et al.*, 2009; Braehler *et al.*, in press). Group CFT targets transdiagnostic processes (e.g. shame, stigma, self-criticism, social avoidance). It has benefited clients with a primary diagnosis of chronic treatment-resistant schizophrenia – including those with mild cognitive impairment and limited literacy skills – as well as clients within the first 3 to 5 years following their first episode and those with other psychotic disorders. Clients with severe negative symptoms, little insight into the fact that they have a mental health problem, severe impairment through co-morbidities or severe preoccupation with delusions were not found to benefit (Braehler *et al.*, in press; Laithwaite *et al.*, 2009). These client groups also show limited benefit from traditional Cognitive Behaviour Therapy for Psychosis (Tai and Turkington, 2009). An earlier study (Laithwaite *et al.*, 2009) found that individuals who were severely psychotic and who were struggling to cope with their psychotic experiences were unlikely to benefit or sustain inclusion in CFTgp. Based on our experience, suitable participants are usually in a post-acute phase of their illness when psychotic symptoms are less severe and they are able to function at a reasonable level. It may be that further adaptations for individuals more debilitated by their symptoms could be successful.

During individual sessions therapists engage clients and conduct a standard psychological assessment including psychotic symptoms (intensity, frequency, content, distress, coping, personal meaning), background (including trauma) and their impact on emotional and interpersonal functioning including any attempts to cope and unintended consequences thereof (see examples in Figure 12.1). People who do not accept the label of psychosis for their experiences (e.g. because they attribute spiritual meaning) are eligible as long as they are able to begin to consider a psychological understanding of their emotional difficulties and have some motivation to work on those. People who experience paranoia and social anxiety need to be sufficiently motivated to work through the initial threat of participating in a group.

Engagement in CFT happens throughout by focusing away from the psychosis onto its adverse impacts and by repeatedly validating clients' coping strategies as their best effort to deal with difficult situations. Although members might vary with regards to their illness models, CFT fosters mutual respect of different ways of making sense by focusing members' attention on their joint goal, their common emotional difficulties and the universality of emotional suffering.

While some clients were able to benefit without having had therapy previously, we would recommend combining the group with individual therapy prior to the group starting in order to make sense of and cope with psychotic symptoms. In some cases we would also recommend individual therapy after the group in order to integrate any emotional issues (grief, trauma) activated through compassion work.

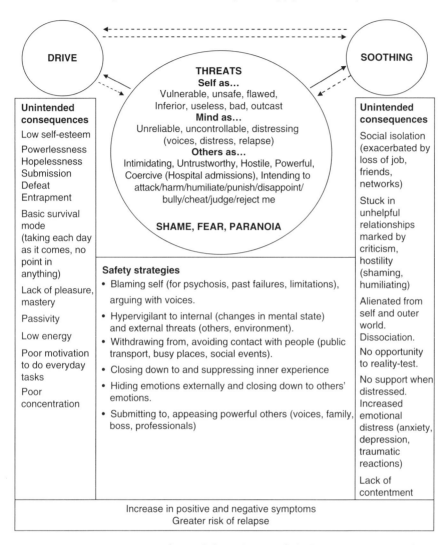

Figure 12.1 A compassion focused formulation of challenges in recovery from psychosis.

Note: ------ dashed lines indicates reduced feedback mechanism

Structural issues

Setting up the group

Further research is needed to determine the ideal format (number of sessions, structure) for running groups with this client group. The present recommendations are based on feedback from our study and on general guidelines for group therapy for psychosis (Yalom, 1983; Kanas, 1996). We recommend delivering the protocol over at least 20 sessions (2 hours per week). A closed format simplifies the key task of developing trust to engage with others. A therapeutic group should consist of at least five and a maximum of eight members since any more would render the setting too complex and intimidating (Bateman and Fonagy, 2007).

A first step towards creating a safe and relaxed environment is to hold meetings in a private, protected room with easy access to smoking areas, refreshments and toilets. Offering informal breaks with refreshments helps initiate informal conversations between members and allows them to take a break from 'hot' topics thereby helping to maintain a therapeutic level of arousal. Members have welcomed a call from therapists prior to the session to deal with barriers to attending such as poor memory, increased distress, low mood or poor motivation.

Structure of sessions

To further reduce anxiety sessions follow the same structure. As members arrive therapists check in with everybody informally. To cue clients' memories, which are often impaired, the session begins by therapists providing a written summary of the previous session, talking through key points and answering any questions. After a brief mindfulness exercise members are invited to feed back on their mental state and their experiences of trying out homework tasks over the past week. Therapists then introduce a particular focus and exercise for each session, which draws on members' current concerns and offers sufficient space for exploration of experiences, exchange and supportive interactions; the latter making up at least half the session. Sessions end with a summary, introduction of homework and final feedback on how members are feeling.

Support outside of sessions

In an outpatient setting, a group format does not always allow for identification of significant deterioration in mental health or risk issues and members are advised to make use of their usual professional and personal supports when necessary. Contact with therapists between sessions is restricted to issues that might affect their group participation.

Role and qualities of the therapist

The therapist's key task is to create a safe and sensitive interpersonal environment (Gilbert, 2010). Through conveying warmth, openness and patience, therapists create a relaxed atmosphere of playfulness, collaboration and mutual acceptance. Therapists require the ability to hold the safe space by maintaining the agreed structure, setting boundaries and allowing sufficient opportunity for sharing and exploration. Personal practice of mindfulness and compassion has shown to improve both therapists' attunement to clients' needs and clients' outcomes (Grepmair *et al.*, 2007; Siegel, 2010). In addition to receiving supervision, having one's own practice to draw on helps therapists to feel confident in flexibly guiding members in working with the compassion/attachment system.

Groups should be conducted with a co-therapist. This helps with monitoring and supporting distressed individuals during and after sessions. In our experience derogatory voices, traumatic memories or blocked grief can be activated during compassion practices. Individual attention and support is critical to help the person refocus on the feeling of safeness, kindness and wisdom, from which they are able to contain the affect. Having a co-therapist also offers an opportunity to model compassionate relating, reframing and reflexivity. The interactions between therapists make transparent their caring intentions towards members, which reduces the possibility of paranoid interpretations and foster a sense of existing positively in the mind of the therapists.

Therapeutic skills and interventions

To deliver CFTgp, therapists need to draw on a host of skills. First, experience of applying a psychological therapy for psychosis such as CBT is essential (Steel, this volume). Second, therapists require training and supervised experience in applying CFT which includes experiential training in mindfulness and compassion (www.compassionatemind.co.uk). Third, experience of facilitating group therapy is helpful (Yalom, 1995).

The therapeutic process itself is rooted in CBT rather than a psychodynamic approach, which would focus on unconscious processing. The format involves guided discovery and guided self-practice using an array of CBT skills such as Socratic questioning, functional analysis, graded exposure and behavioural experiments. Therapists' non-verbal behaviour (slowing down, calm, warm tone of voice, etc.) is a key medium for conveying interpersonal safeness (Gilbert, 2010). While mentalizing abilities in people with psychosis vary, they generally tend to be low (Braehler and Schwannauer, 2011; MacBeth *et al.*, 2011). Interventions and communications should therefore be clear, concise, focus on the here and now and be delivered at an optimal level of arousal such as by avoiding overarousal or intellectualization (Bateman and Fonagy, 2007). Socratic questioning can be useful to encourage people to think about emotions and motives in their mind and in the minds of others (e.g. What do you think might be going through Clare's mind? What do you think she might be feeling? Why do you think she might be feeling this way? How might she deal with this feeling?).

Another feature of CFT is the focus on the body as the seat of emotional experience. Therapists regularly ask members to slow down to attend to their physical sensations to help them tune into their present-moment experience and to approach it with curiosity and kindness. Describing the body's state (sensations, posture, facial expressions, tone of voice), labelling emotions and noticing concurrent thoughts aims to develop metacognitive awareness (Teasdale *et al.*, 2002). By strengthening the capacity to kindly observe our experience we increase tolerance of distress and reduce fear of positive and negative emotions (Linehan, 1993; Gilbert, 2010).

Clinically, we observe that many clients with psychosis have difficulties connecting with affect. They either down-regulate affect or are blunted or show an incongruent expression of affect especially when talking about upsetting events. Findings on attachment (Dozier, 1990; Tyrrell and Dozier, 1997; Berry *et al.*, 2008) and coping strategies (McGlashan, 1987; Spinhoven and van der Does, 1999) suggest that these are important safety strategies. To avoid unnecessary destabilization, CFT therapists introduce compassion practices gradually with playfulness and curiosity. In this atmosphere members can experiment with different exercises and familiarize themselves with the feeling at their own pace.

Group process

Similar to traditional CBT for psychosis groups, CFT group therapy is structured and task-focused. CFT differs from traditional CBT in that it explicitly utilizes the emerging group processes to support the development of compassionate skills and attributes (Gilbert and Procter, 2006). Group therapy naturally provides a social environment where the presence of mirroring minds and group therapeutic factors such as hope, cohesion, universality, identification, interpersonal learning and altruism (Yalom, 1995; García-Cabeza and González de Chávez, 2009) can be capitalized on. If facilitated effectively, the group becomes a lived experience of the caregiving-mentality, which naturally counteracts the isolation, shame and fear members feel. In CFT the group serves as a secure base from which to explore one's inner experience through the minds of others with qualities of sympathy, distress tolerance, empathy, non-judgement, care for well-being and sensitivity (Bateman and Fonagy, 2007; Liotti and Gilbert, 2011).

In our experience, the group atmosphere is at first often marked by a dominant-subordinate mentality between clients and towards therapists due to the high level of threat associated with social settings. Subordinate individuals protect themselves through silence, withdrawing or appeasing other. This hinders exploration and interaction between members and focuses attention excessively on therapists. While more therapist-client interactions in the initial sessions are acceptable, it is the therapists' task to create social safeness and to facilitate co-operative client-to-client relating as sessions go on. This can be done by containing dominant individuals, by openly resolving any conflict and by opening up discussion to others (e.g. Can others relate to John's experience? What reactions did you notice within yourselves as you were listening to John?). Therapists need to both encourage participation while respecting the adaptive use of such safety strategies in some members.

Treatment Protocol

We present the key therapeutic tasks and processes including adaptations for working with psychosis and feedback from clients and therapists who participated in our groups. These are suggestions, which need to be adapted to your setting, to the needs and abilities of the group and the evolving group dynamics.

Formation phase

In the first phase members explore the impact psychotic experiences have had on their lives and formulate ways to overcome blocks to recovery in terms of the CFT model. Members bond over their shared experiences and the compassionate motivation is activated through the insights derived from the model and the setting of a joint recovery goal. The following three steps should be carried out over the first sessions at an appropriate pace for the group concerned.

1 Establishing the group as a secure base
The goal of the first contacts is to begin to create safeness. Prior to the first session, members are sent an invitation outlining the details of the group but also reminding them of how it is normal to feel anxious and that there will be no pressure to speak in the group. In the first session, after a meet and greet where members are given name labels, therapists introduce the goals and structure of the group and remind members that all contributions are voluntary. During an ice-breaker task members work in pairs to find out about, for example, their partner's favourite hobby/TV show/meal and introduce their partner to the group. This reduces the anxiety about introducing oneself. Members' hopes and expectations of the group are shared and ground rules agreed upon. A further task that can be carried out in pairs or triads involves using cards listing negative, positive and neutral feelings to help members share their feelings about coming to the group and how they are finding the first session. This helps to acknowledge and normalize feelings of anxiety and helps to instill hope

and excitement about future sessions. Therapists provide additional support to members who appear anxious and quiet.

2 Learning how the threat system gets in the way of recovery
Formulation involves therapists mapping the psychosis and its impact in terms of the CFT model. Therapists begin by describing common psychotic experiences in basic terms not to educate but to encourage members to share their own experiences and meanings. It is important that group members have a shared understanding of what is meant by psychotic experiences. Often individuals have not had or taken the opportunity to speak about the psychosis and its consequences. Clients often avoid talking about their experiences as staff may respond in an alarming way (admission, increase of medication). The fears surrounding the psychosis prevent clients from making sense of and integrating their experiences. This systematic avoidance also reinforces individuals' fear of relapse, sense of defeat, entrapment and disconnection from others.

The focus of the exploration then shifts to the impact that the psychosis – its symptoms, treatment and emotional distress – is currently having on members' lives. To facilitate this exploration in the group, therapists can use the metaphor of a pebble dropping into water and causing ripples as a way of illustrating how the psychosis has affected their sense of self, emotions, behaviour and relationships to others and society in general (Laithwaite *et al.*, 2009).

Members usually express feeling shame, anxiety and vulnerability. At this early stage members often only connect with *ongoing* threatening experiences as opposed to earlier threat memories as this feels less overwhelming. Some members talk about their psychotic beliefs or behaviours in a light-hearted way while others are merely ready to listen. As members recognize that they all share difficult experiences, they feel huge relief and an initial sense of cohesion, safeness and trust develops. This shared humanity with regard to psychosis (We're all in the same boat) allows others to gradually open up and share some of their often painful experiences. For this same reason members can find this session challenging as it gets them in touch with the negative affect they tend to suppress.

Therapists teach clients about the causes of suffering being rooted in the basic design of our minds and in its evolutionary adaptations. It is emphasized that neither the design of our minds nor the forces which have shaped our mind – society, upbringing and genes - were chosen by us. This concept of 'just finding ourselves here with a brain and mind we didn't choose' is fundamental to beginning the process of de-shaming. Members often blame themselves for the psychosis and their current life situation. They are encouraged to realize that none of this is their fault. By dropping shaming, blaming and fear of stigma individuals can begin to feel less threatened and more empowered in their recovery.

Therapists teach members about how our minds have evolved with three basic types of emotion regulation systems ('3 circle model') and what their functions are (see Figure 12.2).

First, therapists explain how the threat-system is critical for our survival by triggering fast and automatic action responses to protect ourselves. Different threats and ways in which the threat system is trying to keep members safe are explored and validated as automatic safety reactions. Because self-protection is so vital to our survival, threat processing overrides positive emotions. In light of the pervasive threats from self, mind and others following a psychotic episode, it is understandable that the threat system has overruled the drive and soothing/affiliation system. To help clients reduce shame and self-blame it is critical to repeatedly validate the use of safety strategies such as avoidance as an automatic survival strategy.

It is very understandable that you would be feeling frightened and that you would avoid others since you had such negative experiences (e.g. others threatening, bullying you). That makes sense since we all want to protect ourselves from getting hurt or from feeling bad about ourselves. We all want to be safe, so our body and brain automatically kick in to protect ourselves. We didn't design this, so it is not our fault. These safety strategies have been built into our bodies and brains to help us survive over millions of years. There is, however, a downside to avoiding others for longer periods. As you said you still feel vulnerable so that feeling you were trying to protect yourself

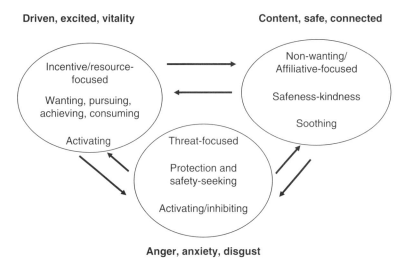

Three Types of Affect Regulation System

Driven, excited, vitality   **Content, safe, connected**

Incentive/resource-focused

Wanting, pursuing, achieving, consuming

Activating

Non-wanting/Affiliative-focused

Safeness-kindness

Soothing

Threat-focused

Protection and safety-seeking

Activating/inhibiting

Anger, anxiety, disgust

Figure 12.2 The interaction between our three major emotion-regulation systems. Reprinted with kind permission from Paul Gilbert, *The Compassionate Mind* (London: Constable, 2009)

from is still there. On top of this you feel lonely, cut off, have no drive, feel even more afraid of others and lose confidence in building relationships.

Next therapists explain the function of the drive system. It motivates us to engage in activities and provides us with a positive feeling of pleasure and reward when we succeed in achieving our goals (e.g. on winning the lottery most of us would become restless, excited and would have racing thoughts).

Third, therapists introduce the soothing and affiliation system. This system is critical for our survival and well-being as it down regulates the threat and drive system through rest, affection, comfort, caring, joy, warmth and play. It motivates us to care for ourselves and each other and to attend to our and each others' needs.

The unintended consequences of the overactive threat system on the drive system such as anhedonia, amotivation, defeat and on the soothing/ affiliation system such as lack of supportive relationships, isolation and increased distress are drawn out collaboratively (see Figure 12.1). In doing so, clients begin to formulate their difficulties as understandable yet undesired consequences of an overactive threat system. Members draw the size of their 3 circles using colours (red/threat, blue/drive, green/soothing/ affiliation) and mini-formulations are drawn out with assistance from the therapists (see Figure 12.3).

It is important to instil hope and a compassionate motivation by introducing the rationale for strengthening the soothing system as a way to counterbalance the threat system ('moving from the red into the green') and to create balance among the three emotion systems. Therapists then use the formulations to validate the fears of developing kindness towards self ('I do not deserve kindness. It makes me weak and vulnerable'), for others ('Others will take advantage of me and walk all over me') and of receiving kindness from others ('People are dangerous and cannot be trusted'). The three circle formulation is revisited throughout the therapy. It evolves and provides a common language with which clients map experience. As trust increases and compassionate skills develop, some disclose and formulate the impact of *earlier* threat memories.

3 Building a shared compassionate motivation to recover
To strengthen the compassionate motivation, a joint recovery goal is developed. The pervasive feeling of vulnerability following a psychotic episode usually hinders people from looking into their future. To avoid dealing with the possibility of one's plans being thwarted by an unpredictable recurrence of symptoms, many adopt the safety strategy of 'taking each day as it comes' (Barnett and Lapsley, 2006; Gumley and Park, 2010). Therapists anticipate barriers to setting a goal – such as hopelessness,

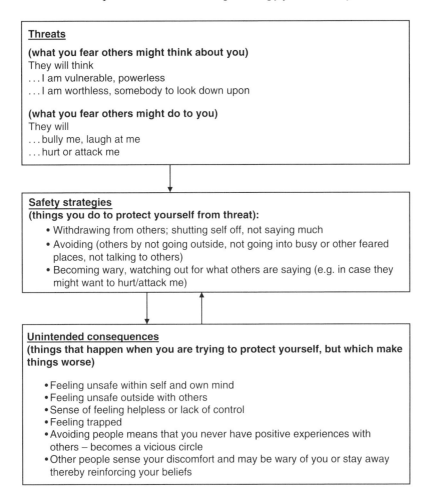

Figure 12.3   Mini-formulation of overactive threat mind

defeat, entrapment, vulnerability – as examples of how the threat system gets in the way of the recovery process. Members are asked to share what recovery means to them; where they are at in their recovery process and what they have already recovered from; and where they want to go. Typical goals reflect the wish for a stronger *drive system* – to be more motivated; to have more energy; to manage everyday tasks better; to live more independently and a stronger *soothing/affiliative system* – to like oneself more; to look after oneself better; to be more accepting and understanding of self and others; to be more comfortable in company; to be more confident in relationships; to socialize more; to develop more peace of mind; to be less frightened of relapse; to be less frustrated by others' stigmatizing views; to think in a 'saner' way.

When asked what they need to achieve their individual recovery goals, members usually become aware of their past barriers at which point fears of compassion are normalized as a sign of an overactive threat system that can be gradually overcome. This naturally leads on to the agreement of a joint recovery goal to develop a stronger soothing/affiliation system. To strengthen self-efficacy, therapists remind them of the progress they have made to date and elicit activities or relationships that have promoted recovery – possibly supporting this by watching recovery narratives on film (for example Scottish Recovery Network, 2008).

To strengthen the *compassionate motivation*, therapists invite members to contemplate insights implicit in the evolutionary model: We suffer because our threat systems are highly sensitive – yet we did not design this. We recognize that the psychosis and other distress is absolutely not our fault but is partly linked to the way our brains have been built and shaped, which we did not choose. There is a potential within all of us to develop a more balanced set of feelings by choosing to cultivate compassion. This gives us an alternative to living in the threat system. Therefore we want to look after our well-being by trying out compassion practice.

As a first step towards developing compassion a basic mindfulness exercise ('How am I?' exercise) is introduced and repeated at the beginning of every session. The exercise begins with a settling of the breath until the person arrives at a personal soothing rhythm. They then ground themselves in the sensations of the body and in the contact between the body and the chair/floor. They are then guided to notice their emotions, mind state and thoughts with a curious, welcoming and kind attitude (allowing what's already there, to be there without pushing it away or getting involved with). If members notice distress or pain, they are invited to ask themselves what the kindest thing is they could do for themselves at this point.

Mindfulness is defined as 'knowing what's happening while it's happening without preference' (Nairn, 1999). Training in mindfulness therefore entails training the observing quality of our minds. The starting point of this training is the development of an embodied awareness of one's physical and emotional experience, which has been shown to be particularly helpful for clients with psychosis (Röhricht, 2009). Our basic mindfulness exercise aims to familiarize the person with their internal experience, which they are often disconnected from as it is the source of distress. Mindfulness is safe to use with people recovering from psychosis (Chadwick *et al.*, 2005; Langer *et al.*, 2011) and has been shown to improve clinical functioning when used on its own (Chadwick *et al.*, 2009) and to reduce symptom-related distress and hospitalization rates when used as part of ACT (Bach and Hayes, 2002; Gaudiano and Herbert, 2006; see Chapter 10 this volume). By sharing their internal experiences with the group, members learn to label, express and validate emotions thereby reducing the need to close down internally. At the same time they are guided to observe the transient and immaterial nature of mental events especially of emotions, which aims to increase distress tolerance (Linehan, 1993). The exercise also allows people to relax when they arrive in the group. Those who are too anxious to close their eyes or to focus on their breathing can focus their senses on the textures and sights of an object they hold in their hand (tennis ball, semi-precious stone) (Gilbert and Procter, 2006).

Middle phase

The majority of sessions focus on the gradual development of compassion for self and others. Compassion practices progress from being grounded in the group, to experiential practices and skills training outside the group. Therapists identify and work with barriers to developing compassion throughout.

1 Grounding compassion in the group: Group mind, interaction

In addition to imagery, concrete ways of accessing compassion in the group are introduced. Members are asked to come up with personal meanings and lived or media examples of compassionate qualities such as empathy, wisdom, courage, kindness, warmth, non-judgment or calm confidence. This helps them develop a shared meaning of compassion. By asking what the strengths and in particular the weaknesses of such qualities are, members identify their personal fears of compassion (e.g. 'The weakness of being kind is that others can take advantage of me.') and therapists have an opportunity to dispel any myths ('Compassion involves strength and courage, which means asserting yourself when others are disrespecting you').

Therapists then ask members to turn their shared meaning of compassion into statements that they write on a poster to form the group's compassionate mind. They could imagine what a wise old person would tell them or what they would have found helpful to hear when they were upset. Members consult the evolving group's compassionate mind to develop compassionate reframes to their difficulties in each session. At this point, it is important to distinguish self-compassion from self-esteem (Neff and Vonk, 2009). Self-compassion has been found to be more predictive of a positive sense of self-worth and less dependent on achievement (drive system) than self-esteem (Neff and Vonk, 2009). Self-esteem in this population is low and has been the focus of specific interventions (Barrowclough *et al.*, 2003). Self-compassion involves treating ourselves with kindness in light of our failings and weaknesses irrespective of achievement (see Box 12.1).

Since members often have negative experiences of help-seeking they are asked to define how they want to support each other. Therapists introduce the idea of members pointing out to each other when they are in threat

Box 12.1   Case example

A male member had experienced a psychotic breakdown after being made redundant following a factory closure. He since maintained that he had caused the closure due to a mistake he believed he had made. Due to shame and delusional guilt he was afraid to go outside or to travel on public transport as he feared the anger of his former colleagues. In the group he mentioned guilt, worthlessness and poor motivation as issues but did not share his story with the group. Instead he was preoccupied by black and white thinking that people were either moral or corrupt. He regularly brought this belief to the group but remained closed off to taking a compassionate stance. Towards the end of the group he shared that he had come to agree with the group's compassionate mind that 'Nobody was perfect' and 'That it is ok to get things wrong'. Therefore he concluded that one was neither immoral nor moral and that a minor slip in morals did not mean that one was immoral. This new flexibility in thinking allowed him to be more accepting of himself and others. A couple of sessions later he reported that he had seen a former colleague on the bus. At first he was terrified but when he realized that this man saw him but neither recognized nor got angry with him, he felt great relief. At the end he felt more relaxed especially when outside. He ruminated less on his self-blaming thoughts and was more forgiving towards himself for having made a mistake.

mode such as being unkind to themselves (self-critical, defeatist) or suspicious of others (e.g. feeling that nobody can be trusted, others will always let them down) and to help provide compassionate reframes for that person. We thereby capitalize on the fact that it is often easier to be compassionate to others than to ourselves. During the interaction therapists guide members to look at each other in order to tune into the gaze, facial expressions of the person talking to them and to open themselves to supportive and kind intentions. This strengthens co-operation and understanding of the model.

2 Developing compassion within self: mindful appreciation,
compassionate imagery

Mindful appreciation   To further stimulate the soothing/affiliation system in a non-threatening way, members are taught to appreciate a pleasant everyday object by slowing down, exploring and savouring it with their senses (e.g. imagining being an alien who has never seen a flower before; Gilbert, 2009, pp. 235–338). Most people are surprised to note that their sensory experiences are more intense and that this helps access positive affect in a gentle way. Members are encouraged to seize opportunities to appreciate everyday activities (eating, washing) and events in nature (birdsong, sunset) and to notice their sensations, thoughts and feelings at the time. This simple exercise stimulated emotional reactivity in some members with blunted affect in our groups.

Compassionate imagery   To further stimulate the soothing/affiliation system we harness the power of imagery. We explain the rationale for using imagery by asking clients to visualize their favourite meal and to observe the powerful physiological effects (increased saliva, stomach rumbling) the image is having on their bodies. The goal of compassionate imagery is to develop a compassionate self, from which clients learn to engage with their problematic parts (angry, anxious, ashamed selves). For some clients an important stepping stone towards the compassionate self is experiencing interpersonal safeness by imagining another mind (real or created ideal; human or non-human) having kind and caring intentions towards them. All exercises begin with several minutes of mindful preparation by providing a sense of being grounded in the body and anchored in soothing rhythm breathing.

A useful first exercise is safe place imagery. Discussions about an actual safe place where members felt comfortable, calm and relaxed can help to activate a helpful image. Unhelpful images are often safety-seeking such as hiding away in bed as opposed to conveying a feeling of safeness free from threat. Another initial exercise invites clients to imagine a soothing colour that has qualities of warmth, kindness, wisdom and strength. They imagine this compassionate colour surrounding them and flowing through their heart centre.

The 'mindedness' of images is gradually increased so that clients familiarize themselves with the feeling of another mind wanting them to flourish. The safe place 'welcomes you and takes joy in you being there'. The compassionate colour 'intends to help and heal you'.

A subsequent exercise involves asking members to first recall a time when they had kind and caring feelings towards a person or pet (as this is typically least threatening) and then to recall receiving compassionate feelings from another. If working with memories is difficult due to lack of caring experiences, members can use fantasy to playfully visualize an image of an ideal compassionate other, which has the following qualities: 1) a deep commitment to you and to helping you to be well; 2) wisdom that comes from a deep understanding of our human condition and of the personal suffering of each of us; 3) calm confidence and strength of mind, which is not overwhelmed by pain and radiates a sense of authority; 4) warmth conveyed by gentleness, caring, openness; and 5) an acceptance of you as you are, not how you think you should be (Gilbert, 2010; p. 188–192). Images might take human (e.g. wise man/woman, wiser older self, Jesus; Mother Theresa) or non-human form (e.g. sunlight, rainbow, old tree). Clients are guided to explore the sensory qualities of the image and in particular focus in on the facial expressions, tone of voice and gestures both of themselves and the compassionate other.

Last, the person begins to develop their compassionate self, for example, by focusing these compassionate qualities on himself and imagining them expanding. Members are encouraged to practice taking on these qualities regularly (e.g. by becoming a wise and compassionate being every morning before getting up) with the goal of being able to access a feeling of compassion flowing through them effortlessly when they are distressed (Gilbert, 2010; pp. 159–164).

All members in our groups were able to engage in imagery. A few members experienced voices or traumatic memories intruding during imagery but were able to refocus on feelings of safeness with guidance and practice. Most were amazed that they could exert control over their minds by generating images at will that induced soothing and connectedness. See Box 12.2 for a case study.

Clients' experiences during the practices are explored focusing in particular on the physical sensations such as warmth and lightness they evoke. By eliciting members' experiences of compassion, threat and drive, therapists contrast the different body states, thoughts, feelings and motivations

---

Box 12.2   Case example

An elderly female was largely housebound due to back problems, paranoia, stigma and fears of having panic attacks when outside. Despite great reluctance to travel to the meetings, she enjoyed the group and engaged well. She used compassionate intentions to eat more healthily and to work towards gradually exposing herself to her fears of being outside. Without any guidance of therapists, she started by going outside to hang out washing and was eventually able to travel to a bigger city by bus to go shopping with the support of a friend. When travelling alone she used her compassionate image of a lifelong friend, which provided her with inner strength, calm, a sense of being at one and greater tolerance of her back pain. Feeling more confident she decided to join a local club and travel more to see family and friends.

that characterize the different states. Attention is drawn in particular to how it feels in the body to be ashamed or defeated vs. feeling excited or driven, competitive vs. feeling safe, relaxed and connected. The shifting between states can be made more concrete by asking clients to step into red, blue and green circles.

3 Practising compassionate skills: Attention, behaviour, thinking
Another skill practice is to ask members to formulate a compassionate intention that they can bring to a routine everyday activity which they struggle to motivate themselves to do. For instance, some chose to say to themselves before and as they were performing the activity 'I'm taking a shower because *I want to* look after myself .' or 'I'm getting up because *I want to* show my family who care for me that I also care for myself'. They were invited to slow down, focus their attention on the intention and the sensory experience, for example, warm water on their skin, and to praise themselves for making an effort to engage in the activity regardless of whether they completed it or not. Members reported an increased sense of mastery, pleasure and ease when performing activities and feeling more motivated to engage in other activities. Other compassionate intentions included getting up before midday, eating breakfast as opposed to not, eating healthily, doing chores and overcoming different limitations, for example, travelling on public transport. Box 12.3 provides an example.

> **Box 12.3   Case example**
>
> A male client had just been discharged from hospital after a psychotic episode marked by persecutory delusions and suicidal despair when he joined the group. He reported feeling 'tormented' by his ruminations over conflicting and unprocessed feelings of anger, shame and defeat in relation to past trauma and humiliation. On the outside he appeared slowed down and flat in his affect. He lacked the motivation to get up or wash and regularly slept until midday. The first change occurred when he imagined hearing the encouraging words and well-wishes of loved ones. This helped him to consistently get up, shower and eat breakfast leading to increased mastery and energy. He experienced the calm and peace of the safe place imagery as a 'revelation' as it was the first time he had experienced relief from his inner 'torment'. Strengthened through these practices he was able to disengage from his distressing thoughts more easily leading to him feeling calmer, more content, optimistic about his future and being more emotionally reactive.

Table 12.1 Example of using compassionate reframe diary

What caused you to become upset?	Immediate reaction?	Shifting to compassionate self	Compassionate thinking:	Compassionate behaviour
Seeing neighbour in street who does not know that I have been to hospital.	*Emotion:* Nervous, upset, ashamed, vulnerable. *Body:* Tense, nauseous. *Thoughts:* He'll ask where I have been. He will know that I have been to hospital. He will think I am a loony and loser. He will look down on me and avoid me. *Behaviour:* Avoid person.	1. Ground myself in body. 3. Slow down breathing. Find my soothing rhythm breathing. 3. Place hand on heart. 4. Put on gentle half smile. 5. Imagine becoming wise and compassionate being.	I am not alone in feeling like this. People who were in hospital with me have to deal with fear of stigma, too. It is understandable to feel scared of others judging me. The psychosis is not my fault, I did not choose it. I do not actually know what he is thinking. The more I will understand my difficulties, the easier it might get to face other people. I am ok as I am.	I will speak to a trusted person about how I feel. I could take a more gradual approach to going out on my own – I could start by going with a friend next time. If I see him next time, I could smile at him to see how he reacts.

In each session therapists guide members to arrive at a compassionate way of attending, thinking, feeling and behaving when faced with difficulties. Out of sessions members practise compassionate reframing of difficulties using diaries as shown in Table 12.1 (Gilbert, 2009; pp. 423–425).

The learning of compassionate responses is 'scaffolded' through the group atmosphere, the support from therapists and members, the group's compassionate mind, the feeling developed in the experiential exercises and finally the everyday life practice of asking during a difficulty 'Imagining being this wise and compassionate being, what is the wisest and kindest thing that I can do for myself at this moment?'. In our groups we observed that the more members developed self-compassion, the more they were able to talk about personal and distressing experiences. When developing helpful responses to paranoid thinking, a distinction between the rational and compassionate mind can be helpful (see Gumley and Schwannauer, 2006).

Neuroscientific research has demonstrated that people high in self-criticism can experience self-compassion as aversive (Rockcliff *et al.*, 2008; Rockliff *et al.*, 2011). Therapists need to explain that stimulating the soothing system can feel unfamiliar at first and can activate negative affect such as sadness or grief, which has long been blocked off. From the start therapists anticipate barriers such as self-criticism, mistrust and lack of empathy for others and explain their function as safety strategies, which now get in the way of recovery. Acknowledging that most of the members share a fear of others and feel vulnerable within themselves helps reduce anxiety (Lincoln *et al.*, 2010). Therapists might also praise them for being courageous enough to come to the group – courage being a compassionate quality. Therapists conduct compassion exercises like behavioural experiments in that they ask members to test out if the feared consequences (of being overwhelmed by distress, becoming lazy, feeling more vulnerable, others intruding, being taken advantage of) set in (see Box 12.4).

Ending phase

1 Compassionate Narratives

During the middle phase members develop safeness to express negative affects in the here and now and learn to relate to it with increasing warmth and acceptance. During the ending phase they consolidate this skill by reflecting on changes in their recovery from a compassionate stance. The construction of compassionate narratives through writing and sharing in the group aims to help members to integrate the psychosis and its impact in order to help them move on and deal with any future setbacks. Since members vary with regard to their cognitive and mentalizing capacities

Box 12.4   Case example

A male group member was apprehensive about developing compassionate responses to his lack of motivation to increase his activity levels. He grew up with a very strong work ethic and was very hard on himself about his difficulty getting things done. Since experiencing psychosis and depression he had become increasingly ashamed and self-critical. He was anxious that being compassionate towards himself would mean that he could 'let himself off' and that he and others would see him as lazy and weak. Therapists supported him to reframe his beliefs about compassion to an act of 'the wisest thing you can do for yourself', which in his case was to gently encourage himself to do a little more each day, praise himself and engage with his critical thoughts in a more understanding way. This assured him and others that compassionate responding required courage and was not an easy way out.

Box 12.5   Case example

A male member entertained a persecutory delusion and suffered from severe depressive symptoms. His affect was visibly blunted. He believed that a newsagent had been deceitful over a winning ticket claiming it for himself. He felt cheated, humiliated and had revenge fantasies with plans on how to kill him, which he felt able to resist. He engaged well with the group and the compassion work, especially with reducing his self-criticism about struggling to accomplish his everyday roles and tasks and improving his self-acceptance. He could shift from ruminating over his delusional belief to reframing it as an overactive threat mind, which had been sensitized in early life. As he shared his life story in the final exercise, he was able to get in touch with grief and sadness about the lack of soothing in childhood. This activation of the underlying grief helped this member progress in individual therapy after the group.

and with regard to the degree to which they have processed the psychosis and any underlying trauma or loss, therapists support them to develop their narratives at their own level – such as focusing on a particular difficulty they have overcome or by taking a lifetime perspective (see Box 12.5).

2 Facilitating transition

In keeping with an attachment perspective, therapists put the same attention into facilitating the ending of a group as they put into setting it up. The ending can evoke feelings of loss, which can lead members to withdraw and close down again. Members are encouraged to integrate their compassion practice into everyday life and to develop a regular practice early on in the middle phase. An individual plan is drawn up for each person to build on what has been most helpful to them. To help members connect with the feeling of compassion, they are given a CD of practices and a compassionate letter from the group mind as a transitional object. To help members build on their achievement of bonding with others in the group, further ways in which they can access social support are discussed. Participants in our groups chose to continue to meet as a group; to attend classes with a similar theme (meditation, tai chi, practical philosophy); to join a mental health club which organized weekly social activities; to engage in regular activities or to attend events with neighbours, friends or family. In the final session, the group reflects on what has been learned and how to maintain the gains. A closing ritual like tearing up a quality they want to leave behind and taking with them a quality they want to grow can reinforce the compassionate motivation.

Working with residual psychotic symptoms

In the case of individuals experiencing distress related to residual psychotic symptoms it is important for therapists to validate the distress people are feeling and for therapists and members to help the person arrive at a helpful way of making them feel safe and respected in the here and now.

In the case of paranoid thoughts the therapist neither colludes nor argues with the content of the delusion but focuses on validating and containing the affect (e.g. It is understandable that you are feeling frightened, if you are worrying about others wanting to hurt you. What might be a helpful way of dealing with this fear now? What can we do in the group to help you feel safe?). If a member feels watched or intimidated by others, they might want to sit outside the circle to observe the group and/or they might want to survey members' (usually benevolent) intentions towards them and feel them by looking at members taking in gaze, smile and posture. Members also tend to feel reassured by supportive and empathic statements from others who have learnt how to cope with paranoia. People are reminded that the threat system is designed for rapid action and will flood us with ideas that are not necessarily true. The compassionate self is interested in separating out the fears and overprotection strategies of the threat system from reality.

Delusional beliefs of a spiritual nature often serve a protective function (against shame from early abuse, trauma or loss) and should not be invalidated but formulated within the compassion model. On further exploration members often experience their spiritual figures as containing a punitive and critical aspect. Those individuals are best guided to a compassion practice which is grounded in reality such as remembering a kind interaction with a member or a pet or developing their compassionate self.

Possible therapeutic mechanisms

Taken together, participants in our groups described improvements in terms of reduced shame and self-criticism, increased self-compassion, emotional resilience, social connectedness and the activation of negative and positive affect, which are in keeping with the goal of CFT and have been observed in non-psychotic clients (Gilbert and Procter, 2006; Gilbert, 2010; Lowens, 2010). The activation of underlying grief facilitated progress in later individual therapy. While not directly targeted in therapy, members also noted improvements in motivation, drive, self-esteem and greater flexibility in their thinking. Several members decided to tackle issues of anxiety themselves, for instance, by gradually exposing themselves to feared situations (travelling on public transport, being in groups, attending events). This has also been noted in CFT for anxiety disorders (Welford, 2010).

CFT appears to help the person develop the warmth and courage needed to approach what they fear – negative affect and affiliation with others (Gilbert, 2010, p. 175). Support for this comes from our finding that clients related more compassionately to themselves and to others and were less avoidant of negative affect when talking about their psychosis and recovery following the CFT group (Braehler *et al.*, in press).

We hypothesize that compassion facilitates the resurfacing of suppressed affect and that it acts as narrative 'glue' that embeds the affect in autobiographical memory. Narratives with a meaningful and coherent sense of autobiographical self are considered indicative of good recovery from psychosis (Lysaker *et al.*, 2003; Lysaker *et al.*, 2005; Lysaker, *et al.*, 2007; Lysaker *et al.*, 2010). It has been argued that the integration of dissociated affects reduces the likelihood of these intruding and destabilizing the self (Liotti and Gumley, 2009).

The specificity of failures in mentalizing in psychosis and how these may be related to the affiliative system are as yet unclear. Mentalizing capacities evolve in the safeness experienced in early attachment and other affiliative relationships (Fonagy *et al.*, 2011; Liotti and Gilbert, 2011). CFT might create the conditions necessary for mentalizing to develop: to provide the interpersonal safeness to venture further into the exploration of one's own mind, the minds of others and of the processes at how we arrive at understanding others' motives, beliefs and emotions.

Conclusion

Psychosis is associated with major difficulties in affect regulation and threat processing. Based on the work described we suggest that group CFT is a promising and evolving intervention for reducing problematic threat processing. CFT also offers a general framework for supporting emotional recovery from psychosis that could be implemented on an individual, group, family and mental health service level.

Note

1   This website is maintained by the Compassionate Mind Foundation headed by Professor Paul Gilbert. It provides information of training in CFT, practical resources for clinicians (e.g. material on psychoeducation, mindfulness, imagery), literature and the possibility to join special interest (e.g. for psychosis) or local supervision groups following training in CFT. www.compassionate mind.co.uk/index.html

References

Bach, P. and Hayes, S.C. (2002) The use of acceptance and commitment therapy to prevent the rehospitalization of psychotic patients: A randomized controlled trial. *Journal of Consulting and Clinical Psychology, 70(5)*, 1129–1139.

Barnett, H. and Lapsley, H. (2006) Journeys of despair, journeys of hope: Young people talk about severe mental distress, mental health services and recovery. *New Zealand Mental Health Commission Research Report.*

Barrowclough, C., Tarrier, N., Humphreys, L. *et al.* (2003) Self-esteem in schizophrenia: Relationships between self-evaluation, family attitudes, and symptomatology. *Journal of Abnormal Psychology, 112(1)*, 92–99.

Bateman, A. and Fonagy, P. (2007) *Mentalization-based Treatment for Borderline Personality Disorder: A Practical Guide*: Oxford: Oxford University Press.

Bebbington, P.E., Bhugra, D., Brugha, T. *et al.* (2004) Psychosis, victimisation and childhood disadvantage: Evidence from the second British National Survey of Psychiatric Morbidity. *The British Journal of Psychiatry, 185(3)*, 220–226.

Belsky, J., Bakermans-Kranenburg, M.J. and van Ijzendoorn, M.H. (2007) For better and for worse: Differential susceptibility to environmental influences. *Current Directions in Psychological Science, 6*, 300–304.

Berry, K., Barrowclough, C. and Wearden, A. (2008) Attachment theory: A framework for understanding symptoms and interpersonal relationships in psychosis. *Behaviour Research and Therapy, 46(12)*, 1275–1282.

Bhugra, D., Leff, J., Mallett, R. *et al.* (1997) Incidence and outcome of schizophrenia in whites, Afro-Caribbeans and Asians in London. *Psychological Medicine, 27,* 791–798.

Birchwood, M. (2003) Pathways to emotional dysfunction in first-episode psychosis. *The British Journal of Psychiatry, 182(5),* 373–375.

Birchwood, M., Iqbal, Z., Chadwick, P. *et al.* (2000a) Cognitive approach to depression and suicidal thinking in psychosis: I. Ontogeny of post-psychotic depression. *The British Journal of Psychiatry, 177(6),* 516–528.

Birchwood, M., Meaden, A., Trower, P. *et al.* (2000) The power and omnipotence of voices: subordination and entrapment by voices and significant others. *Psychological Medicine, 30(2),* 337–344.

Birchwood, M., Trower, P., Brunet, K. *et al.* (2006) Social anxiety and the shame of psychosis: A study in first episode psychosis. *Behaviour Research and Therapy, 45(5),* 1025–1037.

Braehler, C., Gumley, A.I., Harper, J. *et al.* (in press) Exploring change processes in Compassion Focused Therapy in Psychosis: results of a feasibility randomized controlled trial. *British Journal of Clinical Psychology.*

Braehler, C. and Schwannauer, M. (2011) Recovering an emerging self: Exploring reflective function in recovery from adolescent-onset psychosis. *Psychology and Psychotherapy: Theory, Research and Practice, 85(1),* 48–67.

Chadwick, P., Hughes, S., Russell, D. *et al.* (2009) Mindfulness groups for distressing voices and paranoia: A replication and randomized feasibility trial. *Behavioural and Cognitive Psychotherapy, 37(4),* 403–412.

Chadwick, P., Newman-Taylor, K. and Abba, N. (2005) Mindfulness Groups for people with psychosis. *Behavioural and Cognitive Psychotherapy, 33(3),* 351–359.

Cozolino, L. (2007) *The Neuroscience of Human Relationships: Attachment and the Developing Brain.* New York: Norton.

Depue, R.A. and Morrone-Strupinsky, J.V. (2005) A neurobehavioral model of affiliative bonding. *Behavioral and Brain Sciences, 28,* 313–395.

Dozier, M. (1990) Attachment organization and treatment use for adults with serious psychopathological disorders. *Development and Psychopathology, 2(1),* 47–60.

Fonagy, P., Bateman, A. and Bateman, A. (2011) The widening scope of mentalizing: A discussion. *Psychology and Psychotherapy: Theory, Research and Practice, 84(1),* 98–110.

Fonagy, P., Gergely, G., Jurist, E. *et al.* (2002) *Affect Regulation, Mentalization and the Development of the Self.* London: Karnac Books.

Frame, L. and Morrison, A.P. (2001) Causes of posttraumatic stress disorder in psychotic patients. *Archives General Psychiatry, 58,* 305–306.

Freeman, D. and Garety, P.A. (2003) Connecting neurosis and psychosis: the direct influence of emotion on delusions and hallucinations. *Behaviour Research and Therapy, 41(8),* 923–947.

García-Cabeza, I. and González de Chávez, M. (2009) Therapeutic factors and insight in group therapy for outpatients diagnosed with schizophrenia. *Psychosis, 1(2),* 134–144.

Garfield, S. (1995) *Unbearable Affect: A Guide to the Psychotherapy of Psychosis.* Oxford: John Wiley and Sons.

Gaudiano, B.A. and Herbert, J.D. (2006) Acute treatment of inpatients with psychotic symptoms using Acceptance and Commitment Therapy: Pilot results. *Behaviour Research and Therapy, 44(3)*, 415–437.

Gilbert, P. (1989) *Human Nature and Suffering*: New York: Guilford.

Gilbert, P. (1993) Defence and safety: Their function in social behaviour and psychopathology. *British Journal of Clinical Psychology, 32(2)*, 131–153.

Gilbert, P. (2000) Social mentalities: Internal 'social' conflicts and the role of inner warmth and compassion in cognitive therapy. In P. Gilbert (ed.) *Genes on the Couch: Explorations in Evolutionary Psychotherapy* (pp. 118–150): Hove, UK: Brenner-Routledge.

Gilbert, P. (2005) *Compassion: Conceptualizations, Research, and Use in Psychotherapy*. London: Brunner-Routledge.

Gilbert, P. (2009) *The Compassionate Mind*. London: Constable & Robinson.

Gilbert, P. (2010a) *Compassion-focused Therapy: Distinctive Features (CBT Distinctive Features)*. London: Routledge.

Gilbert, P. (2010b) An introduction to compassion focused therapy in cognitive behavior therapy. *International Journal of Cognitive Therapy, 3(2)*, 97–112.

Gilbert, P. and Andrews, B. (1998) *Shame: Interpersonal Behavior, Psychopathology and Culture*. Oxford: Oxford University Press.

Gilbert, P., Birchwood, M., Gilbert, J. *et al.* (2001) An exploration of evolved mental mechanisms for dominant and subordinate behaviour in relation to auditory hallucinations in schizophrenia and critical thoughts in depression. *Psychological Medicine, 31*, 1117–1127.

Gilbert, P. and Procter, S. (2006) Compassionate mind training for people with high shame and self-criticism: overview and pilot study of a group therapy approach. *Clinical Psychology and Psychotherapy, 13(6)*, 353–379.

Green, M.J. and Phillips, M.L. (2004) Social threat perception and the evolution of paranoia. *Neuroscience and Biobehavioral Reviews, 28(3)*, 333–342.

Grepmair, L., Mitterlehner, F., Loew, T. *et al.* (2007) Promoting mindfulness in psychotherapists in training influences the treatment results of their patients: A randomized, double-blind, controlled study. *Psychotherapy and Psychosomatics, 76*, 332–338.

Gumley, A., Braehler, C., Laithwaite, H. *et al.* (2010) A compassion focussed model of recovery after psychosis. *International Journal of Cognitive Psychotherapy, 3(2)*, 186–201.

Gumley, A., O'Grady, M., Power, K. *et al.* (2004) Negative beliefs about self and illness: a comparison of individuals with psychosis with or without comorbid social anxiety disorder. *Australian and New Zealand Journal of Psychiatry, 38(11–12)*, 960–964.

Gumley, A. and Park, C. (2010) Relapse prevention and early psychosis. In P. French, D. Shiers, M. Reed *et al.* (ed.) *Promoting Recovery in Early Psychosis: A Practice Manual* (pp. 157–167). Chichester: Wiley-Blackwell.

Gumley, A. and Schwannauer, M. (2006) *Staying Well After Psychosis: A Cognitive Interpersonal Approach to Recovery and Relapse Prevention*. Chichester: John Wiley and Sons.

Harrison, G., Hopper, K., Craig, T. *et al.* (2001) Recovery from psychotic illness: A 15- and 25-year international follow-up study. *The British Journal of Psychiatry, 178(6)*, 506–517.

Iqbal, Z., Birchwood, M., Chadwick, P. *et al.* (2000) Cognitive approach to depression and suicidal thinking in psychosis. 2. Testing the validity of a social ranking model. *British Journal of Psychiatry, 177*, 522–528.

Johnson, D.P., Penn, D.L., Fredrickson, B.L. *et al.* (2011) A pilot study of loving-kindness meditation for the negative symptoms of schizophrenia. *Schizophrenia Research*, 129(2), 137–140.

Kanas, N. (1996) *Group Therapy for Schizophrenic Patients*. Washington, DC: American Psychiatric Press.

Karatzias, T., Gumley, A., Power, K. *et al.* (2007) Illness appraisals and self-esteem as correlates of anxiety and affective comorbid disorders in schizophrenia. *Comprehensive Psychiatry, 48*, 371–375.

Kirsch, P., Esslinger, C., Chen, Q. *et al.* (2005) Oxytocin modulates neural circuitry for social cognition and fear in humans. *Journal of Neuroscience, 25(49)*, 11489–11493.

Laithwaite, H., O'Hanlon, M., Collins *et al.* (2009) Recovery After Psychosis (RAP): A compassion focused programme for individuals residing in high security settings. *Behavioural and Cognitive Psychotherapy, 37(5)*, 511–526.

Langer, Á.I., Cangas, A.J., Salcedo, E. *et al.* (2011) Applying mindfulness therapy in a group of psychotic individuals: A controlled study. *Behavioural and Cognitive Psychotherapy, FirstView*, 1–5.

Lincoln, T.M., Mehl, S., Ziegler, M. *et al.* (2010) Is fear of others linked to an uncertain sense of self? The relevance of self-worth, interpersonal self-concepts and dysfunctional beliefs to paranoia. *Behavior Therapy, 41(2)*, 187–197.

Linehan, M. (1993) *Cognitive-Behavioral Treatment of Borderline Personality Disorder*. New York: Guildford Press.

Liotti, G. and Gilbert, P. (2011) Mentalizing, motivationand social mentalities: Theoretical considerations and implications for psychotherapy. *Psychology and Psychotherapy: Theory, Research and Practice, 84(1)*, 9–25.

Liotti, G. and Gumley, A. I. (2009) An attachment perspective on schizophrenia: Disorganized attachment, dissociative processes and compromised mentalisation. In M.D.A. Moskowitz and I. Schaefer (eds) *Dissociation and Psychosis: Converging Perspectives on a Complex Relationship*. Chichester: John Wiley and Sons.

Longe, O., Maratos, F.A., Gilbert, P. *et al.* (2010) Having a word with yourself: Neural correlates of self-criticism and self-reassurance. *Neuroimage, 15(49(2))*, 1849–1856.

Lowens, I. (2010) Compassion Focused Therapy for People with Bipolar Disorder. *International Journal of Cognitive Therapy, 3(2)*, 172–185.

Lysaker, P.H., Carcione, A., Dimaggio, G. *et al.* (2005) Metacognition amidst narratives of self and illness in schizophrenia: associations with neurocognition, symptoms, insight and quality of life. *Acta Psychiatrica Scandinavica, 112(1)*, 64–71.

Lysaker, P.H., Dimaggio, G., Buck, K.D. *et al.* (2007) Metacognition within narratives of schizophrenia: Associations with multiple domains of neurocognition. *Schizophrenia Research, 93(1–3)*, 278–287.

Lysaker, P.H., Dimaggio, G., Carcione, A. *et al.* (2010) Metacognition and schizophrenia: The capacity for self-reflectivity as a predictor for prospective assessments of work performance over six months. *Schizophrenia Research, 122(1)*, 124–130.

Lysaker, P.H., Lancaster, R.S. and Lysaker, J.T. (2003) Narrative transformation as an outcome in the psychotherapy of schizophrenia. *Psychology and Psychotherapy: Theory, Research and Practice, 76(3),* 285–299.

MacBeth, A., Gumley, A., Schwannauer, M. *et al.* (2011) Attachment states of mind, mentalization and their correlates in a first-episode psychosis sample. *Psychology and Psychotherapy: Theory, Research and Practice, 84(1),* 42–57.

Mayhew, S. and Gilbert, P. (2008) Compassionate mind training with people who hear malevolent voices: A case series report. *Clinical Psychology and Psychotherapy, 15,* 113–138.

McGlashan, T.H. (1987) Recovery style from mental illness and long-term outcome. *The Journal of Nervous and Mental Disease, 175(11),* 681–685.

McGuire, P.K., Silversweig, D.A., Wright, I. *et al.* (1996) The neural correlates of inner speech and auditory verbal imagery in schizophrenia: Relationship to auditory verbal hallucinations. *British Journal of Psychiatry, 169,* 148–159.

Morgan, C., Kirkbride, J., Leff, J. *et al.* (2007) Parental separation, loss and psychosis in different ethnic groups: A case-control study. *Psychological Medicine, 37(4),* 495–503.

Morrison, A.P., Frame, L. and Larkin, W. (2003) Relationships between trauma and psychosis: A review and integration. *British Journal of Clinical Psychology, 42,* 331–353.

Myin-Germeys, I. and van Os, J. (2007) Stress-reactivity in psychosis: Evidence for an affective pathway to psychosis. *Clinical Psychology Review, 27(4),* 409–424.

Nairn, R. (1999) *Diamond Mind.* New York: Synapse Video Center.

Neff, K.D. and Vonk, R. (2009) Self-compassion versus global self-esteem: two different ways of relating to oneself. *Journal of Personality, 77(1),* 23–50.

Penn, D.L., Corrigan, P.W., Bentall, R.P. *et al.* (1997) Social cognition in schizophrenia. *Psychological Bulletin, 121,* 114–132.

Porges, S.W. (2007) The polyvagal perspective. *Biological Psychology, 74(2),* 116–143.

Read, J. and Gumley, A. (2008) Can attachment theory help explain the relationship between childhood adversity and psychosis? *Attachment: New Directions in Psychotherapy and Relational Psychoanalysis, 2(1),* 1–35.

Read, J., van Os, J., Morrison, A.P. *et al.* (2005) Childhood trauma, psychosis and schizophrenia: a literature review with theoretical and clinical implications. *Acta Psychiatrica Scandinavica, 112(5),* 330–350.

Rockcliff, H., Gilbert, P., McEwan, K. *et al.* (2008) A pilot exploration of heart rate variability and salivary cortisol responses to compassion-focused imagery. *Clinical Neuropsychiatry, 5,* 132–139.

Rockliff, D., Karl, A., McEwan, K. *et al.* (2011) Effects of intranasal oxytocin on 'Compassion Focused Imagery'. *Emotion, 11(6),* 1388–1396.

Röhricht, F., Papadopoulos, N., Suzuki, I. *et al.* (2009) Ego-pathology, body experience and body psychotherapy in chronic schizophrenia. *Psychology and Psychotherapy: Theory, Research and Practice, 82(1),* 19–30.

Rooke, O. and Birchwood, M. (1998) Loss, humiliation and entrapment as appraisals of schizophrenic illness: A prospective study of depressed and non-depressed patients. *British Journal of Clinical Psychology, 37(3),* 259–268.

Russell, T.A., Rubia, K., Bullmore, E.T. *et al.* (2000) Exploring the social brain in schizophrenia: Left prefrontal underactivation during mental state attribution. *American Journal of Psychiatry, 157(12),* 2040–2042.

Schore, A.N. (1996) The experience-dependent maturation of a regulatory system in the orbital prefrontal cortex and the origin of developmental psychopathology. *Development and Psychopathology, 8(1),* 59–87.

Scottish Recovery Network (2008) www.scottishrecovery.net (accessed 29 June 2012).

Segal, Z.V., Williams, J.M.G. and Teasdale, J.D. (2002) *Mindfulness-based Cognitive Therapy for Depression: A New Approach to Preventing Relapse.* New York: Guilford Press.

Siegel, D. (2010) *The Mindful Therapist: A Clinician's Guide to Mindsight and Neural Integration.* New York: W.W. Norton and Company.

Spinhoven, P. and van der Does, A. (1999) Thought suppression, dissociation and psychopathology. *Personality and Individual Differences, 27,* 877–886.

Tai, S. and Turkington, D. (2009) The Evolution of cognitive behavior therapy for schizophrenia: Current practice and recent developments. *Schizophrenia Bulletin, 35(5),* 865–873.

Tait, L., Birchwood, M. and Trower, P. (2003) Predicting engagement with services for psychosis: insight, symptoms and recovery style. *British Journal of Psychiatry, 182,* 123–128.

Teasdale, J.D., Moore, R.G., Hayhurst, H. *et al.* (2002) Metacognitive awareness and prevention of relapse in depression: Empirical evidence. *Journal of Consulting and Clinical Psychology, 70,* 275–287.

Thompson, K.N., McGorry, P.D. and Harrigan, S.M. (2003) Recovery style and outcome in first-episode psychosis. *Schizophrenia Research, 62,* 31–36.

Tyrrell, C. and Dozier, M. (1997) *The role of attachment in therapeutic process and outcome for adults with serious psychiatric disorders.* Paper presented at the Biennial Meeting of Society for Research in Child Development. Washington, DC.

Welford, M. (2010) A compassion focused approach to anxiety disorders. *International Journal of Cognitive Therapy, 3(2),* 124–140.

White, R.G. and Gumley, A.I. (2009) Post-psychotic PTSD: Associations with fear of recurrence and intolerance of uncertainty. *Journal of Nervous and Mental Disease, 197(11),* 841–849.

Wykes, T., Steel, C., Everitt, B. *et al.* (2008) Cognitive behaviour therapy for schizophrenia: Effect sizes, clinical models and methodological rigor. *Schizophrenia Bulletin, 34(4),* 523–537.

Yalom, I.D. (1983) *Inpatient Group Psychotherapy.* New York: Basic Books.

Yalom, I.D. (1995) *The Theory and Practice of Group Psychotherapy,* 4th edn. New York: Basic Books.

Index

CBT for Schizophrenia: Evidence-Based Interventions and Future Directions,
First Edition. Edited by Craig Steel.
© 2013 John Wiley & Sons, Ltd. Published 2013 by John Wiley & Sons, Ltd.